MIND UNMASKED

The human mind has proven uniquely capable of unraveling untold mysteries, and yet, the mind is fundamentally challenged when it turns back on itself to ask what it itself is. How do we conceive of mind in this postmodern world; how can we use philosophical anthropology to understand mind and its functions? While philosophers and social scientists have made important contributions to our understanding of mind, existing theories are insufficient for penetrating the complexities of mind in the twenty-first century.

Mind Unmasked: A Political Phenomenology of Consciousness draws on twentieth-century philosophies of consciousness to explain the phenomenon of mind in the broadest sense of the word. Michael A. Weinstein and Timothy M. Yetman develop a thought-provoking discourse that moves beyond the nature of the human experience of mind at both the individual and interpersonal levels and present a meditation on life in the contemporary world of global mass-mediated human culture.

Michael A. Weinstein was Professor of Political Science at Purdue University from 1968 until mid-September 2015. Weinstein's philosophical work addresses a variety of areas including existentialism, American classical philosophy, vitalism, twentieth-century Mexican, Canadian and Spanish philosophy, social philosophy, postmodernism, virtue, and technology, among others. He was the author of 22 books and more than 120 journal articles and book chapters in Political Theory, Philosophy, and Sociology. Weinstein also extensively wrote international political analyses for a number of online publications, and became widely recognized as a foremost academic authority on Somalia.

Timothy M. Yetman is Adjunct Instructor in Philosophy at Ivy Tech Community College. He has taught courses in research methods, Introduction to Ethics, Introduction to Philosophy, and stepped in during the fall of 2015 to teach his late co-author's classes at Purdue University in Current Political Ideologies and Introduction to Political Science. His interests range from continental philosophy to postmodernism and media studies.

"Weinstein and Yetman offer a fascinating and complex analysis of human existence and consciousness. They create a unique and provocative approach to reflecting on what it means to be 'human', and the rational and non-rational influences that permeate perception."

– James M. Glass, Department of Government and Politics,
University of Maryland, College Park

"From political theory to popular culture, Michael A. Weinstein is, and will always remain, the truly indispensable thinker, a writer of lucid, intense and urgent imagination at the height of his times. His penetrating essays and excurses in *Mind Unmasked* provide a powerful counterpoint to the 'serio-comedy' of contemporary culture by actually bending the fragmented, split postmodern mind in the direction of a new philosophy of life. Here, Nietzsche's *Zarathustra* listens carefully again to this new telling of an ancient story: how do you continue to think lucidly, and in that thinking live ethically, in the midst of the culture blast that is life in the fast, but radically fragmented, twenty-first century?"

– Arthur Kroker, University of Victoria, Author of Exits to the
Posthuman Future *and* Body Drift

"An invaluable inquiry into the phenomenology of mind and its application to contemporary socio-political life. A refreshing critique of totalizing discourses meant to project certainty and security at the expense of an appreciation for contingency and nuance."

– Timothy Seul, School of International Liberal Studies, Waseda University

MIND UNMASKED

A Political Phenomenology of Consciousness

Michael A. Weinstein and Timothy M. Yetman

NEW YORK AND LONDON

First published 2018
by Routledge
711 Third Avenue, New York, NY 10017

and by Routledge
2 Park Square, Milton Park, Abingdon, Oxon OX14 4RN

Routledge is an imprint of the Taylor & Francis Group, an informa business

© 2018 Taylor & Francis

The right of Michael A. Weinstein and Timothy M. Yetman to be identified as authors of this work has been asserted by them in accordance with sections 77 and 78 of the Copyright, Designs and Patents Act 1988.

All rights reserved. No part of this book may be reprinted or reproduced or utilised in any form or by any electronic, mechanical, or other means, now known or hereafter invented, including photocopying and recording, or in any information storage or retrieval system, without permission in writing from the publishers.

Trademark notice: Product or corporate names may be trademarks or registered trademarks, and are used only for identification and explanation without intent to infringe.

Library of Congress Cataloging in Publication Data
Names: Weinstein, Michael A., author. | Yetman, Timothy M., author.
Title: Mind unmasked : a political phenomenology of consciousness /
Michael A. Weinstein and Timothy M. Yetman.
Description: New York, NY : Routledge, 2017. | Includes bibliographical references and index.
Identifiers: LCCN 2017008681 (print) | LCCN 2017031685 (ebook) |
ISBN 9781315160603 (Master) | ISBN 9781351662918 (WebPDF) |
ISBN 9781351662901 (ePub) | ISBN 9781351662895 (Kindle) |
ISBN 9781138064102 (hardback : alk. paper) | ISBN 9781138064119 (pbk. : alk. paper) | ISBN 9781315160603 (ebk.)
Subjects: LCSH: Consciousness. | Philosophical anthropology.
Classification: LCC B808.9 (ebook) | LCC B808.9 .W45 2017 (print) | DDC 128/.2--dc23
LC record available at https://lccn.loc.gov/2017008681

ISBN: 978-1-138-06410-2 (hbk)
ISBN: 978-1-138-06411-9 (pbk)
ISBN: 978-1-315-16060-3 (ebk)

Typeset in Bembo
by Taylor & Francis Books

CONTENTS

Foreword	*vi*
Introduction *Timothy M. Yetman*	1
1 Mind, Narrativity, and the Euro-romance *Timothy M. Yetman*	11
2 Integral Consciousness *Michael A. Weinstein*	64
3 Embeddedness, Serio-comedy, and the Third Ape *Michael A. Weinstein and Timothy M. Yetman*	89
4 Welcome to the Fragmentorium! It's Ridiculous! *Michael A. Weinstein and Timothy M. Yetman*	121
Bibliography	*156*
Index	*162*

FOREWORD

"Everything bears some meaning, refers to something else, but nothing organizes the rest of things into a significant pattern: everything is possible and nothing is necessary, not even the project of making a home of the world, which now merely functions as a bit of nostalgia that sets up a screen between self and circumstance, the better to promote a fragile comfort and a justification for going to work. The civil savage announces that all of the exits from modernity have been sealed, that postmodernity is the stark wish of modern consciousness not to be itself, a hope evacuated of all content, the pure proclamation of the form of novelty projected into an indefinite future."[1].

It was a *ménage à trois* of sorts that brought about this book. Michael Weinstein and Tim Yetman had been having long philosophical discussions about twice a month for several years. They each brought ideas that were intriguing to them at the time, and given that they shared an intimate acquaintance with a very wide range of the greats and should-be greats in philosophy, these friendly chats were exhilarating and left them with further insights. Michael always told me about the content of these interactions on our long walks each week in Chicago. I was, as befits a resident of the Windy City, blown away by many of them. I added my two-cents and posed some questions, but refrained from my usual recommendation to encourage him to write about this material. This was difficult as I thought he was onto something seriously great. Well, I did slip a few times with a "You ought to …" but then caught myself, shut my mouth, and smiled.

He had mentioned that he didn't want to write any other books. In part he'd been spoiled by writing shorter articles on international issues, especially the more than a hundred and thirty rather long analyses of Somalia which garnered a loyal, diverse and responsive audience from those involved with the country. Like his two per week reviews of photography shows, all were published within a day or two of submission.

Of course I wasn't the only one who heard about the ideas that comprise this book. Michael was nothing if not promiscuous, discussing them with all and sundry. Colleagues at Purdue and at DePaul, artists and gallerists, neighbors, and even the security guard at the bank around the corner, had various chats with him about them.

But as the ideas deepened and broadened and even he would admit they were of value, I took my nagging to a newly inventive level. "Wouldn't Tim be pleased to publish a book?" He smiled at my creative nagging, and said, with seriousness, "I'll take it under advisement." He did, and two weeks later he and Tim were beginning to strategize their cooperative effort.

As they finished various sections they gave them to one another for comments. By the time classes began in August of 2015 both had completed all of their parts and commented on them to one another. Early in the morning of September 17th while getting ready for a day of teaching and then driving up to Chicago, Michael died suddenly. The coroner said that he neither had any pain nor could have known what was happening; the ruptured aortic aneurism made for a good death, for him at least. He'd known for several years that it was a good possibility, and that an operation would be very risky and, if he survived it, would probably leave him bedridden. He was fine with this and slept like a baby each night, an existentialist without agony. Tim took over his classes that fall after regular faculty couldn't, finding the students inconsolable. He did brilliantly. Both classes adored him. It took until the following spring for Tim and me to recover enough to think about the book. I said I would help edit it and find a publisher; I'd done this with my books and most of Michael's too. We spent the following months getting the project into shape, including deciphering and typing up the last section Michael had written.

The obvious first choice of a publisher was Routledge. They published the festschrift to Michael edited by Robert Oprisko and Diane Rubenstein in early 2015 (*Michael A. Weinstein: Action, Contemplation, Vitalism*). As the various chapters were submitted to them over the summer of 2014, they sent them to Michael. He was incredibly touched by each of them, and I saw him cry as he read one. They then asked him to write a response of sorts. His chapter was titled "Performing Integral Consciousness: Simulation." It focused on what he had been discussing with Tim, with me, and with all and sundry, and was fully expanded upon in the book you are now reading. Obviously the authors too played their part in making this book possible.

There are others too who also should be acknowledged. Among the all and sundry are Michael and Tim's students, Christopher Lewis, Adrian Leverkuhn, Tim Seul, and Jay McCann. Tim is grateful to his wife, Christine, who helped him shoulder an over-abundance of obligations while working on this book, and to his father, Michael Yetman, for help with early drafts I am indebted to Black Hawk Hancock, Robert Oprisko, Jim Glass, and Tim Seul for their support and guidance on my efforts on this volume. Finally, Tim and I are most appreciative of the effective, efficient and delightfully sweet Natalja Mortensen, Senior Editor at Routledge.

"The quality of life is the quality of desire. The meaning of life is the contingency of its meanings, that is, of the objects of its desires. Everything is possible, but ... *nothing is necessary*."[2]

Deena Weinstein

Notes

1 Michael A. Weinstein, *Culture/Flesh: Explorations of Postcivilized Modernity*, Rowman and Littlefield, Lanham, MD, p. 69.
2 Michael A. Weinstein, "Zero Point," April 15, 1986, unpublished.

INTRODUCTION

Timothy M. Yetman

Articulating reflections and conversations by its authors over the course of several years, this book is an attempt to elucidate the phenomenon of mind in the broadest sense of the word. Taking the insights we develop on the nature of the human experience of mind or mindedness at both the individual and inter-personal levels, we then present a meditation on life in the contemporary world of mass-mediated human culture. Our "method," or approach, is provisionally called radical phenomenology of mind.

In a sense, the starting point for our approach to the study of mind is the same as that articulated by Edmund Husserl in his early (pre-transcendentalizing) work, *Logical Investigations*, which establishes the phenomenological method as the ontologically, axiologically, epistemologically presuppositionless thematization of the data of consciousness as they show themselves in immediacy. Our meditation also draws on thinkers outside the continental tradition who cultivated conceptualizations of mind and its relationship to the world similar to Husserl's such as Charles Sanders Pierce ("phaneroscopy"), Alfred North Whitehead ("actual occasion/entity"), and George Santayana ("intuition of essences"). All of these thinkers contributed to a discourse deeply critical of many of the problematic assumptions of high modern post-Cartesian metaphysics in favor of a more realistic, empirically grounded, unorthodox approach to the study of consciousness in general. Our adoption of what we will here call the "radicalized" phenomenological approach continues the "tradition" these thinkers established of seeking to expunge plainly erroneous and/or useless preconceptions about mind and world, in an attempt to re-encounter the actual world ("to the things themselves") with fresh eyes.

The present work moves beyond these thinkers in so far as it rejects the residues of metaphysical thinking that they all retain, to establish a new approach to the study of consciousness and world that proceeds from a position of ontological

2 Introduction

nihilism. This is therefore a thoroughly "post-everything" (postmodern, post-metaphysical, etc.) work. Although it is conceived in the lexicon of, and participates in, the Western tradition of the life of the mind, it is not undertaken as part of a contribution to the larger Western institutional projects of either philosophy or science. Rather, it is the product of the simple Socratic practice of employing understanding in the examination of (our) life.

Although its "object" is the same as that of other areas of study such as psychology and philosophy of mind, *viz.*, the nature of mind or mindedness as we know it, radical phenomenology of mind, as envisaged and practiced here, is distinguished from these other approaches on the basis of the fact, alluded to above, that it lacks any enduring or overarching aim or agenda beyond the examination of life; outside any particularized, context-specific, immediate, and *ad hoc* concern of its practitioner, it is a cultureless, generalistic, approach to the data of experience. But that doesn't mean that it is incapable of producing insights that may be applicable and of use beyond the specific life-experience and immediate circumstances from which its thematizations arise.

As articulated here, phenomenology of mind constructs its thematizations of experience having taken into consideration, or "inpsychated," to use a Nietzschean expression, as many as possible of the sensibilities and insights developed by an array of specialized disciplines in the human and social sciences, but omits their ontological presuppositions and abjures their system-building aims. The consideration of such a breadth of perspectives allows one to extract insight from each while not taking any of them to be any more or less exclusively "faithful" to the fantasy of objective delimitation than any of the others. The final judgment is something the radical phenomenologist of mind knows to be chimerical. The fact that we have "lost" metaphysical finality (we never had it), doesn't *ipso facto* entail that a practical, working understanding of the actual world, and maybe even ourselves, is entirely lost to us.

As intimated above, one of our guiding notions is that a properly phenomenological approach to any object only takes place from a standpoint rooted in ontological (actual, not ontic) nihilism. Non-metaphysicalist radical phenomenology of mind, then, is the free reflection on mind and world in their actual, living context that results in fundamentally de-ontologized, unsystematic, non-reductive, specifistic descriptions of life. It is undertaken from the point of view of a practically detached, ideologically unaligned, axiologically divested moment of consciousness. The closest thing to systematization, classification, or essentialization it gets is to note continuities, associations, trends, etc., that may present themselves among the forms of experience it surveys over the course of the multiple thematizations that it makes.

Radical phenomenology of mind never settles on anything more than what is consciously affirmed as an always tentative and revision-or-renunciation-ready "fixation of belief," to echo a title from the great American philosopher C.S. Pierce. Science and philosophy have given us a reasonably accurate, or at least practically useful, accounting of the material world we inhabit, but this is not the case when it comes to an accounting of mind. Mind, in as much as it does show itself, does so as an improbable, intractable, immaterial appendage to our material (human) being, which, despite being so essential to who/what we human beings are, calls for further thematization and analysis because it so defies the principles by which we believe we understand everything else we find in our world. If it does nothing else, radical phenomenology of mind demonstrates the uniquely difficult nature of the task that mind sets for itself when it undertakes to know itself.

More than two thousand years of consideration have revealed that the complications and nuances of this tail-chase are legion. Never mind the universe: we are rightly a wonder to ourselves. How is it that, as seems to be the case, mind – that thing or place in which knowledge/experience occurs or arises – is so fundamentally challenged when it turns back on itself to ask what it itself is? It is the unique strangeness and elusiveness of mind that has driven much of the thought that has resulted in the work that follows.

Mind (in the sense of the strictly, uniquely human experience of consciousness) confounds us at multiple levels. First, there is the age-old question of what exactly makes our minds unique. One can approach the phenomenon of (human) mind in quantitative terms as what would appear to be a surfeit of consciousness (relative to other conscious beings), or, alternatively, in categorical, qualitative terms (like demonstrating self-awareness, or having a "soul"). Neither of these gets us very far beyond the initial claim that our minds are different from other kinds of consciousness, whose nature (as distinct "minds") themselves we have even less access to than our own.

Secondly, an important caveat is in order: the above use of the phrase "the phenomenon of mind" is quite misleading, and perhaps herein lies the source of many of the difficulties scientists, theologians, and philosophers have had in pinning mind down. With the possible exception of the individual's awareness of his or her *own* mind (the Cartesian cogito), mind "itself" (mind conceived broadly) is not a "phenomenon" in the standard Husserlian sense of the term, *viz.*, something that "shows itself" to consciousness. The *noesis* can never in real time also be the *noema*; mind cannot "stand over against itself" and be itself at the same time. For this it seems it would need the capacity to exceed the immediacy that constitutes it. Mind knows itself outside of immediacy only secondarily, via its own trace in recollection and in the image of other minds conveyed through language. In both such cases all we ever get is "second hand news" of mind, never the mind "itself."[1]

Beyond the ken of my own self-consciousness mind is only capable of being "known" via the mediation that is interposed between myself and another in second-order re-presentation, and is never a datum of immediacy. It is only the *products* of other mind(s) that can appear as phenomena. So we are left with the same Kantian veil denying us access to other human minds "in themselves" as is the case with other (non-human) kinds of consciousness. The notion that one actual mind is capable of being present to another is, as far as we can tell, a

4 Introduction

conceptual fiction, a placeholder whose attribution is made provisionally necessary by the inadequacy of our perceptual and conceptual resources. On this view, human consciousness is an inexplicable outlier, a strange epiphenomenon of nature, in as much as it seems ironically unequipped to know itself, despite its appearing to have been uniquely equipped to figure out an unheard-of scope of other things about the world in which it occurs. Mind exceeds itself.

For present purposes, then, when we address what we will call the "phenomenon of mind" writ large as a question of philosophical anthropology, we are forced to refer to its artifacts as stand-ins for mind "itself." While neither an understanding of the provenance of mind (*qua* human) nor its availability as a directly encounterable object will ever be ours, there is much material to work with. Ultimately, the only questions we can offer phenomenologically defensible answers to will be those outside the scope of anthropology, the ones that we have phenomenological access to as we "live" mind in first-hand experience. The rest falls into the category of what must simply be called "informed speculation." Eschewing the Euro-romantic rationalist dream of objective knowledge, we can, in a Deweyan or Whiteheadian spirit, still endeavor to paint a more fulsome, if never final, picture of mind generally conceived, based on the extant cornucopia of what we will be referring to as "shared mind:" mind as it is evidenced secondarily in the artifices of human linguistic and cultural traditions.

If there is one thing that is clear about human mind, both at the (radically particularized) first- and (mediated, shared) second-order levels, it is that it seems ever to want to hide itself. In fact, this characterization is already an indefensible reification of mind as something ontologically independent that transcends my own or your own particular conscious experience, which would possess its own kind of agency. It should come as no surprise that we find it difficult to talk about mind without resorting to anthropomorphic language, without the projective attribution of human-esque substantiality and agency to this thing-or-not we are calling mind independent of any hypothesized particular, concrete, actual, individual minds. This hiding/hiddenness of mind has been considered of central significance by many approaches that have come before, among which notably lie the psychological investigations of Friedrich Nietzsche and Sigmund Freud. These two thinkers are signal contributors to the tradition of thought devoted to unveiling mind and all of its complicated and confounding processes and manifestations. At the very least, with these two, we can concede that the "royal road" to mind is one fraught with detour after detour, perhaps *ad (in)finitum*.

Questions specifically devoted to understanding mental life (mind) have been at the heart of the tradition of human inquiry that is central to philosophy at least since Socrates. At all levels, consciousness, as we experience it, has always been the most elusive of things, always one step ahead—and by the same token—behind, itself. Accordingly, when we venture answers to questions about mind, they will not be offered as final resolutions, nor as building blocks to an eventually comprehensive theory of mind, but rather as parts of a mosaic, each of which individually provides nothing beyond what Martin Heidegger called a highly specific "*einblick*"—a flash of insight—into the immediate aspect of mind they are developed to (at least partially and provisionally) illuminate, but which together, hopefully, will present a general picture of mind that can be of some use.

The present work approaches the question of mind by broadly analyzing it at two levels: individual, immediate conscious experience (intuition, presentation); and interpersonal, mediate experience (shared, conventionalized knowledge, or re-presentation). A phenomenological study of mind finds its starting point, by necessity, in a reflection on the experience of mind, or mindedness, from the first person (egoistic) point of view: the relationship of intentionality between my mind and its worldly focus as conceived by Franz Brentano and elaborated on by Husserl. This is because, as suggested above, there is no getting around the fact that the gateway to all experience, and hence, eventually, to reflectively thematized understanding, and then, to an understanding of the structures of shared conventions of meaning, is first-hand conscious experience.

Nevertheless, echoing John Donne's "no man is an island," we aver that mind, as it has made itself historically available to us, would never have happened, nor does it make any sense, in the vacuum of solipsism. So the fuller picture of the phenomenon of mind cannot emerge until the initial view of the radically individuated experience is contextualized in the larger sphere of culture and of life: the study of "my" mind as I encounter it embedded in that larger, transpersonal breadth of mind both in the lived present and across the great span of time and space that is culture with a history, and which is manifested in language.

The issue of the status of mind becomes one of the central, and most recalcitrant, problems in the modern West with Descartes' establishment of the doctrine of dualism, whereby mind, or thought (the "subjective"), is understood to enjoy a distinct ontological status vis à vis material, "objective" entities. The present text lies outside (or after) the confines of the monist-dualist ontological debate and its mind-body/materialism-idealism problems, itself a rich, if problem-ridden, source of insight into the nature of mind and the world in which it occurs. We consider the problems resulting from Cartesian dualism to have been generally satisfactorily resolved (principally through de-emphasis, rather than engagement) approximately a century ago in the work of, among others, Nietzsche, James, Husserl, Whitehead, Dewey, and Bergson, all of whom contributed to a fundamental change in the way we think about consciousness and its relationship to its world.

There still remains much to be fleshed out regarding how we are to think about the conjunction of the so-called "subjective" and "objective" in the concrete actuality of experience, especially when contextualized in what we will call the contemporary, post-modern era of our broader culture. Our guiding notion here is that mind, or mindedness, is the distinguishing feature of human life *par excellence*, and that an elucidation of its forms, mechanisms of operation, and limits is of the essence for any attempt to make sense of human life and existence at any level.

6 Introduction

Much work has already been done in this vein. The philosophical perspective developed here strains the ideas of G.W.F. Hegel through those of Husserl, resulting in the borrowed but completely reconceived expression "phenomenology of mind." We take from Hegel a sense of the awesome power of the human mind, but, following Husserl and the other more recent above-mentioned philosophers of consciousness, we seek to develop a de-metaphysicalized, de-romanticized contribution to the study of mind as it manifests itself writ small (the individual) and large (societies/cultures). Radical phenomenology of mind presents the picture of human life that emerges when one takes a fundamentally free and presuppositionless (descriptive phenomenological, and post-ontological) perspective on all things to do with the extra-material (mental) life of human beings, informed by a serio-comedic attitude. It is pragmatically, but not onto-logically (or any other-wise) anthropocentric, focusing exclusively on *human* consciousness. This is because, even though, as Whitehead maintains, ("mere") consciousness may not be something exclusively human, human beings' relationship with and attitude toward their own consciousness makes of it a qua-litatively different phenomenon than that evidenced in other species. Even in the apparently relatively high level of self-awareness of the other great apes whom evolutionary biology rightly designates as the closest members of our own "family," an accurate and comprehensive understanding of their experience remains strictly off limits to us. As Freud shows us, no other animal has given birth to the kinds of tremendous, complex, and fascinating works that find their origins in the human mind.

In a qualitative leap from our pre-historic ancestors' primeval development of tools and limited verbal communication systems as imaged by paleontology, humankind's unique form of consciousness has brought us, largely as a result of the expansion and practical trans-temporalization of mind that arises with the invention of writing, into a vast and nuanced "second nature." This "second nature" of mind is made up of the values, technologies, arts, religions, political and economic systems, etc., which together make up the great edifice of human culture and inform our most basic shared sensibilities. The "second nature" of mental life that is instituted via shared narratives does not replace or displace the "first" world of materiality and facticity, but arises as an inexplicable complement to the latter whose cultivation and occupation is unique to human beings.

Our discussion of consciousness proceeds from the notion that the human mind and its connection with the world must be understood as manifested in what Whitehead called an "actual occasion." In cultivating the notion of the "actual occasion," Whitehead sought to flesh out all the nuances of William James' revolutionary call for a change in the way we approach studying conscious experience ("radicalizing" empiricism much as we are here "radicalizing" phe-nomenology). James asserted that the latter should not be conceived according to traditional terms as a "subject" encountering a world of ontologically (or any other-wise) distinct "objects," but that the basic datum of consciousness is *experience itself*—a concept that englobes both the traditionally conceived subject and object into its greater theoretical unity.

Mind, as Heidegger and Whitehead both showed us in different ways, cannot be properly understood outside of its connectedness to other minds as well as to its immediate concrete circumstances, both of which constitute elements (which Whitehead called "prehensions") of the "actual occasion" in which we discover it/it discovers itself. Hence, the present work approaches the issue of mind not from within the terms of modern philosophy's Cartesian/Kantian tradition. Rather, our initial approach loosely shares in the phenomenological, pragmatic, and organic perspectives articulated by these thinkers, as generated in a reflective review of mind immediately manifested in concrete, temporally, materially, and culturally contextualized, lived *experience*.

The question of a broader science of consciousness (which would include non-human forms thereof) is extraneous to the approach taken here. The latter would belong to the modern system of disciplinary knowledge as embodied in its tributary sub-systems like zoology, anthropology, sociology, psychology, etc., which are born of, and conducted under, the objectivist ideal of scientism. In equal measure as regards the modern, post-Cartesian rationalist philosophical viewpoint, the present discourse is also developed outside the terms of the modern world-view of scientism. Both philosophical rationalism and modern scientism participate and are grounded in the abstractive notion of the fundamental ontological distinction between subjectivity (mind) and objectivity (world) interpreted exclusively through the assumed law of materialist causality and, most significantly, they are devoted to the pursuit of a universalizable, or at least generalizable, ontological and epistemological schematics, which the present discourse eschews. Hewing to these ontological and methodological presuppositions, modern science proceeds on the basis of what Whitehead called the "fallacy of misplaced concreteness," by which it manipulates what it mistakes for freely encountered "data" even before it pronounces its judgment on them by abstracting, or decontextualizing them as a prerequisite for its procedure.

While the purview of phenomenology of mind coincides, or overlaps, with the subject-matter of these (and other) human sciences, it shares none of their aims (it has no aim beyond thematic understanding) or presuppositions (it has no presuppositions, only findings, or post-suppositions), and is generalistic, not specialistic, in its orientation. When viewed from the point of view of a latter-day phenomenology of mind, the materialist/idealist binary that is the legacy of the modern European tradition decontextualizes mind as manifested in immediacy (as it does with all of its objects), only to reinsert its findings regarding it into a narrative giving voice to a greater scheme of significance which is extrinsic to the data under consideration.

From the Nietzsche-advised interrogative standpoint of radical phenomenology of mind, modern Western philosophy and science are subsidiary contributions to the greater cultural project of *rendering the world meaningful*, and that larger cultural aim is here understood as a product of the grandest of all meta-ideologies (what

8 Introduction

Jean-François Lyotard called "grand narratives") of the West, which we will call the Euro-romance. Rationalism and its offspring, science, as specifically modern Western thought-formations, are deeply rooted in idealism, messianism, and humanism (anthropo-narcissism), all of which are infected with implicit valuations as informed by the legacy of the Euro-romance, and which are therefore not conducive to the development of a clear picture of ourselves and our world.

As we have stated, phenomenology of mind relies for its initial freedom on many of the criticisms of the Euro-romantic tradition of ontologization put forth by the turn of the twentieth-century thinkers we have been discussing. Our discourse also takes advantage of the decisive criticism of the Euro-romantic addiction to meaning that was started by the existential thought of Fyodor Dostoevsky, Søren Kierkegaard, Martin Heidegger, Jean-Paul Sartre, and Albert Camus. This radical questioning of the basic assumptions of Western metaphysics was later brought to devastating completion in the postmodern(ist) deconstructive works of Michel Foucault, Jacques Derrida, and Jean Baudrillard.

Following from the critical call for a radical reorientation of traditional Western thinking after the nineteenth-century disaster of the de-stabilization of ultimate meaning that these contributors made it their business to investigate, our contemporary iteration of the study of mind fits more appropriately into a critical sub-tradition of philosophical, rather than scientific inquiry. However, it is "philosophical" only in the sense that it is but another Socratic attempt to "examine life," and not to establish a system of ideas. Despite all that it owes to the above-named predecessors, the present discourse has moved beyond them all in the sense that our thought is here undertaken in a spirit that is purely illuminative and is divorced utterly from the edifying aims of all institutional knowledge traditions. The idiosyncratic "tradition" we cultivate in this work ("radical phenomenology of mind") can thus be said to be in many ways alien to the basic sensibilities of thinkers of the generation to which Freud and Husserl belong. Despite their contributions to its ultimate decisive undermining, these thinkers remained exemplars of both the scientific and philosophical traditions of modernity. Their invaluable contributions to the critical overturning of many of the modern West's misunderstandings regarding mind came despite the fact that they still worked under the sign of "rigorous" science as an ideal, a legacy of the Euro-romance.

The present work unfolds in a conceptual space that the above-named turn of the twentieth-century forerunners seem not to have been able to occupy, although their work (among that of others) was instrumental in opening it up: the condition of pure ontological nihilism. The potential benefit of improving our understanding of mind writ large in the contemporary world is heightened by the historical fact that the realm of mind and its products has now entirely overtaken the material realm in terms of its significance for human life. Baudrillard's claim that the "real" has been absorbed into, and effectively nullified by, simulation, speaks to this allocation of primacy given to the products of mind over other (real, actual) concerns.

Indeed, the Baudrillardian notion of the threat posed by simulation to the real can be said to be a highly refined and specified application of the powerful theoretical insight introduced by Freud with the notion of the "omnipotence of thoughts:" mind's creative, spontaneous power, manifested in imagination and transmitted in re-presentation (culture), seems to obtain to such a position of significatory dominance and ubiquity that it now challenges the primacy of the actuality (immediacy, the real) that has traditionally been (perhaps mis-)understood to be the initial occasion and context for its works. The power of mind (over itself) is not to be underestimated: it dominates human life. We accordingly here approach mind as something not merely intriguing, but as something Promethean, Faustian, and Frankensteinian. Even though it arises in/from us, the apes who bear and project it, it is not only strange, fascinating, and unforeseeable (it is inexplicable in terms of any of the categories by which we explain other phenomena), but it is also far from inert. *It* "gives" us our world—on/in its terms, not our own. It is interesting to consider this notion of mind as something of an independent force, after a fashion, in its own right, a conception based on the patent fact that, as established culture, it seems nearly always to be out of our reach and control. This kind of unanticipated, uncanny independence that mind (as codified culture) acquires when made public as representation, *becomes a new kind of "objective" datum of experience in its own right*; it takes on its own life despite its having been the product of our concrete intellectual and imaginative work. The independence that it thus acquires is one of the heretofore underexplored aspects of mind that we consider of primary significance in this work. If the human species were to suddenly disappear from the face of the earth, so would mind. We must nevertheless expand our understanding of it as something that is ultimately not under our control once it makes its bid for permanence by asserting itself as something with its own agenda after escaping the immediate concrete human occasion that gives rise to it.

The present project is undertaken in what we consider to be the best tradition of philosophy used in its critical, Socratic capacity to perform an "examination of life," applying the mind's intellectual capacities toward the immanently ameliorative end of living relatively well. In the contemporary world, Socratic philosophy, as the free, seeking, and open reflection on life, is no longer practiced except by isolated individuals here and there.

The falling into desuetude of philosophy as a lived ethos in which life informs thought and thought informs life, *viz.*, as a critical vital technique by which to remedy the perennial barriers to better understanding that are embodied in missing information, lack of perspective, or misleading assumptions that enter into our thinking, reflects the more generally moribund state of the civilization that gave rise to it. Our civilization is dead, we just haven't realized or accepted it yet. In a reversal of the state of affairs suggested in the famous Marxian claim that the dead "weigh like a nightmare on the brains of the living,"[2] we contemporaries are like the ghost family in the film "The Others," who are haunted by the living, unaware that it is actually *we ourselves* who are dead.

10 Introduction

The recent events surrounding the European publications that have repeatedly insisted on depicting the Prophet Mohammed under what can only be described as the willfully naïve notion that they are defending the Western value of free speech are a case in point. These provocations are symptoms not of a Huntingtonian "clash of," nor even a dialogue between, civilizations, but represent an intrapsychic (intra-cultural) struggle taking place exclusively inside the mind/culture of these Western provocateurs. We are mourning the death of our own civilization in a Freudian repetition-compulsion by staging a crisis which would call for a reassertion of our (dead) humanist values ("free speech"). As Heidegger pointed out, following the issue as Nietzsche framed it, the West has long ago lost faith in the force of its own values—in value itself—and succumbed to a negatively conceived nihilism as a self-pitying spiritual disease-state—a kind of despair writ large. Western secularism has lately been so busy asserting its supposed "right" to speak its values that it seems to have forgotten to make the critical initial step of coming up with something worthwhile to say.

Actually living, vital civilizations (although there are none extant) do not seek out straw adversaries to use as foils in an effort to make a narcissistic, purely self-referential show of false vitality for themselves; they are too busy living and building to do so. We will have occasion in the final chapter of this work to address some of these so-called "real-world" events that symptomatize the current state of our (Western-dominated) world. Before that, in Chapter 1, we will set the historical-cultural stage to see how it is that we have arrived at the state (of mind) we are in as a people, laying out a brief cultural history of the rise, climax, and denouement of the Euro-romance as the great narrative testimonial of the modern West. It is followed in the subsequent chapters by articulations of the authors' understanding of the nature of experience, and attempts to illuminate the larger, cultural imaginative space we occupy in the aftermath of the collapse of the Euro-romance.

Notes

1 One of the "giants" on whose shoulders the present work stands, is William James, who addressed these very questions over a century ago in, among other places, an essay entitled "Does Consciousness 'Exist'?" (in *Essays in Radical Empiricism*). In this article, James suggests that we have always taken the same approach to the question of mind as we have to other worldly phenomena and that the incomprehensibly vast difference in quality between mind itself and worldly objects begs a different approach. Furthermore, in a Jamesian spirit, we are not here concerned with the so-called "problem" of the non-phenomenality of mind itself. We just note this fact as part of what must be taken under consideration in attempting to better understand what we are dealing with when we seek to make mind an epistemological concern.

2 Karl Marx, *The Eighteenth Brumaire of Louis Bonaparte*.

1

MIND, NARRATIVITY, AND THE EURO-ROMANCE

Timothy M. Yetman

The Narratological Essence of Mind; Shared Mind and Fabulation, or Transcendence and the Word

All known performances and edifices of mind are ultimately rooted in human beings' fundamental sociality. Cultures, or traditions of sharing mind between individuals, have one seemingly universal characteristic: the production and consumption of stories. Far more than mere fleeting entertainment, these stories give *meaning* to the lives and worlds of their creators and consumers—they are *lived through*. There are solid reasons for both sides of this situation. Before addressing the story of the Euro-romance—*our* story, let's assume the role of philosophical anthropologist and put the specific narrative tradition that the West has cultivated in context, considering the meaning and function of narrativity more broadly. The stories we humans broadcast and receive, we will here maintain, are utterly essential to the way in which mind as an extra-solipsistic (*viz.*, social, or shared) phenomenon has come into being as we know it. In humankind's prehistoric, pre-linguistic past, there were undoubtedly individual minds, but the individual minds that are manifested today cannot but be fundamentally different; they are the products of thousands of years of intersubjective interaction via language, and, although one can only speculatively conjecture, they no doubt have little likeness to their archaic predecessors in the pre-linguistic so-called "state of nature."

By means of narratives, we have all been infecting each other with our cares, thoughts, concerns, fears, and hopes for eons. The notion of a mind decontextualized from larger human culture and society cannot have any real meaning to us. Although our immediate experience is one of particularity, to use a perfectly apt cliché, we are nevertheless ideationally woven into the "fabric" of the general, the universal, of the shared consciousness that constitutes society. I use "society" here in the widest sense, in the understanding that we are members of a species that places a higher stake in the realm of the unreal, of the imagination, of the story, than it does in the concrete, actual, material realm and, accordingly, *remembers everything*. Without memory, mind would lack one of its necessary conditions, and it is memory that adds to the relatively immediate connection between our own particularity and that of other minds, in the here and now of the present, the vast compendium of mind's traces that constitute the abiding edifices of language, literature, and culture. It is a great irony that memory, whose faithlessness common sense has always understood as an enduring source of significant problems, has lately been "confirmed" by science. We tolerate our reliance on memory despite our broad acknowledgement of its consistent unreliability because it is like an abusive partner about whom we have mixed feelings, but cannot free ourselves from, because we are practically dependent upon it: memory is essential to the narratological functioning of mind. It is this "catch 22" that makes cynicism a key component in the standard operation of mind as we generally find it in its mature latter-day manifestation, wherein the search for truth is subsidiary to an initial predilection toward fabricating and consuming/being consumed by, lies.

Addressing the phenomenon of narratology is an indispensable part of the study of mind. One of its immediate concerns is to render phenomenologically as clear as possible the function of mind that is constituted by *faith*. Faith is another necessary condition for the functional operation of (shared) mind; that is one of the reasons it is at the core of Hobbes' concerns, discussed below. For our present purposes, faith, or trust, like memory, is to be considered as an element of shared consciousness that precedes and trumps a concern for objective truth, and has to do more with primordial aspects of (human) mind's response to its experience for which truth is initially of no concern at all. Truth, on this account, is a luxury we are rarely afforded.

This rather Jamesian/Piercean understanding of the search for truth finds the latter to be subordinate to the more pressing quest for reprieve from grief broadly conceived. This grief is precisely the quality of conscious experience articulated by existentialism in the notions of the dread, anguish, and care, as something that makes mind want to escape from itself in proportion to the fullness with which it is manifested, to run away from itself at every turn. Here, incidentally, is a solution to the complication that Freud's concept of the "death drive" posed for his preceding, simpler understanding of human psychology as, among other things, book-ended by the pleasure and reality principles. Mind, on the present view, *simultaneously* and in equal measure, indulges the pleasure principle *and* the will to nothingness (the so-called "death drive") when it seeks comfort in distraction and occupation. Few things have managed more adequately and universally to serve the purpose of imaginative reprieve from both the immediate and enduring experience of suffering in everyday life than the pastime of telling and listening to stories.

Faith plays an essential role in the mechanics of narrativity because, even though in the West it has always been tied to ideas of objective truth (via notions like "fidelity"), it can be argued that its Kierkegaardian passional function as a vehicle for the mitigation of/escape from (Heideggerian) care is more "primordial." We can move beyond this and claim in postmodernist fashion that the truth was never anything of real concern at all to mind. Instead, due to something inexplicable and incomprehensible about the latter, it seems to find itself feeling naked and consequently compelled in the name of modesty to pay cynical lip service to the idea of truth. This reduces the latter to a mere alibi, a conceit on which mind for some unknown reason seems to need to rely in order to function. The escape from itself that consciousness undertakes via the instrument of faith can come just as well from the relatively benign consumption of fairy tales as from the potentially disastrous blind following of orders issued by another—a mentor or a demagogue for example—onto whom we have displaced the dreadful burden of decision and care. Faith, then, is what lies behind the fascination that compels us into the realm of narrativity.

Broadcasting

What is specifically behind the *telling* of stories? First, and common-sensibly, we tell stories because, notwithstanding the fundamentally social nature of humans we noted above, it seems that we cannot help but be first and foremost the center of our own universes. This is a practical explanation of, if not a justification for, anthropo-narcissism. Putting aside questions of truth and fidelity, the functional explanation of stories as mere inert conveyances of information assumed in standard communications theory overlooks the fact that we tell them first and foremost as self-aggrandizing bids for attention, acceptance, and approval. They are projections, broadcasts, or testimonials devoted to satisfying the successor to what would figure in the Hobbesian "state of nature" as the instinct for survival. This instinct or inclination is transformed when the initial material struggle for survival has been superseded by the ideational struggle for significance, or meaning, in the artificial world of shared mind, shared meaning, or culture. The present writing is no exception to this. Even though I share E.M. Cioran's (1987) ruthless acceptance that every human undertaking is baseless, I am nevertheless writing (as did Cioran) with the anticipation that my words will be read by someone in the future, because I have valorized the advancement of a public Socratic critical agenda, even though the deeper thrust of that agenda spurs me to aver that this, like all public communications, does not escape qualification by its own vanity.

We have not yet adapted to the sea-change we have instituted with civilization. The still-active instinct for survival insistently and incessantly throws us back into a comportment that gives primacy to self-interest or at least self-orientation. Despite having largely done away with the ever-present *literal*, material, mortal threats of pre-civilized life, our civilized consciousness remains inevitably cagey, guarding against threats to its (own) meaning. We have sublimated the instinctual energy previously devoted to self-preservation, transforming it into a new tradition of

14 Timothy M. Yetman

performative, self-promoting fabulation. It is by way of this narratological performative activity that all of us, in the mediate or immediate, real or imagined, company of others, engage in civilized life. In the imaginative space of civilization, we now fend off the principally figurative threat we face of being deprived of access to, and participation in, the shared system of meanings in virtually everything we say and do.

This is a hypothetical-historical explanation of what appears to be the universal human tendency to construct and energetically maintain narratives as a function of staking a claim to significance in the secondary (virtual) life-world of shared meaning that is culture. A kind of constitutional (not necessarily a psychological or ethical) self-concern lies at the heart of our most basic orientation as human beings, and the Euro-romantic attitude of anthropo-narcissism is merely the hypertrophied, generalized form of this fundamental self-concern.

One can see in the advent of human mind a later—or the final—stage of a biological continuum where the movement toward complexity accompanies the emergence of ontological, and ultimately mental independence, centeredness, and uniqueness—at the level of the individual. Fleshing out this notion, one can see consciousness as reducible to the occurrence of an entity's reckoning with the world. Wherever there is such a reckoning, there is consciousness. At the most simple end of the continuum, even a virus can be considered a rudimentarily conscious entity by virtue of the fact that it actively reckons with its environment, but in a most direct fashion, when it infects its host and replicates itself, only mutating over generations according to the demands of its encountered circumstances. Such mutations are the result of a mediation between an organism and its world in its least obstructionist, most relatively direct, form. At the other end of this continuum is human consciousness, whose reckoning with the world manifests a dimensionality that is the product of the relatively tremendous detour that is mind's interposition between the material human organism and immediacy. The farther mind takes itself from immediacy with its narrative mediation, the more robust and dimensional mental life becomes.

Immediacy is something we cannot escape while alive; its hold on us is merely obscured by the illusion of distance created by the imaginative work carried out by our exceedingly powerful and ambitious human mental apparatuses. The baseline for consciousness remains the encounter between a singular entity and the world. The fact remains that we can't *actually* walk a single step in another's shoes. The closest we can come is to attempt the imaginative leap of sympathy. Sympathy is only a modified, or hypothetical, modality of the more primordial condition of self-centeredness (in the existential-phenomenological, not moral, sense of the expression). Even the extreme sympathetic pathos of saintliness is in the end rooted in an endeavor to make one's own life and action meaningful, and this meaning, in the context of human society, rests on the mediation provided by socially inculcated sensibilities we inherit from convention. This context is the native home of narratology. The gap between minds is bridged via stories.

The sociable habits of human beings, as we stated above, make possible narrativism and the illusion it lends to us of overcoming the actually insuperable distance between radically separated individual minds. Once a story is born and nurtured, it takes on a life of its own, one whose robustness and durability is proportional to how compelling it is seen to be. Perhaps it must be also noted that a crucial factor in the durability of the life of any particular narrative is the continuity and breadth of its spreading. The re-telling of stories is essential to the longevity of the human narratological tradition.

The phenomenon or "problem" of plagiarism can be explained in light of this analysis: one enhances one's perceived *gravitas* (in the eyes of both oneself and of others) when one participates in the life of a story in any capacity. In the modern Western world, we put a premium on the latter's *genesis*, praising the genius of authorial yarn-weavers because these so-called luminaries participate in the divine aura that attends the mythical revealed Word. Plagiarists are just as driven to take undue credit for others' work by their reverence for those whose work they seek to pass off as their own as by practical expediency. What they are doing is in a sense nothing more than participating in the re-telling, or the dissemination, of what we generally consider to be among the best of our imaginative works. How utterly different is the use of someone's words without citation than with? Given the relatively narrow imaginative breadth of what is considered to be the legitimate purview of most of our disciplinary traditions, how truly earth-shatteringly unique and original are the "exemplary" works published in today's hyper-specialized discourses to begin with? The temptation to illegitimately associate oneself with "greatness" via the mimetic reproduction of another's words is more than likely the same behavior that kept alive many of the pre-graphic oral narrative traditions that gave us the works of the likes of Homer.

One can consider the "problem" from yet another angle. If so-called "victims" of plagiarism are unable to get some level of serio-comic distance from their lives, their work, and the culture in which they operate, they might consider availing themselves of Nietzsche's advice ("what are my parasites to me?"). If nothing else, such a consideration might at least appeal to their vanity, at whose behest they could perhaps accept the notion that having "their" ideas "stolen" from them is a gesture of respect and *only serves to reinforce their already agreed upon status as "genius."* This claim is analogous to Barack Obama's famous statement to industrial leaders that "you didn't build that" as a reminder that *everything* produced in society partakes of and relies on an already existing, shared, public, infrastructure. This applies irrespective of whether that infrastructure is composed of roads or ideas.

For my own part, I maintain no illusion that the ideas I have presented here are in any way "mine." I did not create the language in which they are written, the culture that made them possible, nor the philosophical tradition that refined their elements and made them formally available to me for processing. It would be nothing short of delusional for me to believe that anything I have said here has not already been said in one form or another, and most likely more eloquently,

16   Timothy M. Yetman

by some other thinker. No man is an island; a sense of intellectual propriety has no place in the practice of radical phenomenology of mind.

Receiving

Especially when we take into account that all of the stories that we generate are as much (indeed, initially only) for our *own* consumption as they are for others, it may not seem too difficult to accept the above explanation of our narratological impulse, but it does not account for a second, equally crucial co-condition for the coming into being of the tradition of human fabulation: an enthusiastic audience who delights in the experience of imaginative re-presentation. At bottom, it seems this receptivity may be rooted in our desire for something stable we can rely on in a world fraught with insecurity and uncertainty, and this is where faith plays its crucial role.

Only in the imaginative "safe place" carved out by the narrative, is entertainment—that hypertrophied narratological bugbear that has come to dominate contemporary cultural life—possible. The escapist sense of safety nurtured by narratology provides an outlet for our human desire to indulge in trust. The fact that we are capable of taking something, anything, on faith, flies in the face of what common sense would comfortably describe as our primordial, instinctive tendency to be mistrustful and wary, a tendency rooted in (at least the memory of) actual adversity. This tendency can be said most likely to have arisen in response to what Dewey describes as the "precarious and perilous" nature of human existence: we are rightly vigilant in our anticipation of adversity, and this, as we suggested above, holds true on both sides of the dividing line that is the advent of civilized life.

All of this would seem to weigh against the receptivity that is required for the second, consumptive term in the tradition of narratological relations between human minds. Is it possible that the narratological contrivance of the life of the mind is sufficiently compelling to deliver us from actual material suffering? The power of mind to deliver us from material suffering is evidenced clearly in two fundamentally divergent approaches to life: Buddhism and contemporary Western culture. Both suggest, in vastly different ways, that mind *can* deliver us from suffering, setting aside the otherwise important question of the fundamentally different approach taken by each as to specifically *how* this is achieved (self-overcoming vs. self-indulgence).

The primary form of adversity we faced in pre-civilized life was unchecked nature. After civilization, we face a principally human, unnatural adversity hinted at above: the deprivation of unalloyed faith in, or full access to, the common life of meaning. The most basic form this threat of privation takes is that of deception. In a world of shared meaning, fidelity is at a premium. The ever-present threat of deception and manipulation forces us to spend tremendous intellectual and emotional energy evaluating others' intentions, their loyalties, their usefulness, and, for our own parts, being calculating, conniving, ingratiating, and manipulative, all of which are inescapable in human social life.

The Hobbes-inspired skepticism with regard to others' general trustworthiness would seem to weigh against the practicability of faith that is at the core of the second, receptive term in the narratological relationship we are discussing. So how does one explain it? With reference to the fact that we are exhausted. Navigating the artificial world of civilization can be so difficult that at times we are compelled to wonder whether it has really achieved its hypothetical end of deliverance from, or at least significant respite from, adversity. Ivan Karamazov's Grand Inquisitor may have had a point in reproaching God for his bungled work, but we ourselves certainly haven't made much headway in the task of "correcting" it. In light of this re-engineering job's failure, we are forced to take refuge in trust. Trust arises as the imaginative safe-haven of resignation born of weariness and wishful thinking and finds its archetype in the romantic concept of love. The valorization of trust is the ethical corollary to what Nietzsche called western metaphysics' "will to truth:" an ideal founded on an inversion or perversion of what common sense would seem to call for because, even though having faith in others is irrational, we are willing to take that risk anyway.[1]

Like capricious Nature, others will betray our trust continuously (and it matters little that the vast majority of those betrayals are carried out neither maliciously nor deliberately). Like thirsty desert-wanderers, we are ever looking for an illusory oasis that would provide relief from the memory and anticipation of betrayal.

Historically, everywhere mind comes face to face with itself, when it finds itself alone with itself (the primordial state of consciousness, or "radical separation"), it is overwhelmed and turns away aghast. This is the deep truth about human life depicted in morality plays like *Everyman*, but delved into more deeply by Kierkegaard, Dostoevsky, and Nietzsche, and later expounded on by Heidegger, Sartre, and Camus. What these thinkers showed us is that the separation of minds does not admit of degrees, but is absolute. Theoretically, however, an acknowledgment of the reality of *any* distance between minds shatters the delicate illusion, woven by our narratives, that we can share anything outside the terms of the shared narrative itself, *viz., actually*. Via fabulation, history, tradition, etc., we can all share what appears to be the same world, but in actuality, the radical particularity of our experience denies us that connection, and the many can never become the one.

When one dives deeply into the experience of radical particularity, or dwells alone contemplating the irremediable separation of individual minds, the result is usually what most would consider madness. Madness and evil are of a piece in this sense. This is what drove Hobbes' ardent defense of meaning under the law of *logos* against "absurdity." As seen from the standpoint of shared meaning and its sanctity, madness is precisely the ineluctable outcome of a reckoning with ontological nihilism. Madness and evil, as co-implications of the ontological nihilism that manifests itself in the incapacity of narratology to overcome radical particularity, are what preoccupied Dostoevsky, and that preoccupation came energetically

18 Timothy M. Yetman

gushing out in the form of an eloquent panic attack that spanned thousands of pages of the most riveting stories one could ever read. All of Dostoevsky's works speak to the catastrophic conjoinedness of madness and evil, of freedom ("everything is possible") and anarchy ("nothing is forbidden") in human mental life.

We can also speak of the association of solitude with madness in more everyday terms. When one is sufficiently withdrawn from human culture (something that is ironically a pre-requisite for any phenomenology of mind), one occupies a position, relative to the minds or shared mind-conventions one is surrounded by (including one's own), not entirely unlike that of a "sociopath." This thought came to me a number of years ago when, having already studied mind in a scholarly capacity (via philosophy and political theory) for some twenty odd years, I undertook for the first time to open myself up to understanding my own mind as the first step in taking stock of my life more generally. For the first time in my life, I turned philosophy from an aesthetic, academic curiosity to the practical, Socratic, purpose of actually "examining my life"—or at least took it to a vastly greater level than I ever had. This process involved an endeavor not simply to study myself clinically, from a safe intellectual distance, but to make transparent to myself all that I really was in my unseemly, disordered, and unremarkable actuality as a human animal. Long a student of philosophy, my way down this path of self-discovery most centrally involved diving as deeply and unguardedly as possible into the deeply challenging works of Freud, Dostoevsky, Kierkegaard, Max Stirner, and Al-Ghazālī, among others. After years of merely thinking about and reading, rather than *using* philosophy, I had still yet to fully *live* philosophy, and I only began to do so after taking this "practical turn," which had the added benefit of generating an entirely new way of thinking about mind, one that my own contribution to the present project is the product of.

As I worked my way through these authors' works, a picture began to emerge in my thinking, one that seemed to offer an affective and practical counterpoint to the condition of despair and dismay that attends the experience of radical particularism that is characteristic of much of existentialist reflection, from Kierkegaard to Sartre. It was an idea that I summarily (experimentally) named "benevolent sociopathy." Put simply, it refers to an acclimatization to radical particularism and its ultimate inescapability. *Adapting* to, rather than being driven mad by solitude, the occupation of a mental life that finds itself simultaneously inside of (practically) and alien to (ontologically and axiologically) the common life of mind is what distinguishes this position from that of a "true" sociopath, as the latter is usually conceived. In the next chapter, my co-author will discuss these two positions in terms of the notions of "embeddedness" (dwelling inside the common mind-world) and "reflective review" (dwelling temporarily outside of the common mind-world).

Kierkegaard and Stirner in particular made me acutely aware of what I had already come to appreciate at the suggestion of Nietzsche, *viz.*, that mind, like any object one seeks to know, can only be properly understood from a *distance*. It began to slowly dawn on me that a kind of *absolutely* ecstatic point of view—a complete stepping-outside-of-oneself—is a necessary condition for the development of even a rudimentary self-understanding. As my project of ecstatic self-interrogation unfolded, it coalesced into the broader methodological conclusion that, not only my own, but *any* phenomenological project is doomed to failure absent its being undertaken from an atopic ("positionless") position outside the meaning-space of existing culture. The pursuit of inquiry from the "position" of an "atopia of received meaning," so long as it remains rational and equanimous, is categorically distinct from sociopathy. It is nothing more than a radicalization of Husserl's procedure.

This understanding of a potentially positive aspect to the freedom of mind that comes with the discipline of willfully and deliberately dwelling in an atopia of mind, *viz.*, in cultureless radical particularity, is what distinguishes it from madness, evil, and pathology. It is the approach to mind that mind, as a would-be object to itself, demands. To assume the comportment of radicalized phenomenology of mind in everyday life is to be *among* other minds and mind-systems (meaning systems, ideals), but not *with/within* them (again, crucially, including one's own— one can be as easily expropriated by personal narratives voicing one's unique fears and hopes as by an eloquent speech by a demagogue): that is square one of phenomenology of mind.

Eventually I realized that I was only comparing the distancing experiment of radicalized phenomenology of mind to "sociopathy" because from this position of the deep acceptance of radical separation, one *is* effectively as removed as a "sociopath" from the sensibilities, prejudices, preferences, fears, and appreciations of average everyday common mindedness (what Heidegger called "the they").

By way of clarification, it must be stated that this distance is *purely intellectual*, not affective, and is therefore distinguished from sociopathy by the fact that it not only retains empathy and sympathy for others, but also makes possible an even more *enhanced* form of these. Radical phenomenology of mind allows for this on account of its fundamental freedom from any kind of valuative orientation. It allows for a deeper and more faithful, and therefore more sympathetic, under-standing of what it means to be human. As a practitioner of this approach, one can see clearly that one is every bit as prone to folly and confusion as anyone else. This is no functional madness or elitism: we are all at some level or other, human, all-too-human (or maybe just the right amount?) from this perspective. The only thing different about the phenomenologist of mind's experience of interacting with other human beings and that of those with whom they are interacting, is that they have the added perspective of having put everything in perspective. This frees up the practitioner for affective sympathy with others while refraining from imaginative commiseration with them.

The anxiety-free experience of absolute freedom from all perspectival sensi-bilities that attends dwelling in radical particularity, which we are attempting to flesh out as a condition for the operation of radical phenomenology of mind, is something the "true" sociopathic mind does not know. We have emphasized the non-pathological quality of the experience to suggest that the simple freedom from regnant norms and sensibilities that comes with an ontologically nihilistic perspective, as we understand it, is *nothing other than "raw" experience considered outside of human mediating systems of meanings fabricated and employed by mind, all of which vector to ultimaticity*. On this view, it is the only categorically sensible and sane point of view occupiable, if we take sanity to mean a hewing to actuality: it constitutes the pure realism of radical immediate immanence.

The experiment of assuming the radical phenomenological disposition is eminently sane; it is not a whimsical flight of fancy, but the opposite. It calls for a return to actuality (the "things themselves") that is *absolute*, and this marks it off from the half-baked variant of a "return" that guides Husserl's phenomenological reduction. *Radical* phenomenology calls not merely for a provisional, Cartesian suspension of belief in the assumed reality of our common sense picture of the world, but instead for the embracement of *utter* disengagement from *all* such pictures as dwelling places of mind in an emotionally, existentially, intellectually comprehensive way. A non-pathological acclimatization to the experience of nihilism in radical particularity can be described as a kind of embracement of the original, pre-ontological givenness of mind's actual *Unheimlichkeit*, or homelessness. However, it is a homelessness devoid of nostalgia, because the practitioner understands and accepts that there is not, and never was, any (non-artificial) home for which to long, beyond the unmediated experience of the moment.

Dwelling comfortably, undespairingly, non-nostalgically in radically particularized experience is perhaps the farthest thing from what one generally finds mind actually doing. To say the least, human beings are uncomfortable with being left to navigate experience without the benefit of the sense-making conceptual apparatuses that received sensibilities provide, and to say the most, they cannot survive it. There is no kind of incentive in us, to my knowledge, to abandon shared mind.

Our love affair with narratives is a function of the consolation that they provide as illusory providers of both worldly meaning and human connection. The durability and force of our narratological traditions arise from the fact that they allow us to experience continuous stand-ins for real gratifications, comforts, and consummations when these elude us.

We need others to achieve and sustain this commiserative escape from the unbearableness of our actual solitude, not simply logistically (every storyteller needs an audience and vice-versa), but also psychologically, because it is virtually impossible to accept that a story has a deep significance unless others feel the same way. A story whose entertainment is limited to the mind of a single person is commonly referred to as a delusion.

It's not even so much that we want to believe the specific content of stories, but rather that we simply love the aesthetic of the experience itself. Any story is better than unadorned actuality. It is ironic that despite the comforting nature of this experience as we are describing it, most man-made misery has come as collateral damage in the battles for "hearts and minds" that proponents of and opponents to different narratives have waged. From the broader perspective outside the arena

Mind, Narrativity, and the Euro-romance **21**

of any given competition between narratological regimes, it seems the escape from the aches, pains, losses, disappointment of real life that fabulation provides is what we are after—even if, practically, all it ever seems to do is foment more troubles.

In the modern West, as Nietzsche tells us, truth became king of ideals, and so a modification of the role of faith was in order. Faith's loyalties were now to be restricted to that ideal, hence all the sanctions associated with "bearing false witness." Deception is concretely an act of betrayal of an individual or a group, but, more deeply, it is a violence perpetrated against their shared mind-picture, an offense against the common system of meanings. Hobbes knew this when he warned of the dangers of "absurdity," recognizing the threat to commonly held notions of truth (meaning) that deception, or even the less baleful scenario of confusion concerning shared notions of truth, poses. This threat is occasioned by the actual constitutional separation from "objective" truth that we suffer because of the fact that such a truth can only exist imaginatively, in (always separated) minds. Hobbes here anticipates existentialism.

Politicians, parents, friends, and lovers turn out to be "not the person I thought they were." This very phraseology betrays the fact that these disappointing failings we find in others are rooted in the primordial fact of radical particularity in which our minds find themselves and the consequent fact that we live socially strictly through our narratives. Holding others accountable for betrayal is in a sense ridiculous, because minds never really were able to share themselves properly in the first place: it is a claim that something has been broken that never was whole to begin with.

When we experience deception as betrayal rather than as a simple experience of adversity, we are (at least in part) viewing the offender through our originarily self-centered and fantastic narrative that we impose on them. Radically particularized, we more often than not only understand them as idealized projections of our own making that would embody the refuge from the risks of actuality that we all seek. The framing of such an experience in terms of disappointment and disillusionment is the generally unrecognized mechanism by which *we ourselves actively participate in it*, via our having projected an idealized image onto the other.

Our complicity in our own experience of victimization is never part of the narrative giving voice to the trauma. Transgressions are traumas we passively suffer in the standard view; they are things done *to* us, in which we have no part. The disavowal of our own active role in the experience is made possible by the ready-made narratives from which we can borrow under the sign of the ideal of justice in our system of shared mind. It is thereby rendered not as an experience of generic adversity undergone by a fundamentally isolated mind, but is "taken personally" as a transgression. This narratological personalization of the experience of human-originated adversity can be described as just another manifestation of our tendency to revolt against the fact that actuality is always and everywhere fraught with every imaginable kind of adversity, with pain, with suffering, and death.

Given this understanding, one might be inclined to think that the narrativization of adverse experiences in terms of personal offense would be more difficult to sustain when the experience does not involve other human beings (the event of an earthquake or a plague, for example). The story of Job is but one of countless attestations to the fact that our inherent constitutional self-concern/involvement seems to take most *everything* personally, whether it involves actual others or forces outside of human control. There is usually just about as little practical good that comes from being angry at others for their offenses as there is from taking the same attitude toward God.

Approximately 2000 years ago, Epictetus said the same thing: there is no such thing as a victim that isn't complicit in some way in their own suffering. The thesis of human beings' constitutional primordial self-involvement that we are following here is only reinforced when we consider that the very same inflated sense of personal significance is in play when we experience the *opposite* of adversity—good fortune, and assume that those experiences too, confirm our narratives of our own personal meaningfulness in the world ("God answered *my* prayers," etc., etc.).[2]

Why do we feel distress when our agreed upon notions admit of imperfection? Why do we feel so threatened at the prospect of being left outside the circle of truth? How can it be that this "truth," which according to Western sensibilities, does not rely on the consensus of the human subjects who may or may not entertain it, appears to evaporate when the latter fall into disagreement? We suggest, in response to that question, that there is another, antithetical side to the phenomenon of what would appear to be our instinct or drive for self-preservation/promotion ("will-to-power"): the *unbearableness* of power (freedom), the horror of being left to our own devices, both practically and far more importantly, in the imaginative sphere of mind. It could be argued that the entire purpose of the erection of human societies' systems of shared meaning is to spread the burden of decision over many minds, which keeps at bay the dreadful (in the Kierkegaardian sense) and unthinkable prospect of having to make sense of life and world with recourse only to our own wit and will.

This idea that even while we may behave as though driven by the will to power, we are also fearful of possessing and using it, or at least of owning it, runs counter to Sartre's notion that, at a certain level, we act out of a "desire to be God." Sartre's claim does not account for the observation that, at the radically particularized level, we generally recoil in dread at the thought that when we exercise power, we have only our own resources to navigate its use. It is much easier to exercise power when one "leans" on existing shared norms to legitimize its use. This tendency toward reliance on imaginative support from outside ourselves suggests that individual power is something we do not as a rule pursue. Far from rushing to take God's place, we will seek any means we can find to avoid confronting the fullness of our individual freedom, to avoid acknowledging that, with or without common sanction, we are lone actors whose behavior has consequences. Phenomenologically, a judge with robes and a gavel is doing essentially the same thing as a summary executioner in a war setting or an irresponsible manager making decisions about who gets promoted and who gets fired on the basis of his own personal preferences, i.e., *making consequential decisions, executing power.* By conceiving the use of our own individual will as a mere instantiation of a power outside of or above us (the law, reason, propriety, etc.), we individually and collectively disavow the consequential nature of our own power. It is far easier to act when one sees oneself as the mere executor of some higher will than as a unique material causal force in actuality.

The deflection of the psychic burden presented by the task of making sense of one's life and circumstances that we are talking about here is also manifested in the phenomenon that Freud called "transference." In the therapeutic setting of a psychoanalytic session, the patient's emotional defenses against recognizing and confronting their illness are seen to be freed up by way of a kind of displacement of that burden from the patient onto the therapist. The authoritative status of the therapist functions as an emotional safety net on which the patient, who lacks confidence in him/herself, can rely as an aid in taking on this burden.

According to Freud, although this act of transference is the source of a number of secondary problems, the undertaking of psychoanalytical therapy is almost impossible without it. As imaged by Freud, transference manifests what one might describe as a kind of recalcitrant infantilism in human psychology, one that makes the task of overcoming the desire to cling to our helplessness in the face of adversity (the victim mentality) a preliminary step that must be taken before any real therapeutic reckoning with life can begin. This runs directly counter to, and qualifies, the above-mentioned Sartrean thesis that we generally desire to be God. If not a will-to-helplessness, it at the very least suggests that there is a kind of resistance we display to the challenge of making use of our own power alone to face the difficulties of life.

Twelve-step programs are another case in point: one ostensibly only attains "power" over one's addiction by recognizing that they are *powerless* against it, and inviting another imaginative agency into the mix, often with success. In such cases we see another demonstration of the power of faith (broadly conceived, i.e., not simply of the religious sort) and the pivotal role it plays in human mental life. Phenomenologically speaking, however, such examples are indicative precisely of mind's refusal to act in a straightforward and open fashion. On this view, when those in Alcoholics Anonymous conquer their disease, they seem only capable of doing so with the accompaniment of a narrative that denies the addict credit for that conquest. These are but a few among the countless examples of the ways in which mind tends to need to lie to itself to function at all, and together they are exemplary of the picture we have been presenting of mind, according to which it seems it must take a tortuous path of detours and deflections on its path to self-discovery. Broadly speaking, we abhor the thought of being like a God. From a phenomenological perspective, the construction of all of our complex systems of meaning (the growth of culture) can be described as a common imaginative escape from the pain of consciousness, from the knowledge of good and evil. We are like children who envy the power and freedom from constraints that we naively think our parents enjoy. After the initial "high" we get when finally "liberated" from the constraining legacy of our parents after adolescence, we find, to understate, that there is *a lot more* to the experience of "freedom" than we had imagined there would be in our youth. This is nothing more than a reiteration of Kierkegaard's concept of "dread," which is but a radicalization of the message of Genesis: part of what it means to be human is to deeply regret our ever having touched that accursed Edenic fruit.

Shared meaning is the institutionalization of commiseration in the face of all this. This thought recalls a noteworthy tension in Nietzsche's understanding of the human as torn between the will to power and the aversion to the burden of decision that comes with it that we have been discussing. Consider the United States' invasion of Iraq in 2003: the lesson is that *you need a (non-delusional) strategy for what comes after conquest.* If you're going to kill God, you'd better be ready for what comes after "liberation." Nietzsche suggests that the power/freedom of mind, both in the practical and imaginative spheres, is *as much a burden as it is a gift* unique to the human experience of shared mindedness. He does this by noting, in an anticipation of Freud, that the will to power is not necessarily employed either rationally or effectively in actually achieving its ostensible goal (real power), but that, among other things, it can be used (even if unconsciously) self-destructively under the aegis of spite and despair in the face of the failure to achieve its goals. *Ressentiment,* as Nietzsche referred to it, is the psychic mechanism by which we imaginatively salvage our dignity in the face of its actual loss. It is the effective abandonment of the quest for *actual, practical* power carried out via the half-measure of satisfaction taken in a purely *imaginative* "victory" over one's foes, and Nietzsche understood that it is likely that the most formidable of our enemies lie within, and not outside of, us.

When faced with the ultimate absence of meaning, we suffer what Kierkegaard called the "swoon of freedom," the vertiginous experience of life thrown back on itself, radically separated from all common meaning. Like Nietzsche, Kierkegaard maintained that this separation cannot be overcome by culture ("world-historical" significance). They both held that this is not merely impossible, but that any attempt by culture to remediate radical separation poses a danger because it merely serves as a means by which, individually but together, we conspire to escape from meaning's actual absence, or at least its indemonstrability. A leap of faith, taken from the primordial position of solitude, is the closest we can come to meaning, *viz.,* via simulation. Less audacious, more blindly literalist, versions of this very faith are what hold together the narratives by which conventional meaning is upheld.

Transcending?

In addition to the above, it seems an explanation of the narratological traditions of human mind calls for the inclusion of a third variable, perhaps the most important one—the illusion or effect of transcendence that narratives, particularly after the advent of writing, lend to our experience. We *are* in a sense actually capable (at least for a time) of cheating the constitutional limits of our finitude by way of the creation, relation, and repetition of stories. At this very moment, you, the reader, are in a kind of communion of mind with me, the writer, regardless of time and space that may separate the different instantiations of "this very moment" in which I am writing from "this very moment" in which you are reading. This is the basic mechanism, the "magic," that gives narratology its charm. Stories give an air of permanence to our concerns, and especially if our stories enjoy extraordinary spatial reach (a large audience) and temporal durability (we still read Homer), our testimonies are lent a largesse that our actual lives lack.

Small wonder then, that, as we stated above, the great revealed religions understand their respective truths to have been acquired via "the word." The window into eternity that the word tantalizingly promises us access to is an answer to one of our greatest concerns as finite beings: the imminence of our death. The prospect of our demise has arguably been the single most powerful impetus behind all of our works of mind, both individually and collectively. We dare to think, and even sometimes to speak, of our "legacy." No such concept would be possible without the coming into being of the word, of language, of stories, of which culture is merely a grandiose, elaborate, and broadly shared form.

All literature is merely testimony to the fact that we share the common experience of hardship, joy, and everything in between on the path between birth and death. Every form taken by human storytelling is a revolt against finitude, against imperfection and inadequacy, against the figure shadowing the Everyman that reminds him that time is limited and that sooner or later, the accounts must, and willy-nilly, will, be brought current. Stories are our way of sharing the lies we tell ourselves, because even when their content is brutally true to life, they offer the illusion of refuge in commiseration, which, although powerful and even exquisite at times, ultimately is no real power over the inevitable. This, undoubtedly, is the principal reason for the durability of the narratological tradition, which, since time memorial (there is no time *im*memorial—such time can by definition be part of no narrative account) always has been, and enduringly will, be central to common human life as we know it.

(A Narratological Narrative about) the Euro-Romance: (Our) Mind Isn't as Special as it Thinks it Is

The Euro-romance is the story of Western civilization. It is the binding agent connecting the minds of its people to each other and their world. It is a fantastic, ongoing, solo dance with a partner not of the actual world—a hoped for, imagined transcendence. It centers on the project of establishing an understanding of the ontological status of humankind with specific attention given to the question of human freedom. As an issue and a concern, the question of freedom (whether there is such a thing, how it is to be conceived, and what different answers to the latter mean for ontology and axiology) is a pivotal leitmotif connecting the Modern Western epoch with its Ancient and Medieval predecessors, as well as its post-modern successor. The following meditation is devoted to a reconsideration of the Modern Western "grand narrative" (the Euro-romance) from the point of view of radical phenomenology of mind, one of whose results is an explosion of that narrative's facile grasp of the extra-rational and perhaps inscrutable nature of the entity it presumes to make transparent, and the consequences of what its misguided understanding of that entity's "freedom" entails.

The Modern West, as the Russian thinker Lev Shestov maintained, has been largely defined by the dual legacies of Athens and Jerusalem. These bequeathed to us not only the respective traditions of reason (philosophy) and faith (Judeo-Christianity), but also the sense of tragedy and the quest for redemption, that have been so central to the Western worldview from its origins through its current phase. It is the synergistic play between these two traditions that gives rise to the Euro-romance as it unfolds throughout the history of the West. The vicissitudes of how the question of human freedom is framed throughout the course of Western thinking provide a window into our most basic sensibilities as a culture, and, by one measure, it demonstrates that the West has reversed the traditionally assumed developmental trajectory, going from a state marked by more wisdom in its youth (less anthropocentric, more humble) to one increasingly naïve in its later stages.

Whether it is looking forward in hope or dread, or looking back with nostalgia or regret, the Euro-romance comes into its dramatic own in modernity, amidst a series of fitful "growing pains" associated with the transition from its tragico-fatalist origins to its messianist-*cum*-technological humanist maturity. It is a tale of hope, fear, projection, and narcissism that spans over two millennia that has fundamentally touched all the significant events that have occurred in that time. It has by now profoundly altered the nature of global human life and the planet on which it unfolded over those 2000 odd years, as many of the social and political norms, industrialization, and the anthropoforming technologies that were its products have been exported everywhere, establishing a monolithic globalized material culture.

Although non-Western societies retain their distinctly non-Western sensibilities and traditions, and have their own idiosyncratic stakes in today's globalized technological-economic-industrial system of human intercourse, the platform on which all terrestrial human interaction takes place has its roots almost exclusively in Western-derived systems of organization and activity (perpetual technological advancement and pan-capitalist exchange). In light of this, Western culture could be described *a posteriori* as a kind of fatal force that shaped our species' global destiny, simply by virtue of the historical dominance of Western civilization.

This notion of a kind of historical fatal power exercised by the implementation and universalization of the West's technological and economic *ethos* is intimated in the later Heidegger's understanding of technology as a new kind of "destining." Processes initially put in place by human beings have broken free from their executors and now coldly operate under their own momentum in the post–metaphysical cultural void of late modernity. Technology, on this view, is the material complement to human consciousness, in so far as it constitutes the same kind of interposed mediation between life and world that we described above as the *modus operandi* of mind at the ideational level. This understanding of the Western technological orientation to the world as something that has brought about a kind of artificial meta-nature, which increasingly becomes the actual context of both material and ideational life was more fully elucidated by Jean Baudrillard in his assessment of contemporary Western culture under the sway of a "fatal strategy" that confounds the traditional epistemological, ontological, and axiological compass of modernity. That compass was calibrated according to the now obsolete Euro-romantic myths of Truth, Finality, and the Real, and has now become quixotic in its anachronistic inadequacy. The culture of the West, or its ghost, constitutes the undead horizon of terrestrial life today.

The simple fact that Western civilization became such a dominant force in the world does not mean, as one of its own ideological products would suggest, that it is intrinsically (ontologically) superior, or that its rise to hegemony was a function of its being the "fittest" civilization *vis à vis* others that have made some show in history. History, as they say, is written by the victorious. It is no coincidence that thought-formations such as Darwinism, like its sibling capitalism, have by now become part of our most basic orientation to our world. They are founded on more fundamental Euro-romantic onto-ideological presuppositions such as the intrinsic value of competition and the inevitability of meliorism. These thought-formations are products of the one culture that came to largely dominate the world. From outside the terms of this and all other value schemes (from which vantage alone is it possible to make comparisons), the attempt here is to pass descriptive (phenomenological) judgment on the West as just another formation of mind, intrinsically neither inferior nor superior to any other, with its own unique qualities, but one that is plainly, entirely, and predictably, human.

Before Freedom

The regnant worldview of pre-Socratic ancient Greece, to which Socrates (and later Plato) responded with the cultivation of reason as an instrument to be used for mundane, human ends, was dominated by the spirit of tragedy. The tragic sensibility that had been narrativized in the mythological traditions of Hesiod and Homer was at once entombed and thematized in the literary works of the great dramatic playwrights and the philosophical ideas of the pre-Socratics of the ancient Greek world, who gave intimations of a revolutionary proto-humanism that would forever displace the tragic Greek worldview.

The tragic *weltanschauung* voiced a lamentation about humankind's essential powerlessness before inscrutable fatality. Among the philosophical exemplars of tragedy, Heraclitus, in particular, is a spiritual forebear of the present work. Although his

28 Timothy M. Yetman

project, like that of the others in his cohort, was one of proto-ontology (asserting that all being is becoming), it lacked the naïve hubris that made possible the grandiose and comprehensive metaphysical visions entertained in the later phases of European philosophy. Pre-Socratic ontology does not (yet) aim at what Emmanuel Levinas describes as the mature Western ontological goal of "totalization," so much as a rudimentary grasp on the nature of things.

The pre-Socratics were transitional figures: they discovered the life of the mind whilst dwelling in the midst of a culture characterized by the still regnant tragic sense of caution and humility; they underwent the experience of wonder with a healthy sense of fatalistic awe that tempered the burgeoning spirit of curiosity. Heraclitus in particular saw us human beings as sitting agape in the face of a cosmic phantasmagoria indeterminably and incomprehensively vast in scope in every sense, and whose essence was one of non-essence or at most enduring evanescence. Standing on the threshold between the relatively quietistic tragic mindset and the interventionist search for comprehensive conceptual and practical control that would come to define our thinking in modernity, the pre-Socratics constitute the institutional baseline of philosophy.

In contrast to the subject matter dealt with by the tragedians, philosophy was relatively free from the urgencies and sanguinary concerns of political life. Philosophy's turn away from the generally grim historical realities of practical human affairs toward the other-worldly concerns of metaphysics marks the beginning in the West of the cultivation of the life of the mind. Broadly speaking, this pursuit can be seen as the first step down a path that walks, and makes apparent for the first time, the fine line between the efflorescence of human artistry and the quest to escape from the realm of the real into that of the imaginary. Perhaps there is no distinction to make between these two things. The pre-Socratics were not able to fully appreciate the fact that by merely pondering abstract metaphysical questions about the meaning of life and world, they were already breaking into entirely new "territory." This move, enacted in the life of thought, would eventually turn out to be as fraught with dangers, albeit of a different, unprecedented sort, as the practical world of war and politics. With Plato's subsequent reconceptualization of metaphysics under the governance of *logos*, the transition becomes decisive.

The playwrights viscerally exemplified the tragic worldview even as they turned it into a museum curiosity by reenacting in the simulacra of dramatic productions the actual experience of fatality that seems to doom human interaction to the incessant repetition of our role in the same grim drama. The classical Athenian tragedians gave voice to a wistful but resigned protest against the very real experience of this ongoing trauma by giving the sense of the ineluctability of the vicious cycle of the *lex talionis*. The trace of sobriety that marks the works of the tragedians tempers the emergent tendency toward wonder pursued by the philosophers. It is solely in virtue of this remnant of the spirit of gravity that, despite its relative lack of experience, it would appear that the ancient—especially pre-Socratic—period of Western thought can in one sense be ironically described as the least naïve of the three stages of our culture's history. At least lip service to a spirit of humble resignation in the face of something beyond human power was being paid, and even if that spirit was already quickly becoming atavistic, its morality emphasized a sense of the importance of appreciating and respecting human limitations that distinguishes it from subsequent periods.

Freedom with Palpable Training Wheels

Plato formally inaugurated the Western development of thought as a valued pursuit on the basis of the newly formed fantastic premise that our human minds are the key to escaping our materially-felt fatality. Platonic idealism tremendously deepened the Western concept/experience of mind in virtue of the fact that it was the first great compromise-formation in Western thought. It began what Nietzsche would later interpret as an attempt to flee from material, concrete reality into the realm of imaginary perfection but did so by convincing itself that it had a sound alibi for the cultivation of its metaphysics, purporting that the latter alone could satisfy the human need to make sense of the world of concrete becoming.

The Platonic project gives birth to an inchoate, but emphatic, sense of the significance of human freedom, attributing to humankind an enhanced ontological status in virtue of its possession of reason. *The Republic* perfectly embodies this compromise, with its establishment of the theory of Forms on the way to the would-be practical aim of developing the template by which we would organize communal human life under the state. In order for the state to be successful, it would have to be erected according to the timeless principles of reason, but the resulting edifice as envisioned required (and thus made conceivable the feasibility of) human *intervention*. Platonism walks the path between freedom and necessity.

A remnant of the pre-Socratic classical world's tragic fatalism remains at the heart of the Medieval Christian perspective on the world in the binary of sin and redemption, which continues the compromise-formation of Platonism. Christianity places humankind in the paradoxical position of being the inevitable manifestation of the occasion for evil, whilst acknowledging an emergent sense of freedom, via the nuanced, two-sided idea of human freedom it develops. By way of combining the front-loaded conception of freedom-as-human-capacity-to-understand-and-choose-the-good with the retroactive idea of atonement, it makes a move toward the relative centering of the human, while still deferring to the priority of the divine (the absolute), through whose grace alone comes ultimate deliverance. If we look at the unfolding in history of Western mind through the specific lens of the rise to prevalence of anthropocentrism (or anthropo-narcissism) as a function of the changing nature of the way freedom is conceived, we can see the medieval as conceptually, not just chronologically, mediating between the pre-Socratic tragic *weltanschauung* and the modern world-views of the West. While the medieval period still privileges fatalism over freedom (in the idea of the inexpungable nature of original sin, among other things), the Christian theology (theo-ontology) that it rests on makes a profound move away from the fundamentally fatalistic pre-Christian *mythos* that preceded it.

Not only are we human beings promoted in significance in the medieval by virtue of the fact that we are, practically, called upon to be instruments of a divine will (via morality), but also conceptually, in virtue of the central idea of Christian theology: that God undertook to take human form, suffer, and even die as we humans do, via the immanentizing figure of Christ. In the post-classical West, the everyday human world becomes a concern for the divine in an unprecedented way. Neither the Divine as conceived by the Greek or Judaic traditions ever spent a moment thinking, let alone *agonizing*, over what it feels like to be abjectly human. The post-classical change in the conception of the divine from something distant and inscrutable to a being who is deeply invested in the mundane—specifically in the human—is the second part of the thought-revolution effected by Christianity. This change marks a substantial step on the path toward a shift in Western thinking that progressively sees human life as the center of things.

The medieval begins a process by which the question of freedom becomes more central and consequential, muddling the qualitative distinction between divine and human agency. Perhaps this would be better described in terms of the notion that in both Platonism and Christianity, (the) Go(o)d shares with us, for the first time ever, his (its) power. If we were to evaluate this decision taken by (the) Go(o)d in Freudian terms, it would appear that He Himself is not immune to the will to self-annulment. Once humans come into the knowledge of good and evil, which God, we are told, made possible in the first place, the divine's conceptual monopoly on power is broken.

Even if we are conceived as entities beholden to a metaphysics that is greater than us, it is now understood that we hold some capacity for intervention, which deals a blow to the absoluteness of pre-Socratic classical fatalism. It is only by virtue of the remnant of structure provided by the notion of the divine will and the attendant concept of morality that there remains anything but raw human causal power in this thinking. As Nietzsche emphasized, the fast-fading force of this imaginary structure will come back to haunt Immanuel Kant in his ethics and his reflections on the so-called "problem of evil."

Modernity: Freedom with Strictly Imaginary Training Wheels

Despite its ultimate apotheosis of freedom, a re-activated, complicated, form of the ancient tragic sensibility (a fixation with fatality that comes, now, in the form of a simultaneous collusion with, and rebellion against it) is behind modern secular humanism's reformulation of the medieval narrative. Modernism still not only seeks, but also groundlessly anticipates, deliverance as an article of faith. This time however deliverance is to come in a fully immanent form, via the prospect (ideal) of a civilization that rests on an expanded but nuanced (impossible) conception of human freedom. In modernity, human freedom comes to be no longer understood simply as one term in the no-win situation represented in medieval morality plays such as *Everyman*, according to which we are the lynchpins of moral accountability even while we are in the end unable to do anything more than face eternity with a clear conscience. Put another way, from the medieval perspective, we are free to choose between good and evil, but we are not free to recuse ourselves from this choice. Contrarily, the modern West undertook to boldly (if vainly) confront the tide of history and put an end to what had until then been seen as the ineluctably senseless barbarism and misery that has always haunted the common human experience.

By returning with a vengeance to the Platonic identification of the question of the human with that of reason, the modern West sought to turn the bugbear of what Shestov called "invincible necessity" on its head. In the ancient and medieval worldviews, "necessity" is precisely what is at work behind the *lex talionis*: fatalism as a mysterious force to which we are subject but that can be neither understood nor opposed, and which therefore makes no room for a concept of human freedom of any meaningful sort (at least for us moderns).

In contrast to the tragic understanding of necessity as represented in the ancient mythocentric worldview, which casts it in fundamentally baleful terms as the virtual guarantee that life is defined by ineluctable and inexplicable suffering, modernity re-tasks necessity under the onto-theodicean auspices of *logos*. By wresting the idea of necessity from the obscurity of *mythos* and placing it into the light of *logos*, modernity inverts the valuative meaning of necessity, making it into an essential theoretical tool in the cultivation of the idea of meliorism, a conversion manifested in thinkers from Leibniz to Hegel. Necessity now has a name and a *modus operandi* that we not only henceforth can confidently understand, but without which we would also be lost.

The modern idea of human free will makes a giant conceptual leap from fatalism by imagining—indeed, anticipating as inevitable—an unbounded, unconditioned, and undetermined world of possibilities—a "perpetual peace" in Kant's vision of the "end of history." It is at this point that actual freedom for the first time becomes a problem, because the only thing standing in the way of this vision of a world expunged of evil-as-contingency is the human problem of evil. Kant "solved" this problem by recourse to what amounts to a reiteration of the classic Christian idea that freedom is the capacity to choose the good—only this time, the good is equated with our innate rationality, to which we have access without divine assistance if we, in the famous words of Locke, "but consult it."

The consequent change in the meaning of human freedom in modernity that redounds from this recasting of necessity from mysterious and terrible to clear and beneficent is founded on what Derrida might call a "dedoublement," wherein two (or more) often incommensurable meaning valences are sustained under one concept. On the one hand, it relies on the dream of an escape from necessity-as-fatality to inspire us. To this end, the aspect of the broader concept of freedom connoting indetermination—or at least under-determination (betokening an escape from fatality)—undergirds the cultural sub-theme of meliorism that is essential to modern Western thinking. History cannot progress, enlightenment is not possible, barbarism is inescapable, if this absolute, positive element of freedom is not in play.

On the other hand, the specific way in which human freedom is to be embraced or enacted in practice is through a kind of ultimate relinquishing of one's will, a giving over of oneself to the "law of reason," or necessity-as-rational-structure. With Kant, one "uses" one's freedom to *restrain* oneself (a kind of freely undertaken (in one, shallow, sense) refusal of freedom (in another, deeper sense)) by "choosing" the categorical imperative. Although Kant was perforce conservative in terms of the claims he made about rational necessity, recognizing that the universal moral law implied by reason has no intrinsic force (this would vitiate freedom), he still exemplified the ebullience born of modernity's faith that reason provides us cause for a positive response to the question: "What can I hope for?" The problem with this is that "hope" recalls tragic powerlessness, not inevitable progress. In the end, modern rationalist ethics, as embodied in Kant, is unable to make good on its claim that necessity is among its holdings: it is essentially a game of make-believe. It begs the question whether or not reason can be understood as a transcendence with truly practical causal force, ultimately settling for the admonition that we must act "as if" that were the case, rather than demonstrating it. The problem of evil's insolubility lies in the fact that our actual, constitutional freedom (as understood from a phenomenological perspective), which occasions it, is incommensurable with anything law-like.

Imperatives are fundamentally conceptually at odds with the positively conceived aspect of freedom on which modern meliorism relies, but wants to qualify at the same time. *Real* freedom—freedom conceived outside of metaphysics, which englobes and annuls the very meaningfulness of an imperative—causes an uncomfortable "swoon." Unconditioned freedom at once raises and renders insoluble the philosophical "problem of evil" because it is absolute and comprehensive, in contradistinction to rationalism's limited notion of freedom as simple in-determination hovering over the safety net of an assumed transcendent operative necessity. Freedom as understood purely immanently, from the point of view of ontological nihilism, throws us back on our own devices. It renders vain and comedic the very idea of necessity. It is the nothing and nowhere that gives rise to Kierkegaardian despair, to Sartrean nausea, to Camusian consternation, to Dostoevskian apoplexy. It is the difficulty of this aspect of freedom for which, as Nietzsche maintained, we are perhaps not yet ready. To dwell in the pure determinationlessness of ontologically nihilistic freedom, it would seem necessary that we become something more, or at least other, than what we are.

This is why Nietzsche looked beyond the horizon of our humanity, of mind as it has shown itself in all its limitedness historically, to the so-called overman. He was one of a handful of thinkers who at least vaguely understood that at some

Mind, Narrativity, and the Euro-romance **33**

level we are simply apes who, in a theme elaborated on in Chapter 3, would seem to have been the product of some kind of malfunction or a Frankensteinian experiment. He suggests that our unique and distinguishing essential feature among other worldly entities is not that we are simply and monolithically rational, but are instead, in Max Scheler's language, "maladaptive," beings. Bafflement at how an animal so apparently irremediably unfit for this world came to dominate it is at the heart of this strain of thinking.

As Kant tells us in "Conjectural Beginnings of Human History,"[3] everything (as far as speculation would suggest) seemed to be going fine on earth before the advent of "reason," by which he referred to "mind" in the broad sense in which we use it here. Every animal in its niche, living peacefully alongside brute necessity-as-fatality with nary a concern to overcome it, nor a complaint about its demands. It is unlikely there were too many *fusses* made before mind as we know it came about.

Kant broaches the question regarding mind: whence and wherefore? He offers, has, no answer. With the advent of mind, we arrive at this new situation where mankind finds itself in opposition to the natural order, indeed, in *rebellion* against the ineluctable necessity-as-fatality that it has always suffered. This amounts to a change in our role, a role assumed when, as Scheler says, we as a species say "no" to the iron law of necessity that all entities experience at all times. This refusal, as Scheler understands it, is manifested in the maneuver of distancing that we carry out naturally in the simple act of consciousness, of ideation, which holds the world momentarily in abeyance as an object encountered rather than a force undergone, a problem to be solved rather than a limit, a game to be played rather than a fate to be suffered, a workshop of the immanent imagination rather than a phantasmagoria to be awed by. No other animal appears to do this.

Modernity's repackaging into new bottles the old wine of the promise of deliverance is demonstrated in Kant and Hegel, two exemplars of modern rationalism's inherited messianism. It is interesting to note that despite their comfortable enthusiasm about reason and its purported guarantee (necessity-as-rational-structure) that freedom founds our human power to wholly remake ourselves in our own (albeit proper) image, they also were serious (honest) enough to leave room for skepticism in their thinking (especially Kant). They both noted in puzzlement the striking incongruity between what their respective understandings of what rational necessity would/must bring about (the inevitability of progress and/or enlightenment) and the empirical historical record—the data of the human world's known past and present, which seemed by all accounts to unambiguously belie the assumed necessity of reason's immanentization.

This is why Kant, in one of his most promising but least followed-up ideas, suggested that enlightenment, if it is to come about, will at the very least require some level of *audacity* on our parts. It is rarely asked how poorly the simple assumption that we humans would intuitively follow our rationality for the simple reason that it is "its own incentive" (per the *Critique of Practical Reason*) squares with the

34 Timothy M. Yetman

more profound anthropological Kantian idea that it is audacious to be wise, and that wisdom involves deep freedom (autonomy). It should not be surprising that Kant never elaborated of this proto-Nietzschean insight that moves methodologically beyond mere description, making imaginative room for the importance of accounting as much for what is *missing*, for what would appear as functional deficits, as for what is simply among the given, when studying something. Modern rationalism's faith in the inevitability of reason's revolutionary correction is in a certain way fundamentally of a piece with the Christian worldview's anticipation of the second coming of Christ. It was another iteration of a hope founded on the anticipation of a kind of miracle—and also an alibi for its self-proclaimed urgency.

The Euro-romance and Anthropo-narcissism

If we think of the above discussion in terms of the trajectory of the coming to prominence of Western anthropo-narcissism, we can see that it was a story about the progressive stages of the "discovery" of our unique importance, the Kantian understanding of human beings as "ends in themselves" being the unprecedented fruition of this idea. How does a universal eschatology, one that would seek to account for the "end of *all* things" (my emphasis), issue in this highly specialized form—that of the human being as an "end in itself," unique among other considered "ends"—except by the assumption of an ontological exception with regard to human beings?

The privilege Kantian ethics accords to human beings is the logical transposition of the assumption implied by the "deduction" of the Categories in the *Critique of Pure Reason*: that the world's very ontological structure accords with the human mind. Kantianism makes clear that, even if we did not create the world, we humans are necessary conditions for the meaning and value of *everything*. The modern Western mind, as exemplified in the thought of Kant, gave priority of place for the first time to the question of what it means to be human because of its understanding of the latter as uniquely important among all other entities.

Can we really be blamed for having done this? Would any other kind of entity, were it to assume a mindedness like our own, have done any different? We may have mistaken ourselves for demi-gods, but we have always been animals. The question of forgiving ourselves for having indulged in this wishful exceptionalism is moot. What matters, at a descriptive level, is that by way of this joining of the question of reason with the question of the human, modernity brought to fruition the incipient rationalist revolution begun by Plato in the face of the fatalism that preceded the "golden age" of ancient Athens. It was thought in modernity that the anomaly of free human consciousness must hold the key to breaking the cycle of suffering and madness to which our earlier worldviews took a more sober, more resigned approach, and we are now living with the legacy of that assumption's consequences. Perhaps, in the face of evil, *anything will do* as a means to reprieve.

It is, I suspect, not a coincidence that it is *we* who so deeply appreciate *our* own uniqueness. We have no others (a requisite jury of non-identical peers—Richard Rorty's "antipodeans," for example) to whom to address this question, and it seems unlikely we would seek such consultation if given the opportunity. From René Descartes all the way to Heidegger (even despite the latter's anti-humanism), the question of what it means to be human is considered *the* question that trumps all others in modern thinking. Wouldn't standard scientific or philosophical probity suggest a possible red, or even yellow, flag here? Can we be absolutely, rather than merely relatively, important? If there's only one case of this kind of specialness in the universe (the human kind), as the modern Euro-romance maintains, then you cannot demonstrate that specialness in any way except through tautology, not unlike Descartes' cheaply bought proofs of the existence of God (which proved the exact same thing, since the latter's concept of God is merely an idealized projection of the *cogito*). The modern period, which took from Plato and Aristotle the opportunity of recourse to reason as its guiding principle, but left behind all traces of the ancient world's respect for humility and the vigilance that that sensibility called for, marks the coming into fulsomeness of the anthropo-narcissistic attitude: the arbitrary and empirico-rationally unfounded attribution of an exaggerated intrinsic importance to human life and existence vis à vis everything else.

At bottom it appears to be little more than wishful thinking rooted in two fundamental and empirically ubiquitous forces driving human behavior: hope and fear, both of which undergird the Euro-romance, as they do all romances. If, with Rousseau, looking backward, we are but able to shed ourselves of bad habits and institutions, or, with Kant, looking forward, to audaciously undertake to supersede the condition of "tutelage" by opening our ears to the compelling voice of reason, so the story goes, we may avail ourselves of a power native to our being, one we are called to employ in a cosmic righting of things. This is the essence of the Romantic strain that is the "passion" driving reason's rise to dominance in our modern thought as a specifically human destiny.

The depth of the passion is demonstrated when we contrast it with a more sober, Hobbesian or Machiavellian view. The latter perspective would simply explain our sense of self-importance as little more than an extension of our practical/imaginative quest for self-preservation. Hobbes' sense of the importance of the human doesn't extend very far beyond mere survival. The above-addressed Kantian-Hegelian view, contrarily, does not merely see us as practical beings who wish to make our lives more commodious and less nasty, brutish, and short, but couches our story at the center of a larger one of cosmic, universal, and ultimate significance.

The Euro-romantic Mind in Post-ontological Perspective

After some 2000-plus odd years, the jury is in: we are not, nor have we ever been, who we think we are. Our minds, largely at the behest of our hearts, have

36 Timothy M. Yetman

tricked us into misunderstanding ourselves fundamentally. The historical record flies wholesale in the face of this crucial misrecognition made by the flight of fancy that was Western rationalism. It seems to have thought that it could imagine its way out of the doom of fatality, of destiny, of the cycle of life and death, of the ineluctability of blood for blood. It is a rejection of the ancient wisdom that would suggest that fundamentally we are not so terribly different from the other apes, indeed, from all other life forms, even from the inanimate. Like Heidegger, who at the end of *Being and Time* concluded that our most essential characteristic is "care," Whitehead argued that our relationship with the future is a fundamental and inextricable part of who we are, and our failure to see this has been collateral damage wrought by the modern West's Euro-romantic misconception of ourselves in an abstract, idealized image.

The thought that we may not be fundamentally different from other worldly entities, which was not at all outlandish to the ancient likes of Heraclitus, nor to the more recent likes of Whitehead, has been unthinkable for the mainstream of modern Western thinking. This unthinkableness is a function of both vanity and sloth. Vanity because it represents a heavy blow to our self-image, and sloth because it is also a function of the way thought-and-value systems (shared mind conventions) generally operate. Once in place, they displace perspicacity, imaginative and practical receptivity to hard (in two senses) data, and a pragmatic disposition, in favor of aesthetic narratological coherence. The content of all thought-and-value systems, including modern scientism and rationalism, are held together by the unseen formal aesthetic element provided by dramatic narrativism. We have always thought we were simply looking at the world, but at no time have we ever really done so, because by the time we look, our heart-infected minds have already robbed our myopic gaze of the capacity to do such a thing. The very idea of encountering that world as comprehended object is just a part of that narrative.

As the medieval Muslim thinker Al-Ghazālī reminds us, the very same world looks entirely different depending on where and when you are born, each time/place having its own set of traditions, values, and sensibilities: the bugbear of relativism. It is baffling that such a simple and plainly visible truth has gone, and continues to go, so completely and widely unappreciated. In his memoir *Deliverance from Error*, the eleventh-century Al-Ghazālī penetrated the intellectual sclerosis that had already established itself in the Platonic-Aristotelian-influenced Medieval Muslim tradition. He suggested not only that all such worldviews are rooted in "error," but that their untrustworthiness is made apparent by the insecurity with which they are all scandalized by any other system, actual, historical, or theoretical, that they encounter with a significantly different world-picture.

The aesthetic dissonance between divergent narratives that Al-Ghazālī makes note of drives something that appears *a posteriori* to be more or less universal among human thought-and-value systems: exclusivism. As Louis Althusser, and later Foucault and other postmodern critics of mind have shown us, the modern West has come up with perhaps the most elaborate, nuanced, and effective set of

Mind, Narrativity, and the Euro-romance **37**

mechanisms by which to practice this exclusivism. It protects, entrenches, and perpetuates its thought-and-value regimes (or *epistemes*, as Foucault calls them) by the inculcation and enforcement of its worldview in the minds of its natives. Foucault's thought announces the self-cancellation of narrativity, the rendering impossible of the enchantment on which it relies for its efficacy (*too much* knowledge of good and evil, as it were), and hence, the end of the West(ern Narratological Epoch).

The breaking open of the rigidly closed circuit of Western thought and practice that postmodernism (deconstruction) performs reveals the previously unseen truth that "truth" is nothing more than a function in a dramatic narrative. Postmodernist discourse demonstrates that the Western narrative (the Euro-romance) was perhaps one of the best conceits mind has ever come up with by which to hide from itself the fact that this, like every other truth, was not something it found in the world, but was of its own making. The modern West created its own unique narrative about itself and its world, just like every human culture that preceded it, has co-existed with it, or will succeed it. By virtue of the conceit of the ontology it generated, Western mind fooled itself into thinking that it had left the primitive minded world of mystery, of metaphor, of figurativity—of narrativity itself—and graduated to the plane (both civilizational and epistemological) of the Truth.

The self-referential nature of Western mind as manifested in its ontological and ideological systems has been variously described by late twentieth-century thinkers from Adorno to Althusser to Derrida, as "totalizing," "hegemonic," or "enclosed." The first two of these dreamed of exploding/exposing the artifice of late modern cultural life in the West via the critique of ideology. The third of these was among a cohort who disclosed that there was nothing "real" or "true" to return to once that explosion took place, nothing, as it were, "outside the text" that constitutes the narrative terrain that is ideology's (shared mind's) vehicle. Althusserian ideology critique is an offering made as part of a critical theoretical struggle with Western capitalism not from a position outside of ideology, but from a "competing" thought-and-value system within the Western mind-world. It relies on scientism (by claiming that there is an underlying material reality that ideology ultimately rests on) for its claim to legitimacy, and it is therefore as much of a piece of the Euro-romance as capitalism. As a technique, however, ideology critique is a form of phenomenology of mind.

It is no coincidence that the above sentence, as part of a discussion devoted to the phenomenology of mind, is reminiscent of Foucault's famous statement about Marxism in *The Order of Things*. Although I am here acknowledging Althusser as a phenomenologist of mind, I am also firmly rejecting the weak thread of materialism that Althusserianism, at least a little cynically perhaps, holds on to even as it claims that there is no such thing as an "extra-ideological discourse." The discourse being articulated here is undertaken in the radically phenomenological spirit of refusing to ignore the "obvious" supremacy of the imaginative over the material, practical realm for human life. There *is* indeed an "outside" of ideology:

ontologically nihilistic phenomenology of mind carried out from the perspective of a radically particularized moment of consciousness.

When we consider the elaborate "disciplinary" mechanisms described by Foucault, via which (a given particular iteration of) mind enforces recognition of its exclusive truth, we are reminded of Nietzsche's criticism of the "will to truth" at the heart of Western thinking. The latter, as Nietzsche takes great pains to explain, is a form of rebellion against the practical immanent absence of enduring and reliable principles by which the world would work (the emptiness of Kantianism), and it is a function of fear—specifically, fear of our own insignificance. A realistic (radical phenomenological) picture of ourselves and our world as apparently devoid of intrinsic logical purpose or moral justifications has simply been too harsh for Western mind to accept.

An honest look at the human world reveals that our intolerance for insignificance and meaninglessness is written all over everything we do. Our un-exceptionalness has been staring us in the face the whole time but it was too difficult to see. (Again, can we be blamed?) The unfiltered look at the actual data of human history shows that, despite the distorted picture of us that the Euro-romance painted, we Westerners are empirically simply one among many other human tribes, and that more generally, we humans are just another strain of ape, and so on, and so on. For practical purposes—phenomenologically—we are the same as all the others, and, like America, the only thing exceptional about us is the fact that we *think* we are thus.

Mind, as modern Western history shows, doesn't know itself, but it is unaware of (seems not to want to be bothered about) its ignorance in this regard. This is the unintended consequence of human overconfidence that was fomented by the Euro-romance as it forewent the aim of an actual, frank description of the Human in favor of a celebration thereof—a kind of metaphysical "selfie," if you will. And as the entire corpus of human literary testimony plainly, if always belatedly, tells us, the deadly combination of excessive confidence and naïveté can pose one of the greatest threats to the possibility of understanding. Modernity's promise was that mind would finally outgrow its liability to fall into the traps that life always seemed to be setting for it. Like all promises, this was but another trap—in this case, one of its own making, revealing the fact that mind may be its own worst enemy. Mind always just beyond itself.

The Story of the Euro-romance

Although its content is that of reason's revelation, the principal form taken by the human storytelling tradition in the modern West is the romance. Like all forms of fiction, the romance is a kind of lie; lies are the exclusive province of mind, of the human. One could even say that the lie (representation) is that wherein shared mind (as we experience it) is occasioned, whence it gains its unique dimensionality. The Euro-romance is the specifically Western form of the

Mind, Narrativity, and the Euro-romance **39**

common lie, born ironically of reason's fetishization of the truth. Comically, this fetishization is itself irrational, but it seems to have been the only means reason could find to rid itself of the burdensomeness of the knowledge of good and evil (like a kind of nervous laughter).

The Euro-romance is the song reason sang to itself as it misrecognized itself as having outgrown faith, the need to believe, the propensity to be a sucker for a compelling story. It is the compensatory idea erected in modernity when reason deferred or avoided a reckoning with this truth about our simultaneous human guile and gullibility, reenacting both of these qualities via a self-consoling story about its own destinality, its inherent necessity. (Irony of ironies: Soren Kierkegaard: did you know that Reason felt exactly the same way as you did? It took the advice that you gave but couldn't take yourself because you were incapable of lying to yourself. It threw caution to the wind in an indefensible leap of faith in the immortality of its own soul!)

The story, as we all know, depicts the mundanization in history of ahistorical "necessity" just like the figure of Christ in Christian theology: an echo of testimony to the search for transcendence-in-immanence and vice versa. Once the Euro-narrative has been established as the exclusive schematic from within which everything is given significance, the story makes perfect sense, but from outside its terms, reason appears to have made the same mistake of taking the figurative for the literal that the pre-modern *weltanschauung* was guilty of. Setting aside its suppositions, rationalism's *pre*-supposition was to thoughtlessly assume the inevitability, the pre-givenness of its own truth. Tautology is reason's best and only real achievement.

Reason's assumption of its own necessity is itself not founded on rationality, but is driven by what Kierkegaard called its "passion." Obligatorily disavowing passion, reason perpetrates a preliminary version of what Baudrillard would later call the "perfect crime," effectively obliterating the absurd, the incomparable, the incalculable—reason's other—from its scotomized view. The passionate leap of faith that buoyed the so-called "age of reason," by which Western mind achieved the implementation of its will to power, is unrecognizable, incomprehensible in terms of that very world-view's most essential premises.

Modern Skepticism as the Ally of Certainty, or Freedom-as-Rational-Structure (2.0)

Modern rationalism's disavowal or oversight of the passion that drove it and secured the closing of the loop of its mind is commenced concomitantly with the advent of the new epochal *weltanschauung* in the thought of Descartes. In the latter, Western mind preemptively shielded itself from subjection to the very critical disposition it claimed to champion and practice. In Descartes we see the construction of modern rationalism's alibi, its establishment of a sub-culture of explanatory thinking that would give to it its subsequent power to dominate all

40 Timothy M. Yetman

other approaches to thought up through the zenith of modernity and into the present by virtue of its striking aesthetic seductiveness.

It is not our present purpose to argue the merits and weaknesses of Descartes' ontological and epistemological claims on rationalist terms, but rather to suggest that what his thought does is not so much to establish the certainty of his own new findings or to debunk prevailing dogmas, as to establish rationalism as the exclusive methodology for interrogating the world and mind. The term "rationalism" is here used in the broadest sense, referring to both the general metaphysical understanding that the world and human life are ultimately governed by a transcendent order, and the unquestioned resort to inductive and deductive reasoning as the final courts of appeal that transcend both "rationalist" and "empiricist" sub-traditions within Modern Euro-romantic philosophy's cultural apotheosis of reason. Founding his "first philosophy" on what remained after ostensibly subjecting all his ideas to the crucible of doubt, Descartes, no doubt in good faith, thought that he was effecting, or at least participating in, a revolution that would ramify toward the eventual liberation of Western mind from the wilderness of error. Behind the trees of argumentation and theoretical demonstration, however, we see planted the seeds of a new forest, another in a long line of world-views claiming exclusive rights to our attention and devotion.

It's easy with the benefit of four hundred years of hindsight to take Descartes to task for his naïveté, for the ease with which he so quickly abandoned the cautionary discipline of doubt. He immediately declared philosophy to have been rescued from uncertainty by the chain of reasoning that moves effortlessly from the datum of one's own consciousness to what seem now to us post-Euro-romantics as relatively simplistic, metaphysical leaps of imagination. We are not accusing Descartes of having been disingenuous. He was, like all his contemporaries and many that came after, working under the residual sway of the medieval *weltanschauung* and lacked the imaginative wherewithal to honestly entertain the thought of God's absence, even as he worked to replace the Medieval God with modern metaphysics. The early moderns did more than that: they established the rationalist worldview as a durable tool that would give us a false sense of security in our thinking for centuries following.

The argument that forgives Descartes for the facility with which he re-built after purportedly clearing the ground, one which takes into consideration his having occurred only in the relatively naïve adolescence of the West, holds less water when one compares his procedure to that of the medieval Muslim thinker Al-Ghazālī. After an illustrious intellectual career, the latter was drawn to the spiritual life of Sufism. Like Kierkegaard, Al-Ghazālī was a defender of faith not as an alternative to the benightedness of human ignorance, but as a preventive against the folly of *hybris* that comes with the burgeoning of curiosity and false confidence born of human acumen, embodied in the Platonic tradition. He *was*, not surprisingly, seeking God. And yet he brought skepticism to a far greater level of rigor than Descartes himself did, and did so some five hundred years before

Descartes. Had Al-Ghazālī returned from the dead in the seventeenth-century, he would no doubt have suggested that we do more research into the reliability of the contractor who was to build the foundation for the mind-home in which we and our family were to comfortably shelter into the future.

Encountering, and giving fair consideration to the work of Descartes, Al-Ghazālī would have perhaps concluded that the "incoherence" of philosophy had not only retained its sway, but that the unfounded confidence—the naïve arrogance—that he was concerned about had come to rule the day. Al-Ghazālī was specifically concerned with, and might have predicted, what will be discussed in more detail below, namely the destabilizing or destructive consequences of the logocentric trend he saw in human intellectual culture and the threat it posed to the idea of the very availability of an unquestionable final truth. This prospective loss is not the result so much of a correctable error intrinsic to rationalist thinking, but a warning that the latter's critical/demystifying strain could eventually result in the untenability of faith in *anything* absolute. This indeed came about at the end of the Euro-romance.[4]

Al-Ghazālī foresaw that this anthropocentrizing trend could lead to dire consequences because rationalism's exclusivism made no room for anything outside its narrow terms, and thus presented an inadequate imaginative model for picturing life and the world. His concern was that the false enlightenment born of reason was too likely to only reinforce the "servile conformism" in our thinking that both he and Descartes ostensibly sought to move beyond. He undertook a radical, comprehensive skepticism that would, chips fall where they may, once and for all establish whether or not our minds are capable of escaping from the illusions that they generate, and attain to something actual, something truly given.

The seriousness of Al-Ghazālī's search for the divine drove him to practice skepticism in a way that was anticipatory of existentialism. This involved really going out on a limb, dwelling not merely in a contrived state of intellectual onto-theological suspense, but embracing also the harrowing experience of spiritual disorientation and despair that must result from ultimate doubt, from truly unmooring oneself from all received reference points by which to navigate life. Al-Ghazālī dove headlong into skepticism in the spirit of one resolved to remain there even if no way could be found out of it. He felt, and embraced, the "swoon of freedom" that Kierkegaard speaks of, which pertains precisely to the questions of faith vs. reason that are at stake in both his own thought and that of Descartes, indeed in the mind of the modern West generally conceived.

Unlike Descartes, in whose thinking the initial step of doubt figured as little more than a perfunctory hurdle to be cleared, for Al-Ghazālī, as for Kierkegaard, *everything was on the line*. After discovering Sufism, Al-Ghazālī was able to "find God," (escape from illusion) but it was in a Kierkegaardian rather than Cartesian spirit that he did so. He was a Jerusalemite, not an Athenian. Basing his "discoveries" about the divine more on an alternative notion of meaning as something found in faith and devotion rather than in demonstration, Al-Ghazālī maintained the intellectual

42 Timothy M. Yetman

wherewithal to appreciate far more deeply the nihilistic implications of relativism and the limits of the human mind's capacities than Descartes (who did no such thing). He therefore serves not only as a useful methodological counterpoint to Cartesianism, but as an unintentional pioneer in thinking through nihilism. This makes him another of the central forebears of the present work.

Al-Ghazālī's uncompromising skepticism with regard to the divergent regimes of mind he encountered, like Kierkegaard's much later, points furthermore to a crucial inversion (or perversion) of the concept of human freedom carried out, beginning with Descartes, by modern rationalism. The "freedom" referred to in Kierkegaard's expression, the "swoon of freedom" is a radicalization of that concept that comes with a Ghazālian questioning of all received truth. This radical questioning anticipates and contributes to the phenomenology of mind as we have been articulating it in these pages. It is the saying to oneself that the only thing certain is that all the competing world-pictures can't be exclusively true, which points us in the direction of the thought that comes at the end of the Euro-romance, *viz.*, that *they are all just stories*. It is a freedom from reliance on the idea of (logocentric) necessity itself. It is also precisely the freedom from all presuppositions and sensibilities that we have been claiming as a prerequisite for properly conducted phenomenology of mind: ontological nihilism.

Evaluating the modern West's worldview from a phenomenological vantage point that "brackets" its presuppositions and sensibilities reveals that the break with its predecessor that modern rationalism considered itself to have achieved is not absolute. The phenomenological view allows us to see that, while the contents of the new narrative are different than the old, at a more fundamental level, it is merely a continuation of the human tradition of telling and re-telling stories to oneself.

This kind of "subterranean" continuity bridging superficially divergent worldviews is what Foucault's radicalization of Husserlian distancing brought to our attention—a kind of phenomenology of "knowledge" whose execution makes necessary the quotation marks that I just put on either side of the word "knowledge." Foucault shows us that the substance of narratives serves as diversion or distraction from the deeper continuity of narrativism as the principal mode to which human mind appears to generally default. Accordingly, the only really significant difference between the modern and medieval narratives is revealed not in the structure of the new narrative but in the deepened nuance of the rhetorical techniques it employs in establishing itself. Modernity takes an extra step in the creative storytelling process, committing to oblivion (disavowing) the pre-historical (pre-conscious, preliminary, pre-thematized) leap of faith that it makes by assuming (not showing) that necessity is *itself* demonstrably necessary *a posteriori*, i.e., actually. Another way of saying this is that modernity came to understand itself by weaving a narrative about itself in which it is featured as the first example of mind having moved beyond mere storytelling and into a reckoning with the meta-narratological realm of Truth. One can retrospectively explain history, human nature, and apparently anything else, worldly or otherwise, via the keystone notion of rational necessity (just as Judeo-Christianity did via the concept of God's will), but as Kant admitted, one cannot account for the advent of reason itself, one cannot escape the latter's apparent arbitrary occurrence, or un-necessity. The ancient and Medieval world-views were more honest, more modest, in their stupefaction.

Modern Scientism as a Function of the Euro-romance

Darwinism is an excellent case by which we can simultaneously perform a demonstration of radical phenomenology of mind and illuminate the modern phase of the Euro-romance from the particular angle of how it expresses itself in the worldview of scientism. The worldview itself, or as Althusser and Balibar call it, "the seeing," rather than the "sight," comes into view when, as we did above, one juxtaposes it from a phenomenologically disciplined distance to previous Western worldviews. Foucault made the case that each of these successive paradigms constitutes a distinct iteration of the enduring practice of promulgating a place in the system of meanings (a signifier) for any given worldly phenomenon. As Foucault sought to show, although the content of each epochal worldview presents fundamentally disparate and incompatible pictures of what is ostensibly the same world, the one thing they all share is the fact that they exemplify the same human tendency to form comprehensive, exclusivist meaning-and-value schemes through which to define and interpret the world.

Scientism generally, and Darwinism in particular, participate in the modern West's hierarchy of valuation in the same way as does every durable cultural form in any given human thought-and-value regime. The theory of evolution, at bottom, is another conceit in virtue of which Western mind imputes to or perceives purpose in the world. Purpose in this case comes as a variation on the (anthropo-projective) assumption of *logos* in nature. Evolutionism can thus from one angle be described as Platonic, as it contextualizes the "many" represented by individual biological mutations that occur in the process of becoming into the larger continuity of the "one," represented by the law of natural selection, which law itself biology sees as eternally valid.

If one were merely to expand the scope of that kind of thinking from the particular to the more general, the logic underlying evolutionary theory could be used to support a larger theory. According to this expansion of the theory, one could hypothesize that perhaps it is not only individual organisms or traits that are selected to continue while others are eliminated, but that what we understand to be the current "laws" governing terrestrial life could themselves be subject to the same kind of process of retention and elimination. From this viewpoint, the "law" of natural selection is relativized on the basis of the very logic on which it is premised, and is subject to the possibility of a kind of deeper change according to which entirely new kinds of meta-"laws" or patterns might displace existing variants on such "laws."[5] There is no way to argue against such a possibility, since science deals strictly with the concrete, the *a posteriori*, a realm to which, as Hume showed us, pure *a priori* necessity does not apply.

The phenomenology of narrativism suggests that, just as we assume that everything *we* do we do for a relatively straightforward reason, Darwinism assumes that everything that happens in nature happens for a reason. As in the former case, when we (or others) can't immediately determine a reason, we come up with one (a justification or explanation). This view, which relativizes Darwinism by evaluating it from an extrinsic perspective, remains true even if one accepts that empirically, the theory of natural selection appears to be extremely good at explaining biological data.

The radical phenomenological view maintains that, at bottom, by its own admission, science can vouch for nothing but data. Like all scientific theories, evolutionism does more than that, retroactively super-adding a kind of theoretical (metaphysical) purposefulness onto the stream of otherwise inert data. Putting aside the more devastating de-absolutizing critique we made above, whereby no "law" of any kind can absolutely be guaranteed to hold sway, even the standard function of explanatory description that evolutionism would undertake is fundamentally undermined by the fact that the fuller meaning-context it provides (the "law" of evolution) is a *speculative retrofit of mind*. Accordingly, the notion of the "survival of the fittest" is not a descriptive concept, but rather an interpretive, narrative one. It presupposes and *sees* a method to the madness of nature's overwhelming panoply of multifarious entities and processes, a method (*logos*) that, most likely not coincidentally, is implicit in many of the same assumptions that capitalist economic theory makes about human economic activity. Despite its adamant contentions to the contrary, science has, and can have, no coherence as a cultural form in the absence of the gap-fillers that theories like that of evolution provide. Theories are by definition never among the given; they are the imaginative complement to and binding agents of the data themselves, and they are only found in minds.

Within the context of any given science's epistemological culture, theories provide a narrative, if merely tentative and hypothetical, that contextualizes and makes sense of raw data. There is another, sociological, layer of narrativity that must be considered in the phenomenological study of any science and its specialized sub-disciplines (of which there seems to be an unending proliferation) in the larger context of the culture in which they occur, one whose purpose is legitimization. Scientific thought-and-value conventions like biology's evolutionism, are never simply set down and left alone once they are promulgated. They are not mere inert collections of so-called "knowledge" whose sole value is in their applicability in solving problems on the way to improving the quality of human life. Setting aside the fact that the normal life of any science is ongoing and subject to continuous revision within its own terms, as creations brought about by human beings, much of the attraction and durability of scientific theories and paradigms owes itself to the fact there is more to our relationship with our knowledge-edifices than simple

Mind, Narrativity, and the Euro-romance **45**

use-value. They are sustained also by the fact that they are fetishized by their creators and devotees. How does one determine which is the more powerful between the very different kinds of incentive a scientist has in the humanitarian goal of curing cancer, and the self-aggrandizing goal of "recognition" among his or her peers, or, better yet, the fantasy of being awarded a Nobel Prize?

Freud's relationship with the psychoanalytic school of thought he founded is a perfect example of this fetishism as one among the decidedly un-scientific, often irrational motivations that institutional status and legacy-building provide within the competitive culture of science as a whole. In a deep irony, the ostensibly principled devotee of scientism who, clearly in good faith, sought to (and did) unearth new truths about the human mind, showed his own exceedingly human colors unabashedly when it came to the direction the "official" psychoanalytic movement, once established, would follow. He engaged in political games regarding who he considered "legitimate" members of his intellectual community and who he considered illegitimate, among other things.

Freud eventually drove many of his most devoted and brilliant followers to pursue their own paths because of his lack of tolerance for approaches that "innovated" on his own. It is not just the short-sightedness of this kind of un-scientific emotional attachment to something larger than oneself that is ironic about the case of Freud's relationship to psychoanalysis. Relatively soon after Freud's death, psychoanalysis fell into disrepute in the broader culture of psychology on account of its being considered too "subjective" and not conducive to a quantifiable kind of knowledge about the human mind. If it were still acceptable to use classical psychoanalytic terminology, one could explain why the discipline of psychology, like all the other "soft" human sciences, took the behavioral, quantitative turn in the mid-twentieth century by suggesting that it suffered from an "inferiority complex" vis à vis the so-called "hard sciences." This disciplinary envy is a function of the rise to supremacy of scientism as a valued institution in the larger culture of the modern West.

The example of Freud's aversion to free inquiry when it challenged his personal sense of orthodoxy is a fairly extreme and isolated anecdote illustrating the emotional attachments we form to ideas, but it is exemplary of a broader, deeper tendency. As Thomas Kuhn argues in *The Structure of Scientific Revolutions*, once mind-systems are firmly established, they become self-sustaining and increasingly closed off from attempts at radical revision. Like political and religious world-views, they eventually develop robust defense mechanisms against challenges, which are vicarious manifestations of the human will to self-preservation and, needless to say, serve only to impede the free development of fresh inquiry. Despite the usual pretense, we never simply get raw reportage of the data themselves, or even the modest theoretical explanation of specific phenomena, but an overarching "grand narrative" about the meaningfulness and indispensability of the science or sub-field itself. This grand narrative is itself utterly un-scientific. It is rather a rhetorical performance by which a given interpretation of a set of data, the theory that explains them, and the discipline that generated the theory are all given the

46 Timothy M. Yetman

gravitas of a larger meaning by advocates who fulfill the role of evangelical apologists both for particular theories or schools of thought, and scientism generally.

An example of this kind of apologetics appears in the recently re-made PBS Series *Cosmos*, hosted by Neil deGrasse-Tyson. Roughly half of the script of the first episode of this series is devoted not to a summary of the current state of our astrophysical knowledge, but instead to a propaganda production whose purpose is to defend scientism and its axio-epistemological regime against the challenge posed by its having been lately dethroned in the contemporary post-modern world of post-scientistic culture. We will later elaborate on this understanding of our contemporary culture as a "fragmentorium" in which no conceptual or valuative scheme any longer holds a position of supremacy. This substantial, defensive, sub-theme featured in the new production of *Cosmos* was another story being told, one about the struggle that secular-scientific thinking has grudgingly had to put up in modernity (and apparently still has to) in order to establish what it considers to be its unimpeachable legitimacy. Like the religious propaganda of the medieval Church, it celebrates its prophets (Copernicus, Newton) and mourns its martyrs (Galileo, Bruno).

The Unraveling of the Euro-romance

As our cultural-phenomenological history aims to suggest, the Euro-romance, of which Darwinism is a product, is a romance with transcendence, with ultimate meaning. Its progression, or unfolding in history, reveals a continuous effort to plumb the depths and scale the heights of the mystery of life undertaken by a tribe of apes who were unsatisfied with all that is denied to them in their existential and cognitive finitude. The trajectory is one of progressive demystification, concomitantly with the centering of humankind in the ontological picture it develops.

The Euro-romance and its anthropo-centrizing arc reached its zenith in (especially the latter-half of) the 1800s. Nineteenth-century Europe witnessed the coming into its own of the West in the widest sense of the expression. It was a unique and glorious fructification of mind never before seen, the climax that set the stage for the catastrophic denouement of a two-thousand-year-old "error," as Nietzsche put it. The nineteenth-century brings into stark relief the two principal achievements of Western mind. First and most fundamentally, the edificatory: the creation of a body-of-knowledge-as-a-way-of-life. The West had finally arrived as a self-confident and self-sustaining, living storehouse of mind whose tangibility and seductive power had given us a way to own, rather than simply suffer, the world, so we thought.

Secondly, as Nietzsche made us aware, perhaps the more crucial development of Western mind, that which ultimately proved its undoing, was criticism, or demystification. Demystification, the final achievement of the flowering of Western mind, is the master-signifier for the late modern epoch in the West. It is

Mind, Narrativity, and the Euro-romance **47**

mind going beyond itself—manifesting its highest essence (as critical interrogator) and undermining itself (as producer and consumer of stories) all at once.

From the perspective of the contemporary post-Euro-romantic, the occurrence of someone like David Hume can be confusing because, given his brilliant, uncompromisingly critical insight and intellect, and his radical claims of our mind's steep limitations, we contemporaries may find it difficult to understand that he could have retained a belief in the existence of anything transcendent. We are left to assume that for Hume, like Descartes before him and his contemporary Berkeley, and the pre-nineteenth-century West in general, the idea of God was simply so deeply ingrained that there was no imaginative or emotional capacity for comprehending the world without some reference to or reliance on the divine, either as religiously or metaphysically envisaged, even despite all the things that Western mind (especially empiricism) was actually telling itself about its world. It could be argued that without this operative incapacity to comprehend the non-existence of transcendence, we would never have seen such bold moves as those made by Hume: his criticism was safeguarded from the dreadfulness of its own nihilistic implications and made sustainable by the unconscious assurance provided by assumed transcendence.

What was revealed directly behind the "fourth wall" that tenacious thinkers like Hume unwittingly breached was simply ignored, because their (our) eyes hadn't been trained to look there, and their hearts weren't ready to allow for the rupture of the dramatic narrative they were engrossed in. The event of nihilism was a trauma already underway in the Freudian sense. It was something, as Nietzsche's madman famously said, for which even the brilliant likes of Hume were "not yet ready" even though, partly at his own behest, it was already a *fait accompli*.

Hume set the stage for the denouement of the Euro-romance. Responding to the radical skepticism of Hume, Kant's thought embodies the shift in the task of philosophy that comes inevitably with the metaphysically erosive consequences of demystifying criticism. Continuing with Nietzsche's metaphorical reference to us having "swallowed the sea" and revealing the "infinite horizon" of meaninglessness in the absence of the transcendent, we can recount the collapse of the Euro-romance via the allegory of a maritime excursion ending in disaster. From the Renaissance through the eighteenth-century, the modern Euro-romance had been on a mind-mission of *exploration* and discovery that mirrored the seagoing proto-imperialistic adventures of the likes of Cook, Raleigh, and Columbus. With Hume, that mission becomes reclassified as a "*search and rescue*" operation. With Kant, it is altered to the all-too-common and tragic follow-up in the wake of the latter's failure: a mission of "*search and recovery*."

Kant took to heart the defensive position that rationalism now faced as a result of its own critical overreach. All the constructive, positive work was over, and now reason set about the task of determining what little was left it could hold on to. This salvage operation that Kant undertook was like a finger in the dike holding back the coming tsunami of metaphysical and ontological nihilism; it

48 Timothy M. Yetman

worked for a while, and that is why Nietzsche referred to him as the "great delayer."

Kant's antinomies don't serve as an example of where reason will lead us astray (they lead us precisely nowhere) so much as evidence that the truth it can deliver to us is not monolithic, which is more than enough to be disastrous. The fracturing of what it had been thought was simple (truth) that Kant brought to light was a blow to the Euro-romantic tradition's sensibilities, and it was a fracturing brought about by the same continuum of mind that had serially elaborated that supposedly monolithic truth. The One is well on the way to being irretrievably lost amidst the infinity of the Many.

It was Nietzsche who brought the Euro-romance to an explicit head. Applying the notion of the will to power to the living dynamics of the larger mind-sphere that is Western culture, Nietzsche revived the spirit of Al-Ghazālī. He suggested that perhaps modern rationalism behaves no differently than any other human narrative tradition when it justifies its self-promotion as something more than that alone, as something larger, something necessary in some way.

Nietzsche effectively declared that henceforth Euro-romantics could only be such strictly in a ridiculous, nostalgic sense, since that romance would now be formally and broadly recognized as dead, a thing of the past. This meant that whatever the path forward, the West would perforce recognize and *own* the human, all-too-human legerdemains by which its story had theretofore gained its position of narratological hegemony at the ultimate expense not only of other narratives, but of its own vitality, and, for purposes of our present discussion, of an accurate understanding of us human beings as we actually are. Nietzsche supplies us with a tool for evaluating the rise of rationalism and scientism from outside the culture and terminology of rationalism itself. From the Nietzschean point of view, rationalism appears as but another worldview asserting its will-to-power, competing against others to establish its exclusive legitimacy.

The understanding of Western rationalism as just another example of a human story's endeavor to assert itself can only come from a cultivated position of imaginative distance, which is the bedrock of the practice of radical phenomenology of mind. Nietzsche deeply appreciated, and tried to pound into our thick skulls, the immensity, the absurdity, of what Western reason was asking of itself. He did this despite the fact that, in his heart of hearts, he was himself stricken with the same passion that drove the Euro-romance. Although he was the modern West's greatest native critic, he himself was mired in the conditional, in hope, in value, in an idea, the dream of "overcoming."

The problem for Nietzsche had to do with perhaps yet another complication that ramifies from the "untimely" quality of his own thinking, from the fact that he "sounded" more deeply and thoroughly the (empty) structures of Western metaphysics. He was ahead of his time, but he, too, was not ready for what that entailed. As in the case of Kierkegaard, Nietzsche's "soundings" eventuated in the finding that Western thought and culture had failed to establish human access to

Mind, Narrativity, and the Euro-romance **49**

the transcendence, certainty, and reliability that it thought it had achieved with its "discovery" of the *logos*. This left him bereft of the kind of (requisite) faith that had sustained his predecessors, and hence all that seemed left to him was disappointment and dismay. Bewildered by the first daring, unobstructed look at the scene of the trauma of nihilism, Nietzsche was unable to fully inhabit the comic attitude—essential to the notion of serio-comedy as we discuss it below, which is the gift given to us after the hope that Nietzsche had for something better had later finally been extinguished. This "trauma" is given expression in Nietzsche's wit. The resort to wittiness is the last gasp of the disillusioned romantic; it indicates the failure or incompleteness of the radically free spirit of comedy more fulsomely conceived. Absent the serio-comic sense of life (discussed in depth in Chapter 2), the witty failed romantic mourns for a lost future in a kind of reverse nostalgia for that which never would come, given the double datum of nihilism as a fact and the incorrigibility of the human refusal to live with that fact. This eminently witty practice of expressing nostalgia for a "lost" future that never was is also at the heart of the spirit of bemused dismay that would later characterize Baudrillard's biting postmodernist cultural criticism.

Nietzsche took the Euro-romance to task, seeing it as the host who threw a gala and then pooped on its own party, which, however reluctantly, he attended himself. He rightly chided rationalism for its blindness, but also for its hypocrisy. The former is a criticism in the vein of radical phenomenology of mind; the latter is rooted in value, and ironically places Nietzsche's thinking, or perhaps more accurately, his feeling, within the confines of the narratological field of the Euro-romance—if only as a bereaved survivor. Heirs to Nietzsche, we can today see Western civilization, which flowered under the Euro-romance, in terms that are truly beyond good and evil, namely, phenomenologically. With neither romanticism nor disappointment, we can claim that, whatever else might be said of it, Western civilization may be the single most impressive feat of human imagination ever to have occurred. The West took the art of the lie to never before seen levels of complexity and involvement, and, at least in that sense, it still remains at the vanguard of the genre.

As Heidegger appreciated, Nietzsche went beyond merely criticizing rationalism for its inconsistencies and unsustainability at the level of the ontological picture it created. He moved on to consider this unsustainability at the level of meaning and value: the problem of Nihilism as a kind of apocalyptic event resulting from the "death of God," or, as Heidegger put it, the loss of the "supersensible" realm and the blow that this loss constitutes to the psychological stability of the Western mind broadly conceived. Nietzsche admonished the West not merely for bemoaning the death of God, but for refusing to recognize that it was the Euro-romance's fatal combination of arrogance, ignorance, and drivenness that occasioned the event itself. In the famous passage from the *Gay Science* making the "announcement" that "God is dead," Nietzsche makes it clear that the latter did not simply die, but that "we" killed him. This refers to precisely what we

50 Timothy M. Yetman

stated above as the fruition of the West's blind, monomaniacal pursuit of Truth via the path of rational-empirical demystification.

Unsatisfied with indirect, figurative truth as "revealed" in religion, the Euro-romance endeavored to bypass the divine, to "find out for itself" the deeper truths of life and world. What it found was a void that it mistook, as Rorty says, for a mirror. Nietzsche was the great inaugurator of the era of knowledge beyond good and evil, wherein Western mind found that all it had left was criticism-turned-back-on-itself after the great stories of the mysteries of Being turned out to have always been mere cathartic narratives meant to assuage our collective imaginative hopes and fears. His suggestion that we weren't emotionally prepared for a life that we would forever be doomed to navigate without the "metaphysical comforts" of imaginative reliance on God or subsequent onto-theological replacements for God has proven true. He brought to our attention the fact that if one wants to really find out the truth, one can by definition not know what to expect, and that what one finds may not be mere value-neutral facts, but may be instead a disastrously destabilizing understanding that there never were such things. Nietzsche points us in the direction of the idea that knowledge of good and evil, once the fruit is digested for a millennium or two, becomes indistinguishable from the knowledge that there is no such thing as "good and evil," just brute consciousness alone in the world.

Following the protestations of Kierkegaard and the apoplectic fits of Dostoevsky, Nietzsche was the first to coherently and clearly define the precise nature and depth of the problem that nihilism posed to the sustainability of the Euro-romance. His thought made it clear that the Euro-romance, with its unchecked anthropo-narcissistic strain, its overconfidence, and its ambition, would quite likely lead to the West's own undoing as a living culture. In the thought of Nietzsche, the Euro-romance belatedly found itself on the far side of a crisis, *the* crisis of the modern West, that of how—and if—the culture could find a path forward without ultimate meaning.

While the Euro-romance arrogated to humankind the role of being the sole gateway through which that meaning could be made available in the actual world, it left itself forever sundered from the fruition of that process.

Nothing was the same after Nietzsche. He went where Hume and others wouldn't/couldn't go, and in doing so, made it nearly impossible for a serious mind to return to a faith in transcendent meaning of any sort. Such a return would hereafter constitute a cynical act of Sartrean "bad faith." Modern Western rationalism was in essence a spoiler of all stories, a would-be deposer of the figurative realm itself.

The Euro-romance is a narrative like any other. This particular enchanting story about the Truth does not escape the rule by which *all* stories gain their force from aesthetics and nothing else, a rule that cannot be incorporated into or tolerated by the rationalistic perspective because that perspective has always misunderstood itself to have been working in a different genre, beyond "mere" aesthetics.

Mind, Narrativity, and the Euro-romance **51**

With that thought in mind, let's look at how Western ontology and metaphysics imploded in the period between the nineteenth and twentieth centuries and made way for post-ontological, radical phenomenology as we understand it here.

Existentialism: The Terminal Diagnosis

The first great instantiation of the fully conscious terminal self-diagnosis of the Euro-romance was existentialism. Dostoevsky and Kierkegaard were scandalized by, but not afraid to speak of, the absence or unavailability of ultimate meaning. Heidegger and Sartre reckoned with radically contingent personal finitude as the sole actual horizon of human life. In both its early and later instantiations, existentialism can be described as a bi-polar thought movement vacillating between despair and exultation in the face of the concrete, actual nature of our lives as simultaneously doomed and free agents. This strange, paradoxical fate is perfectly expressed in the Camusian idea that we must learn to live with, to even embrace, absurdity: we are doomed by death's practical refutation of transcendence, but that makes room, in theory, for a life that can live concretely for itself rather than for an idea.

The nineteenth-century existentialists shared with their immediate successor, Nietzsche, a perspective on the devastation that psychological reliance on the great narratives of transcendence that comprised the Euro-romance can have when those narratives collapse. Although much is made, as we have discussed, of the disaster that the loss of ultimate meaning (negatively conceived nihilism) has caused, what Nietzsche's existentialist predecessors did was to give us substantial reason to consider that perhaps it was not the "event" of that loss itself that caused the situation, but rather, our seeming human incapacity to receive it. Like their contemporary, Baudelaire, they gave voice to the ages-old human sense of outrage in the face of the fact that we are so construed as to seem to need meaning, even while we are denied it in this life.

Kierkegaard in particular contributes to the undermining of the Euro-romance's charm with his deeply unsatisfied reaction to the gloss-job that is Hegelian idealism. He took issue with the cheapness of its empty promises, which like the Christian doctrine of the Second Coming, offer no plain due date, and serve as a kind of secularized theodicy, an assurance that unhappy consciousness will cease to exist at the end of history. Kierkegaard felt that such an assurance was meaningless for any given *me* in any given *here and now* (radical particularism). Kierkegaard shared with Dostoevsky the sense of *personal* offense in the face of the apparent absence of meaning in the immanent, and the travesty of human reason's failed endeavor to remedy that void.

These two thinkers narrowed our focus on the ramifications of the fact that transcendence is A.W.O.L. in the actual world. They forced us to consider that this lack we experience implies that regardless of whether there is something wrong with the universe, or the fault lies with us human beings, *either way, we*

52   Timothy M. Yetman

suffer and perhaps more importantly, *there is nothing that can be done about it.* They were pioneers of modern nihilism, and were as yet not able to see that it may be possible to live without the idea of the eternal *concretely.* Kierkegaard's existentialism exposes the hollowness of modernism and its reliance on universality for its force, insisting that all we truly possess is the radically contingent, concrete experience of the finite, historical individual, and that anything else is strictly a matter of faith. This not only throws into question the practical value of the grand narrative of Euro-romantic rationalism, but it crucially points in the direction of what we have described in these pages as the fundamentality of singularity or particularity.

The focus on particularity is central to the twentieth-century's second phase of existentialism as embodied in Heidegger, Sartre, and Camus. These thinkers worked in an intellectual space in which the idea of meaning had already largely lost its claim to ultimaticity, in which the concrete (facticity) had become understood as the sole context in which meaning, if it was to be found (or generated), could sensibly lay any claim to actuality, although the quest for something beyond the purely arbitrary remains central in their thinking.

As for Heidegger, the abandonment of strictly transcendent meaning was for Sartre not without a connotation of liberation, a chance to cultivate meaning in the immanent. By arrogating to the human the task of creating significance, Sartre sought at once to shed the impossible burden of transcendence and the stultifying claims it has made on finitude, while at the same time retaining for thought and life the centrality of meaning in some form or other. Although Heidegger rejects Sartre's humanism on the way to his own post-anthropocentric meditation on human finitude as a function of concrete "fundamental ontology," he retains the sense, like Sartre, that meaning is still a thing of paramount importance, and that it can arise "authentically" from finite human life in its "projective" existential comportment.

It was no doubt the two wars that cut Europe to ribbons both materially and culturally that weighed so heavily on the second phase of existentialism. Anticipating the full-blown nihilistic resignation of Baudrillard, Heidegger's endeavor to salvage meaning thoroughly collapsed in his mature reflections on technology and nihilism. Like the latter, Sartre and Camus, to risk oversimplification, can be said to have embodied in their thought the continued quest to sustain meaning regardless—in spite—of the understanding that such an undertaking is vain, to find meaning in unmeaning, as it were. Freedom was still too dizzying. Because they had not yet discerned the primordially purely narratological essence of mind, they were unable to conclude, as we have here, that meaning collapses when it is stripped of the very force that makes it compelling—*viz.*, its purported transcendence. They gave us no "closure," leaving us only with an empty ritualism by which the lack of traditionally understood meaning made itself keenly felt, a prescription for "going through the motions" in its absence. This only confirms what Heidegger finally recognized as the West's incapacity to live without ultimaticity, i.e., the supersensible; the idea that we are not up to the task of standing in for, or even merely living without the idea of, God, which, one must infer, is what the thirst for any and all meaning ultimately consists of. We are, according to the latter, hopelessly addicted to transcendence and powerless in its absence.

The lesson to be drawn from twentieth-century existentialism is that the ontological and axiological absolutes that we always misunderstood as holding sway were never objective to begin with, but lay solely without our minds and hearts as fantasies. There is no actually losing something that never was. The event of the "loss" of the metaphysical realm calls not for a renewed (and vain) search for a replacement (Heidegger's call for a return to the question of Being undertaken "properly," or Camus' taking up the mantle of an absurd freedom), but rather, simply an adjustment of our expectations. This is the partly Nietzschean bottom line that late existentialism did not take up. Rather than lament, as Heidegger did, our being consigned to the impossible situation where "only a god can save us," Nietzsche challenged us to forego the idea of salvation altogether, to live within our actual spiritual means as a species and accept that all meaning is—because it always was—strictly of our own making; *that's what we had been doing, anyway*, over the millennia, when we lied to and believed ourselves about the reality of absolutes to begin with.

Postmodernism: The Autopsy

Postmodernism comes after the erosive effects of Western criticism itself finally rendered its own metaphysics largely laughable. It made a case for the ridiculousness of trying to do the impossible—give a satisfying answer to the question of the one and the many, trying to reconcile things that cannot be reconciled. Postmodernism reveals the absurdity of the demand for coherence among the tremendous variability of the component systems making up the existing labyrinthine web of thought-regimes that Western thinkers have cobbled together over the life of the civilization.

Postmodernism is the first step taken by thought outside the traditional mind-frame of metaphysics in the history of the West: an open acknowledgement not only of the fact that ultimate meaning ("authenticity," "autochthony," "finality" the "real") never was, but that all notions of being and value must henceforth be recognized as radically contingent and historical.

Postmodernism can be contrasted with another approach, namely critical theory, which, being also in the "continental" camp of recent philosophy, made it its business to rescue some semblance of a civilizational foundation after the collapse of metaphysics, the baleful aftermath of what had been described in the early twentieth-century as the "crisis" in modern thinking and the fading of the dream of something universal that can give us the sense of meaning we have always been looking for.

Critical theory also mounted a radical cultural critique, one that focused on the "barbarism" of the twentieth-century West's technocratic and artificial mediated culture. Walter Benjamin, Theodor Adorno, Max Horkheimer, Herbert Marcuse, and eventually Jürgen Habermas, all inherited the same sick patient as the postmodernists did. Both critical theory and postmodernism can be juxtaposed according to their different responses to the diagnosis of technological nihilism that Heidegger had promulgated in his later thought. They sought to respond to the madness of mass society, consumerism, and technology worship with the only tool they had any faith in: reason. Habermas argues that even in a "post-metaphysical" world, it is still possible to establish a functionally "just" society through the use of "immanent" reason.

Postmodernism goes a step beyond the radical claim made by Horkheimer and Adorno that the Western history of *logos* is merely another cultural fulguration within the more primordial, more enduring, Western narratological habit rooted in *mythos*, which they understand us never to have escaped from. With the endeavor to salvage a more sane, practical form of rationality—to point to the possibility of a way to eventually redeem reason—critical theory still constitutes something of a holdout for the feasibility of a kind of authentic meaning that would sustain a civilized alternative to the late-to-post-modern destiny of barbarization. Postmodernism, alternatively, is thoroughly nihilistic in its uncompromising wholesale rejection of *logos* and its culture. It came to prominence later than critical theory, and recognized for the first time that, at the end of the millennium, all the unconscious cynicism of the Euro-romance is laid out in the open and is now an almost fully conscious cynicism. As theorists following after postmodernism, we now live outside of any particular narrative, finding ourselves in a sea of disjointed, coexisting, overdetermining, overlapping, sometimes competing, sometimes cooperating, idiosyncratic narratives. We therefore occupy a "position" (by definition, it is positionless) beyond or outside of the meaning-space of either *logos* or the *mythos*, which itself was all that kept alive the dreams of the Euro-romance. All we seek to do in this work is to lay bare the fact that this is the mind-terrain on which we all operate today, regardless of what we may tell ourselves to the contrary.

If existentialism on the whole can be likened to a physician making a terminal diagnosis regarding the Euro-romance's incurable late-stage illness (exemplified in Heidegger's exclamation that "only a god can save us"), postmodernism is the West's forensic pathologist, and Jean Baudrillard is its principal exemplar.

The fact that we have lost ultimaticity, or given up on it, doesn't mean that we are not still profoundly driven entities who appear to need not only to busy ourselves no matter what, but to know that that business is "not just any" such business, if you will. We are now living (are we living?) in the phantasmagoric fragmentorium, in Baudrillard's fourth-order simulacrum, the axio-ontological nowhere in which all palpable traces of reference to, or even nostalgia for, the real (ultimaticity), is gone. If we take to heart the lessons of Baudrillard's thought, it would appear that we never needed ultimaticity to begin with. Industrious, minded apes, we are more than capable of manufacturing its effects artificially. Who cares if we are not gods? "He" never set a very good example, anyway, did he? We were always the masterminds of the mind-world (and hence, simply, the

Mind, Narrativity, and the Euro-romance 55

world as we encountered it) in which we lived to begin with. It's just that now we have no one else to blame for the situation we find ourselves in.

Postmodernism suggests that we are not merely denizens of a time after the end of meaning, but one in which it has been rendered impossible, comic, in the human world, a sordid archaeology of not merely dead, but mockingly dead, significance: the Fragmented States of Zombietopia. If you think I'm being flippant by framing this serio-comic situation—our situation—in such terms, turn on a reality TV show—any such show—and give your honest answer as to whether the people featured on that show are at all joking around. All the featured human apes on latter-day reality TV fall far more easily into line *without* a script than with one, precisely because they *are* apes (bonobo-chimpanzees) doing what they (we) do best: creating and exacerbating stupid, juvenile drama for an audience to simultaneously identify with and (cynically) distance themselves from. "Reality" TV is considered, in today's culture, a manifestation of "authenticity," the very same "authenticity" that drove support for the Trump and Sanders campaigns in the 2016 election cycle. We are leering, rubbernecking, prurient gawkers at the event of our own train wreck. And all seems as well as ever.

Never mind so-called reality TV shows: just because they are such perfect examples of the "obscene" as Baudrillard conceives it in *Fatal Strategies*, i.e., an exaggerated, buffoonish immodesty, that doesn't mean they are fundamentally different from any other sector of public life. Is the "serious business" of politics any different? No, it's fraught with the same drama. Is the sociological space of your office any different? No, it's riddled with drama. Is the argument you have with your estranged friend any different? No, it's the product of some kind of stupid drama, I suspect. What about sports? Is that any different? No, it's a drama. The fact that Russian Foreign Minister Sergei Lavrov has felt compelled to weigh in in defense of Russian athletes involved in doping scandals is confirmation of, and heightens, the dramatism of sports.

We are so deeply and naïvely invested in these dramatic spectacles that we are all astonished, in equivalent measure, every time we hear about "betrayals" like the ones perpetrated by John Edwards when he had an extramarital affair, by Lance Armstrong when he used drugs, by Brad Pitt when he abandoned Jennifer Aniston for Angelina Jolie. What precisely does that astonishment say about us? Everyone knows that sports, like the rest of our culture, is thoroughly infected with the Nietzsche-diagnosed disease that is hatred of the immanent flesh, and therefore manifests the broader cultural endeavor of replacing that inadequate flesh with a technologically enhanced version of it. For our part, we are excruciatingly ambivalent about the way the spectacles of sports, entertainment, and politics are conducted. We want purity and are disappointed when cheating occurs. Would we, the audience, truly be as engrossed with the relatively boring scenario of a scandal-free, "honorable" spectacle as we are in the "dirty" version thereof? Without these, we would have to forego the excitement of waiting in line at the grocery store, where all the magazine covers are plastered with stories about these spectacles.

Postmodernism may be the documentary of the Euro-romance's aftermath, but even it is still tinged to some extent with a Nietzschean nostalgia for what the West might have been, a sadness in the reckoning with our intransigent human, all-too-humanness (bonobo-chimpanzee-ness), in as much as the latter means an ape who prefers the artificial, imaginary world of the mind to all reality.

Postmodernism's most realistic exemplar is Baudrillard, who swallowed every bitter pill he found about the West and its deeply diseased (or, more clinically put, deeply confused) state. He can be credited for his refusal to take the path of the likes of Derrida, who, notwithstanding his own contributions to the revelation of ultimate meaning's farcicality, appears to have been looking at the end of his career to salvage some kind of left-leaning, *"engagé"* purpose for theory, bringing back a Marxian "sensibility," or pondering an impossible quasi-Levinasian post-metaphysical ethics of the "gift," and even going so far as to talk about "justice." The attitude of dismay and scandal in the face of the "loss" of the real that Baudrillard displays throughout his work puts it outside the bounds of ontological nihilism and radical phenomenology of mind. Radical phenomenology of mind evaluates criticism with no regard for "gutsiness" or "stamina," or any such thing, but only for the extent to which criticism respects actuality.

Despite its residual romantic nostalgia, postmodernism can be said, among many other things, to have made plain the multi-faceted ways in which the mature West carried out the decision to annul itself, an annulment that has not merely taken place in the immaterial realm of mind. Postmodernism confronts us with the fact that, in mass society, there is no other significant means of social intercourse than mass media, and that may well be due to the fact that the latter-day human bonobo-chimpanzee is apparently no longer satisfied with merely imaginary fantastic satisfactions, but has undertaken to rebuild the actual, physical world in the image of those infinitely manifold fantasies. We have created a technological cocoon divorcing and protecting us from the actual world of finite material existence. Exposing the idea that our aversion to finitude and particularity, to pervasive unmeaning, is so deep and powerful that we are willing to do anything to escape from it, is one of postmodernist criticism's signal accomplishments.

One of the consistent themes one finds in Baudrillard's thought is the idea that everything about the human itself is on the way to disappearance together with everything else that is (or once was) "real." From a radically phenomenological perspective, one asks, why should we lament the prospect of the end of the human—either as an idea or a physical organism? Why should it matter that the human may be yet another casualty in the overall program of replacing things real with things made up? Would that not manifest a trace of the Euro-romance's anthropo-narcissism? Why should the possibility of the evanescence of our species be considered lamentable, especially considering the fact that each and every concrete one of us certainly *will* evanesce? In 100 million years, it will be of no consequence whether we will have destroyed ourselves by making the planet inhospitable, by the self-induced coming plagues of the post-antibiotic era, or by the sun's eventual scorching of the planet into carbon. Postmodernism laments the coming of the post-human, but there is no cause to do so from an ontologically nihilistic perspective.

After the Romance: Ontological Nihilism and Radicalized Phenomenology of Mind

Shestov's *Athens and Jerusalem* makes a case against the tyranny of rationalist universalism in the modern Euro-romance, proposing that we human beings have before us two alternative approaches to the search for ultimate meaning: reason and faith. In the spirit of Kierkegaard, Shestov holds that we do best to choose the second of those two. The present work offers a third alternative: the abandonment of the search for such meaning altogether.

Such an abandonment is what we mean when we "found" our reformulated concept of the phenomenology of mind on the "principle" or "finding" of ontological nihilism. Ontological nihilism is the state of mind that surfaces from the abyssal sea of despair in the face of meaninglessness when the romance of modernity's fantastic hope, born of its tragico-fatalist heritage, disappears, leaving pure value-neutral openness to actuality. This actuality includes as part of it the mind-world of infinitely proliferating and disconnected (non-ultimate) meaning in the phantasmagoric fragmentorium of contemporary mediated life among human bonobo-chimpanzees. Ontological nihilism is the ironic (serio-comic) "regulative ideal" of radical phenomenology of mind as a practice. It is a freedom of mind that is achieved when mind finally finds that it has no resting place, when it understands and accepts the absoluteness of relativity.

The practice of post-ontological phenomenology of mind has as a necessary, if not sufficient condition, a dwelling in, or habituation to, the condition of ontological nihilism. The meaning of the experience of nihilism as we understand it here must be clearly distinguished from its negative variant, or nihilism-as-disease (as understood by Nietzsche and Heidegger). Nihilism, as it is understood and embraced here, is just what it would seem to be: the detached, divested experience of consciousness in a value-neutral mode. This (Zen-like) variant of nihilism is a state of spiritual and epistemological freedom (radical immanentalism), not a philosophical school of thought. The distinction between this latter "free" variant of nihilism, which we consider a *sine qua non* of radicalized phenomenology, and the Nietzschean/Heideggerian understanding of nihilism, has to do more than anything else with the way in which the fact of valuelessness and meaninglessness is *received*. The late modern reception of nihilism as "disastrous" (echoing Blanchot) is itself not at all nihilistic (in our present sense), as "disaster" is hardly a value-neutral concept. The conception of nihilism in catastrophic terms derives its "negative" cast solely from a misguided nostalgia in the West for the illusory plenitude of transcendent meaning that never was to begin with, except as a figment of mind.

58 Timothy M. Yetman

Another way of expressing the divergence between the present writing's understanding of nihilism and the traditional one is that ours is not a privative concept, but rather a "positive" one in the sense that it finds meaninglessness to be a value-neutral datum. Post-ontological phenomenology of mind is, as far as we can tell, the only way in which one can hope to approach a reasonably true-to-life description of the state of mind writ large in the undead condition that is cultural life in the twenty-first-century contemporary West.

Even though we live in what we have referred to as an "undead" culture, it is nevertheless the case that the present authors could never have arrived at this essential thought (that of the necessity of performing philosophy from the stand-point of pure, positive nihilism), without our having occurred at the end of a multi-millennial tradition of thought and practice in the West, which we call philosophy. Philosophy is "practiced" here not in an edificial sense, but rather as a practical, always applied, critical evaluator of life and thought at all levels.

If it is the product of a dead or dying civilization, then technically speaking, as an institution, philosophy, is also dead (or dying). At either the personal or institutional level, philosophy is a practice possible only in the luxurious space opened up as the fruit of all the work done by history, as Hobbes understood it, to pull our lives out of the dreadful and moribund "state of nature" and into the "commodious" circumstance that is the end-purpose of civilization as it is usually understood. Ironically, as it turns out (now that it has become far too commodious), Western civilization has brought about its own *literal* spiritual end.

We qualify our statements about the nature and function of philosophy with a reminder of Hobbes' sensibility for purposes of sobriety. Hobbes underscores the serious side of the bivalence in the notion of serio-comedy. His thought gives us a sense of the improbable achievement of civilization, reminding us that the negatively conceived material freedom from basic wants and, later (and much more importantly), the positively conceived imaginative freedom of open reflection and self-examination that civilization afforded, was nothing inevitable whatsoever, but the product of excruciating effort and deep sacrifice.

The confusingly protracted process of decomposition that our civilization is experiencing prods us into an absurd revision of the standard notion of the decisiveness of death. This protracted, zombie-like state our culture is in is symptomatic of nihilism in the negative, or pathological sense of the expression we discussed above—a failure to adapt to the "disaster" of ultimate unmeaning.

The idea of our culture as something "undead" brings to mind the scene from the film "Monty Python and the Holy Grail," where a man attempts to prematurely rid himself of his not-quite-but-almost-dead familiar to a body-collector, spurring an argument about the rigidity of the collector's rules (he will only take *completely* dead people). The man demands that the collector take his familiar because he is *almost* dead and insists that he shouldn't be refused on such a small technicality. The scene can be understood as allegorical in a deadly serious, but still hilarious way, regarding the deep truth about the baffling nether state that the West occupies between being alive and unambiguously dead as a civilization. It also brings to mind the currently prevalent practice in contemporary America of sending our elderly out to proverbial pasture, ridding ourselves of them by dumping them in nursing homes.

Both the current state of post-Euro-romantic Western culture and the scene I refer to above give voice to an idea of death as somehow not absolute, but admitting of degrees. The depth of the irony here is great, for it was always the refusal to accept death and all its mementos that drove the Euro-romance, and nevertheless, our culture is not unlike a terminal hospice patient who has no vitality remaining, has declined all extraordinary measures that might be taken for revivification, but also refuses to (completely) die. Like disinterested presiding physicians, we are capable now of recognizing the unique and epic phenomenon that has been Western civilization, but we are only able to do so from the point of view free enough to understand that, despite what it may have achieved, it is essentially a relic of the past, and therefore, is something no longer (vitally) to be reckoned with. Yet there is still this sordid mess. It seems befitting of any formulation of nihilism, one supposes, that it must be premised on an acclimatization to the lack of the prospect of "closure."

Nihilism only appears disastrous from the point of view of one who had entertained the illusion of ultimate meaning to begin with, and the event of this despairing reception is something strictly native to the entertainer of such illusions and not to the fundamental fact of nihilism itself. The "negative" valence of nihilism is thus descriptively (not merely logically) made to appear as something extrinsic to the true nature of nihilism as a simple anontological (ontic) datum. When considered simply (phenomenologically), from outside any of the ontological, epistemological, and moral schemata developed by civilization, the understanding/acceptance of the fact of nihilism can only be seen as a positive development.

The experience of "actual" (non-disastrous) nihilism involves, at a personal level, an embrace of a self and its circumstances that is fully understood to be ultimately meaningless, contingent, accidental, radically de-centered, and superfluous—*and finding, seeking, needing, nothing to do about it*: freedom without the swoon. From the perspective of radical phenomenology of mind, the very ideas of meaning and purpose are just that: ideas. They lack any ontological status.

The neutral, free, reception of nihilism in this sense is necessary for a phenomenologically faithful thematization of experience, both internal and external to the seeking mind that would look to develop such a thematization. Post-nihilistic phenomenology is the province of mindedness freed from entanglement in any and all inherited, borrowed, or fabricated sensibilities and suppositional comportments. It is born from the ashes of the ultimate criticism (culturally), the ultimate skepticism (epistemologically), and the ultimate doubt or despair (spiritually). It is the (imaginative) nowhere that one lands after a leap of faithlessness into the ontic world of actuality. It is the aftermath that follows the empty echo that has always responded to the deep needs that give rise to faith. It

60 Timothy M. Yetman

is a leap beyond the mindset in which such notions as faith, conviction, evidence, and truth have any relevance, a step outside of all iterations or products of mind and their seductive but expropriative siren songs. The immensity of the undertaking involved in the attempt to step completely outside one's prejudices and presuppositions has chronically been underestimated. It's easier said than done. That said, it must be emphasized that our understanding of the "status" of one who occupies the state of nihilism is nothing like Nietzsche's "overman." The latter concept is too idealized, perfect, and enduring for any actual human to embody. At bottom, all that ontological nihilism and radical phenomenology of mind entail is the notion that, in certain moments, one finds oneself at ease with radical particularity, contingency, and immanence.

Ontologically nihilistic phenomenology is a state of mind or consciousness that finds, or perhaps places itself outside of, or *after*, the experience in which mind lives in a world it mistakes for something meaningful, the latter being a state of only semi-consciousness, ever distracted and under the sway of its own creations/notions. Ironically, the value-neutral reception to nihilism that we propose here makes space for the ontic in all its fullness, bruteness, and multifariousness. It is thus truly the "absent" foundation from out of, or in spite of which, pure phenomenology grows, because it is the product of a *total and permanent* "epoché," one more complete and rigorous than Husserl's. It places its entertainer beyond the (Euro-romantic) imaginative attitude that holds science and its universalist/transcendentalist aims at the top end of the table of values. The sacralization of the institutions of science and technology is but another in a so far unending series of human sacralizing fetishizations. To the ontologically nihilistic phenomenologist of mind, nothing is sacred, and nothing is profane; they simply are what they are until further perspective or insight can elaborate on them.

Husserlian phenomenology sought to build a reliable storehouse of ontological meaning using the mind as its gateway to timeless, ahistorical essence. This is why Husserl urged that we practice philosophy "as a rigorous science." The creation of a pure arena of mind in which not just the "things themselves" (this or that immanently intended object), but their *being* itself was to be made available, was the Holy Grail promised by Husserl because its product (timeless essence), although occasioned in an engagement with the concrete, is itself transcendent, eternal, and unconditioned.

Radical phenomenology of mind is not occupied with such traditional edificial epistemological and ontological concerns. These concerns are themselves the products of a thought-and-value regime that, although alien to actuality, artificially provides a context of significance in which philosophy is practiced (they tell us why we do so) and hence, also a context of significance for the objects of our world and for our engagement with those objects. All meaning-contexts are idiosyncratic, historically and culturally specific functions of mind. Even if one were to grant Husserl the transcendence he so valued à propos of the essences revealed in the phenomenologically rigorous intentional experience as he conceived it, the latter-day radical phenomenologist of mind asks, "What good would the fact of transcendence do me when I myself am not of it, when I am instead irremediably immersed in immanent duration?" Not only have we eschewed the fetishization of ahistoricalism that Husserl's "transcendental" turn cleaves to, but in doing so have endeavored to radicalize Husserl's reductive method, to take the "epoché" even further than he did, to *permanently* elide all valuative and conceptual comportments entirely in our approach to making sense of the world. The radical phenomenologist of mind, accordingly, *never leaves* the confines of the perspective that "brackets" all received mind-sensibilities.

We have in this work embraced the relativism that is the inevitable complement of ontological nihilism, having cultivated a sensibility vis à vis the workings of received mind that come from the insights of the likes of Freud and Scheler, both of whom urged us that mind cannot be trusted, that it is infected by the heart, among other things. Scheler developed the notion of "philosophical anthropology" and was central to the development of the discipline of "sociology of knowledge," both of which, like Althusserian ideology critique, are forms of the phenomenology of mind: cases of mind stepping outside of itself to see how it goes about its own business. Sociology of knowledge proceeds on the understanding that it is not merely the "things themselves" that our mind has deprived itself of access to, but that a remedy for such a deprivation cannot be hoped for without subjecting the operations of (our own) mind itself to a ruthless and thorough interrogation.

Post-ontological, nihilistic, radically immanentalist phenomenology of mind is an austere affair that claims for itself nothing beyond an immediate, ephemeral insight. It does nothing more than observe, ponder, and thematize world and life from a spatio-temporally unique moment of consciousness, always with the understanding that each of its insights itself is as radically fraught with specificity and contingency as the objects and moments it thematizes. It is the strictly focused, free study of the world as filtered through the activities and artifacts of the mind itself in all its manifestations, in so-called "real time," and nothing else. The concept of phenomenology of mind we put forth here is a hybrid product that engages in what Weinstein has referred to as "love piracy."[6] Love piracy takes advantage of an immanently critical approach to existing thought to borrow concepts from others in the construction of its thematization. In the present case, the phenomenology of mind takes only the valuable methods and insights developed by approaches like phenomenology, pragmatism, process philosophy, existentialism, and postmodernism, while eschewing any and all metaphysicalist strains, explicit or implied, manifested by any of them. Phenomenology of mind is not invested in any greater project than the expanded self-awareness of mind and its immediate world (which includes the (never objectively reliable) memory of its past), and has no desire to establish the absolute validity of its findings for an ontology. It also makes possible, and perhaps necessary, the adoption of the serio-comic attitude, which will be discussed in detail in the next chapter.

One of the ways in which the phenomenology of mind puts aside, or overcomes the desire to ask the question of ontology is by the embracement of (or aspiration to) a non-appetitive attitude on the part of the would-be practitioner: it ostensibly results in a laying out of the nature of essence as something not possessable by the knower in any kind of durable way. Husserl tried to obviate the Kantian problem of our being denied access to essence by tying the latter to specificity (the moment of intentional communion between *noesis* and *noema*). Husserlian essence, even though dramatically dressed-down, remains essentially Kantian because it is transcendental, and this is precisely where the present approach parts ways with Husserl. Maybe there is eternal essence, but we will never commune with it because we can only ever experience it in duration (cf. James, Bergson, Santayana), and it can't be abstracted from its concrete connectedness to other things (cf. Whitehead). My intuition of an essence in an intentional experience will be a unique event in itself: it forms and exhausts its own ontology.

Radical phenomenology of mind, as conceived here, proceeds in a spirit that is akin to that promoted by Zen: it seeks involvement with the world as a panoply of particular immanent wonders or concerns, not as an enduring possession that might have some currency; the will to ontologization is nothing more than another confirmation of the second Noble Truth of Buddhism. We want more than what experience alone provides; we want it all to be meaningful in some sense, in *any* sense, to have been so for a reason. All of these desires have exclusively to do with *us*, not the world we find ourselves in.

We Westerners sought to take imaginative ownership of our world by naming it. From the point of view of my own experience, both the "essence" of the world and of myself as figured in a radically phenomenological experience are evanescent: the frame of their "being" only holds for the moment. In the next moment they may be framed quite differently. The name I therefore give things of that world will only have already expended its significance (its currency value) when I try to hold on to that name for any reason not directly related to its limited thematization. My desire for something enduring can have nothing to do with the thing I have named nor the moment in which it came to my explicit attention. This does not imply idealism but simply a recognition that I am finite and my experience is not enduring and ahistorical.

Unillusioned and, to the extent that one's humanness will allow, free of appetite for more than the given, the radical phenomenologist of mind accepts that she doesn't "own" anything but merely sustains a life deeply connected with thought via the cultivated idiosyncratic perspective-engendering habits by which she thematizes her life and world, which she also recognizes as not her own.

Santayana begins the first chapter of his *Skepticism and Animal Faith* with a statement to the effect that we always find ourselves "*in medias res*," always in the midst of things already underway, as it were. This thought, which coincides with Heidegger's notion of "thrownness" (*geworfenheit*), is just another figuring of the form of human experience as irremediably always already lost, devoid of the metaphysical landmarks that the Euro-romance took for granted as givens. In the next chapter we will present a meditation on experience as a "phantasmagoria" that will serve as an example of post-Euro-romantic radical phenomenology of mind that is informed by this sense of experience that Santayana proposes. The meditation will undertake to cultivate a "serio-comic" sense of life as an alternative to Miguel de Unamuno's tragic sense of life on its way to articulating the notion of "integral consciousness" as a kind of serialized, radically immanent, momentalist experience.

Notes

1 Cf. Michael A. Weinstein's *Structure of Human Life* for a fuller discussion of the ineluctability of the quest for control in human life.
2 Despite the blunt, simple-matter-of-fact tone that I have employed in combing through these universal human behaviors and attitudes, I would not dispute the likely near universal retort asseverating that sustaining a life that is free of any or even a few of them—even if only briefly—is nothing short of a herculean achievement. But let not the fact of difficulty turn us from a frank appraisal of our humanness in all of its manifestations, for how are we to get anywhere in the quest to improve life, if we begin that quest with an initial refusal to reckon with patently practically effective truths? I acknowledge that the ineffectuality of the present words will be proportional to what may appear as their superciliousness. What purpose is going to be served by presenting the findings of my reflections regarding this species and the works of its unique consciousness? I will say no more in my defense than to remind the reader that we have seen where the shared madness of the late twentieth-century West's communal flight from the above-mentioned reckoning has taken us.
3 In *Kant: Political Writings*.
4 The translator of Al-Ghazālī's *The Incoherence of the Philosophers* states, quite interestingly, that the Arabic word *tahafut* in Al-Ghazālī's title, "… has been variously translated—for example, as '*destructio*' by the Latins, 'inconsistency,' 'disintegration,' 'collapse,' as well as 'incoherence' by modern scholars" [xxvi]. These connotations of destruction and undermining presage what we will discuss below as the eventual consequence of rationalism in the Euro-romance: the Derridian idea that logocentrism "deconstructs itself" by demystifying so completely that it destroys its own implicit foundations.
5 This de-absolutizing of what we consider the laws that govern the material world echoes Quentin Meillassoux's "principle of unreason" or "factiality" in his *After Finitude*.
6 Michael A. Weinstein, *Culture/Flesh*, vii.

2

INTEGRAL CONSCIOUSNESS

Michael A. Weinstein

The present reflection comprises a survey of the most important terms and their relations to one another that are relevant to describing the structure of experience from the position of life as apprehended by a finite conscious center with no ontological commitments except for the renunciation of ontological commitments.

Experience

Experience is the medium of conscious life; to risk a misleading characterization, it is conscious life's substantial form.

There is no way around such a characterization. There cannot help but be a comprehensive term for that which englobes conscious life, and it cannot merely be an abstraction, so long as one acknowledges—as is done here—that the conscious center does not exist alone.

Experience simply "is," as William James wrote, and in his words, "leans on itself." For James, that characterization led to the ontological doctrine of "neutral monism" suspended between idealism and naturalism. There is no reason to resort to James' expedient in the present reflection, since that reflection has renounced ontology. It is enough to say that experience is the medium of conscious life, opening the way to what James called "radical empiricism," which, switching to the phenomenological vocabulary, designates everything that appears to the conscious center without prejudice to ontological status, such as real or imaginary.

There is much to say about the appearances and the forms that they take in general and particular; there is less to say about the medium, which, since it is a comprehensive term, cannot be defined in terms of something else that includes it. Nonetheless, there are two characteristics of experience that define it for a post-ontological reflection.

Firstly, when it is considered in a reflective review that is grounded in remembrance of many moments of experience, the latter is indefinite in regard to its spatio-temporal boundaries. The conscious center acknowledges that it is within experience, since it is entertaining it, does not belong to it altogether. The acknowledgment of the indefiniteness of experience makes the lack of its ownership by the conscious center obvious, the conscious center does not know where experience ends in time or space, or if it ends at all; there is simply the acknowledgment of an undefined beyond.

The moves by which the indefinite can be symbolically determined are familiar from Kant's antinomies, for example, the finite and the infinite. A post-ontological reflection makes no such moves and, as a consequence, forecloses any meaning for experience as such, which renders experience to be a moving mass of appearances with no discernible overall direction. Perhaps some appearances can be strung together into meaningful patterns, evincing purposive development, but those coordinations occur within the moving mass that is consubstantial with the medium.

Secondly, the conscious center is decentered by the acknowledgment of experience. That the reflective review undertaken to describe the structure of experience is performed from the position of centric consciousness, which stands over its other remembered moments of experience, does not indicate that the conscious center's position is privileged in any other sense than that it is the transient position from which experience is thematized. Post-ontological phenomenological reflection acknowledges that it is one position among others, the one that yields the kind of philosophical judgments that are sought in the present reflection.

The reflective review of experience is a mode of what José Ortega y Gasset called the movement to *"ensimismamiento,"* being in one's "self-sameness" as opposed to *"alteracion,"* the movement towards loss of centric consciousness in that which is other to oneself. It might be that when one is deploying a philosophical discourse, one feels and expresses the judgment that one is most oneself, and it is surely that feeling and judgment that informs the present reflection as it is being written. Yet what is one to think about one's memory of communing with one's lover, for example, or of having been reduced to abjection, or of just losing oneself on the road when one is driving or losing oneself in food that one is preparing, and so on indefinitely. The declaration-deed made by Ortega that "my life is the radical reality and all other realities are rooted in it" does not hold beyond the moments in which it is made.

Yet simply to acknowledge that the reflective review, in which the conscious center remembers experiences, imagines other possible experiences, and tries to coordinate them into meaningful patterns, is one position among others does not seem to exhaust the subject of decentered experience and is attended by my dissatisfaction.

That dissatisfaction might be attributed to my operating inside a philosophical discourse and my affirming myself as the subject-(position) of that discourse. I will not deny that, yet I remember that the reflective review directed to describing the structure of experience is simply the most general and intimate solitary reflection that I experience, my experience of reflecting on the structure of (my) experience. The reflective review is only the most philosophical of the wider range of experiences that make up home discourse, the mode of *ensimismamiento* in which I converse with myself about whatever subject-matter appears. I cannot help but feel and judge that I am most myself when I am performing home discourse, and that is because it brings intimacy to its fullness, intimacy with myself.

Home discourse, for me, is a philosophical discourse, which it is not, I imagine, the case for many other people. I have spent decades cultivating the art of talking to myself in a discourse that is governed by certain rules that originate in philosophical discourse; my converse with myself is comprehensive with regard to its theme, as accurate and precise about its object as I can make it, and aware of consistency and inconsistency of judgments. In addition, I intensify the feelings that attend and presumably generate my thoughts about the theme under consideration. Practicing thought according to those and related standards has become the way that I habitually and spontaneously think, my self has become identified with it. It is, I suppose, a variant of a philosophical life. It has a privilege for me; other kinds of lives have privileges for others.

Now it is possible to return to the decentering of centric consciousness, having understood why I privilege and valorize centric reflective consciousness; I do it for myself, but I know that it is a position alongside rather than above others—a phase of the moving mass of experience that I have cultivated, expanded, made precise, and deepened; but a sector of experience—the most intimate sector, the most private recess that, as philosophical reflective review, yields shareable judgments that others can consider in their own reflective reviews if they happen to run across my thought.

There is a humble arrogance involved in undertaking a reflective review of experience as a structural phenomenology. It is humble because all that I have to work with is my particular and intensively enculturated experience, my portion of what I acknowledge to extend beyond myself into the moving mass, which has no definite boundaries. It is arrogant because I am presuming to offer that fragment to others with their own portions to consider.

Phantasmagoria

Considered formally, experience is a grab bag of everything that the finite center of (a) life might intend or entertain—Samuel Alexander used the word "enjoyment" for having an experience, which is going a bit far on the positive line. That sack of squirming items is full of holes; indeed, it is not clear that it is a container at all, since experience "leans on itself." James pointed out that even when considering experiences that could be called plausibly mine, most of them are not (self-)conscious; they are buried in *alteracion*. He suggested the term "sciousness" for the way in

Integral Consciousness 67

which most experiences are intended. Beyond sciousness, which can sometimes be reclaimed by reflective review through remembrance, is an acknowledged space-time, though it is not experienced directly by the finite center, that eng-lobes the conscious center's life, penetrates it, and constitutes (most of) it. Think of concentric circles with broken lines: the nucleus is the finite center's present intentionality, surrounding it is sciousness-subconsciousness (James), and surrounding the latter is experience-at-large. That is the way a conscious center conducting a reflective review can intellectually imagine the structure of experience revealed/yielded-by the review.

Experience is, as has been stated, formed contents, not merely abstracted form. The question arises of what to take out of the grab bag to begin a description of the (formed)-contents.

One/I could presumably start with any intentionality of any phenomenon/appearance, since the form of experience provides no indication of what formed-content "should" be privileged in the reflective review by being made the starting point. I cannot escape the judgment that any starting point will be arbitrary.

I will follow a Cartesian hyper-reflexive path by starting with my present doubt about which "possible" starting point to "choose." In doing so I place myself in the position of the circus rider described by Oliver Wendell Holmes, standing and watching the horses circle the track before he decides to jump on one of them and begin his adventure-performance. There are all these experiences and kinds of experiences that come to mind now. I need to imaginatively enter one of them, thematize it, and exclude the others.

I will dwell on the experience of the before-I-make-a-commitment to a theme, and I will thematize that experience.

The ideas rush through my mind. I might begin with the most fully elaborated, complete, and multi-leveled kind of experience. Alternatively, I could consider beginning with some kind of more "primitive" experience, if indeed there is any such. Maybe I should start with some extreme experience that indicates boundaries, limitations … and, perhaps, their supercession. What about something from the range of "average everydayness?" I could key myself into axiology and select an experience that I valorize or, alternatively, that I loathe. Just listing those possibilities—and, rest assured, there are many more—lightens me. The whole pursuit of a starting point becomes all of a sudden something that it seems much better for me to defer; there is no insistency about making a commitment. I will simply relax and observe the ideas fly by and record the structure of observing-the-ideas-fly-by. My position is similar to what Jean-Paul Sartre described as the *decalage*—the suspension that precedes making a commitment; but it is not attended by any fear and trembling, nausea, fatefulness, or the sense that I am about to lock myself in a prison of determination in which I will be stripped of my "freedom." There is nothing "tragic" about the "human condition;" the Holmesian suspension is comic, albeit serio-comic.

68 Michael A. Weinstein

The experience of the indetermination among ideas to thematize, which I presume is shared at some time by many, if not all "philosophers," is one mode in which the *Phantasmagoria* appears. Taken "together," the formed-contents of experience are a phantasmagoria. Indetermination-over-the-formed-contents-of-experience reveals a shifting and changing sequence of appearances-scenarios, and here I am appealing to the "ordinary" definition of phantasmagoria with some tweaks. The sequence is not orderly; it is disjointed and is a mixture of illusions and actualities, all thrown together and fused with diverse emotional responses: jumble, hodgepodge, confusion, medley, agglomeration. It would be disorienting if one was inside it rather than observing it and recording it. Indeed, if one encounters the phantasmagoria in other contexts than reflective review, the experience is often quite unpleasant. Doubt about a starting point for a philosophical inquiry is tame, but think of what one/I sometimes experience when I get up in the morning. As I enter wakefulness, I am assailed by a welter of apparently disconnected thoughts—suddenly I feel apprehension and anxiety about something that I am supposed to do or undergo that day; it is quickly succeeded by a lingering dream image; then the thought of someone I know; then part of my to-do list; then my attention is drawn to the papers on my night table; then I think of getting a cup of coffee; and so on. Moments of self-satisfaction are succeeded by feelings of depression; violence and sexual fantasies crop up and are displaced by aches and pains, and thoughts of what they might mean. I am driven to try to commit myself to one line or another, if only to get the day started and sweep away the confusion, which is as close as I get to what Krsna calls the "universal vision" in the Bhagavad-Gita. Krsna warned the seeker Arjuna against asking to experience the universal vision and the latter pleaded to get away from it as soon as it appeared.

The phantasmagoria was exquisitely described by Holmes as a "Bedlam of Ideals;" the madhouse that is experience before a part of it has been sectored off from the other intending experiences. All I have to do to escape the madhouse is to devote myself to one of its sectors; it will do simply to walk to the kitchen and prepare coffee—the effort will take my mind off other concerns and then I will be ready to surrender to habit or a presently overriding interest and take up the next concern.

There is, surely, nothing more genuine about the phantasmagoria, that is, foundation or primitive, than there is about more orderly experiences. It is simply the experience that engenders the serio-comic sense of life because it shows that there are times when order is shown to be a pretense or, if one prefers, a construction. There is no reason why I have to respond to the phantasmagoria comically, as ridiculous, absurd. I could just as well be horrified by it, as Arjuna was when he was drawn more closely and intensely to it. I respond with the serio-comic sense of life because the phantasmagoria shows me that life—for me—can be nothing other than play. Its appearance shows that seriousness fails in Bedlam, even though so much that goes on there is taken with "deadly" seriousness … for the moment, until something that seems to be more serious comes along. One is contemplating doing a good deed or even in the process of performing it, and then one stubs one's toe. The phantasmagoria always seems to be there, if one is attentive to the sequence of experiences as they take place from present moment to present moment. The phantasmagoria levels importance. The shifting standards of importance themselves constitute a phantasmagoria.

Serio-comedy

The serio-comic sense of life is the subjective response—as Alfred North Whitehead called the subjective component of an "actual occasion" or "drop of experience" (a moment of intentionality)—to the phantasmagoria. It is the base-line mood through which life is felt and judged in the present reflective review of experience.

As an object of intentionality, the phantasmagoria is an abstraction and construction that answers to the remembrance of all sorts of moments of experience or, in George Santayana's term, "intuitions of essence." In reflecting on those memories and thematizing their structure, the reviewing consciousness finds that they compose disjointed sequences, and that judgment evokes at the very least a smile in me, and often a rueful laughter.

A sense of life refers to a summary feeling-judgment on life-experience (life/experience). It is at the antipodes from primitive or fundamental experiences, yet its object is composed in great part of memories of the former, in all their variability, levels of intensity, harmonies, and oppositions; that is, the phantasmagoria. At least that is how I am coming to and at my sense of life.

There are alternatives to tying the sense of life to the phantasmagoria. Indeed, my impetus to deploy the term "sense of life" is Unamuno's "tragic sense" (*sentimiento*) of life, which seems not at all to have been based on a reflective review of experience, but, instead, on his desire not to die encountering his "rational" judgment that he would die and disappear altogether. I am not faulting Unamuno for his judgment that life is structured by an especially painful and disquieting (an understatement?) frustration. I have been through Unamuno's experience and, for me, it led to what I called at the time "the hatred of existence." Tragic life takes the failure of life to meet the requirements of the conscious center when it is seized by the "hunger for immortality" as some sort of wound or injustice. The thought of one's dying and death becomes horrible to entertain; it can be immobilizing; it tortures. Resentment about it is likely to be felt. One feels insufferably imprisoned in one's body, yet all that the conscious center wants is to keep its body intact and functioning forever.

The above is how I remember experiencing the tragic sense of life. I have no wish to explain it away through psychological criticism, for example, to call it narcissistic or egotistical. Indeed, for me, neither of those conditions speaks against the hunger for immortality. It still comes upon me now and again, and when it does, it is as Unamuno says, agonizing. I just cannot sustain it for very long anymore; it has become part of the phantasmagoria, standing alongside Ortega's "sportive sense of life" and the Mexican philosopher José Vasconcelos' "happy pessimism" (*pesimismo alegre*), the latter of which finds comfort in entertaining paradisiacal dreams in full knowledge that they are illusory and, perhaps, because they are illusory, which is an attitude that would seem to be alien to Unamuno. I have experienced them all, and now they have fallen into the disjointed sequences.

The reflective review has a rhythm, it dips into the phantasmagoria, taking up a memory, inspecting it, and reliving it imaginatively; and then it returns to contemplating the phantasmagoria, placing the memory that it has thematized into one or another sequence or, as Georg Simmel put it, a web, in this case a torn web.

I find that as I have been considering the tragic sense of life, I have been smiling, and that the smile has become broader as the reflection has proceeded. No doubt, the tragic sense of life is excruciating when one is living through it, but I am not living through it now and, as part of the medley, it is a cause for amusement. I can only remember stalking around my house in solitude in the early hours of the morning, agonizing over the thought of my death and feeling my skin crawl from the hatred of existence, with the feeling-judgment that I am a ridiculous figure. What has happened to me since then?

It seems inescapable to me that the shift from tragedy to comedy is a result of the decentering of the ego and its resultant status as a position within an englobing experience. Whitehead based his later reflections of the category of "importance," that is, which intentionality pops up at any given time is attended by a sense of the importance of its object. If I give my real assent to the proposition that feeling-judging that I am at the center of my life, to the point that I might even believe, momentarily, that I am in command of it, is simply a position, then that feeling-judgment is relieved of any overriding importance. Right now, my consciousness is as centered as it ever is, yet I judge that experience to be transient. Recurring to Holmes' image of the circus rider, I am atop the horse of reflective review, but I know that I might be thrown off that horse at any moment or that I might decide or feel impelled to jump on another horse. When I die it will not be "myself" as some entity or even function that disappears; what will be obliterated is the possibility of my taking the position in which I make the declaration-deed that "my life is the radical reality." Much as that position is highly valorized when I assume it, it has no standing beyond that. Centricity is becoming a throwaway. I will surely get tired of conducting this reflective review, the thoughts will become stale, and I will find something else to which to give myself over, if only going to sleep. Such is the phantasmagoria; it keeps changing—I can be hyper-reflexive and then I will doze off.

It is not funny to experience the fear of imminent organ failure or organ failure itself; the same goes for being alienated from a loved one or grieving, and so on. Those are serious experiences, but to repeat, they are all within the phantasmagoria, and, considered that way, are items in the variegated jumble. They are serious moments within a comedy.

Serio-comedy is, as a form of drama, a comic situation or plot that is presented in a serious form. The serio-comic sense of life adheres to that definition: life observed through the phantasmagoria is a comedy, here specifically a comedy of confusion, that is presented here in the "serious" form of a philosophical meditation governed by received standards that have penetrated and suffused my home discourse.

When Sartre reached the conclusion that he wanted to be the in-itself (*en soi*) for-itself (*pour soi*), which he acknowledged was impossible, he was seized with the thought that he was superfluous, and that caused him great consternation. The serio-comic sense of life is far more comfortable with the acknowledgment of the conscious center's superfluity; it makes all pretense ridiculous and can even be considered sometimes as liberating, because superfluity can be joined to play under almost all conditions.

Serio-comedy, as understood here, is not the burlesque of serious concerns, as it is for comedians like Woody Allen who spoof existentialism in order to lighten the tragic sense of life. The serio-comic sense of life has, instead, replaced the unremitting tragic plot of the Euro-romance with the phantasmagoria, which has no plot, no grand narrative, as Jean-François Lyotard would have it, only petty narratives leading nowhere discernible, intertwining and untying. Serio-comedy does not spell the end of seriousness, only of what Sartre called contemptuously the "spirit of seriousness."

Serio-comedy of Confusion

As the object/subject-matter of a reflective review, the phantasmagoria appears/ is-named specifically as a comedy of confusion, which works by the humor involved in the breakdown of expectations, the failure of plans to be fulfilled, relations among actions that defeat their respective purposes, misunderstandings of intentions, miscalculations of the relation between intentions and extant situations, inadequate perception and judgment, and the inability and/or unwillingness to sustain order within consciousness or the world, among innumerable kinds of disconnections and lapses. Those situations engender uncertainty and disorientation in the self, which are the subjective elements of confusion. One loses one's bearings.

There is no reason why confusion has to evoke laughter. The Canadian philosopher George Grant deployed the image of being lost in a pine forest as a metaphor for the human being's existential situation, and, for him, it was a terrorizing depiction. The turn to comedy occurs when the conscious center contemplating the phantasmagoria concludes that, absent the guidance provided by an ontological commitment, being lost is simply the condition to which one always returns as one's baseless base of operations. It is not that I got lost in the "pine forest" and will at some time, perhaps, return home to a life structure by actionable interests; the opposite holds: orderly life, for the conscious center contemplating the phantasmagoria, is an excursion from which I return to the Bedlam of Ideals.

The lack of any overarching meanings and their replacement by the moving mass of experience(s) leaves the serio-comic sense of life with the feeling of relief that comedy can bring; here I am back in my mental den, having done this and that, and I take comfort in my knowledge that I will be doing it all over again tomorrow (as long as I am still alive), and what I do then will matter no more than what I did today. For the time, in my den, I can sit in the mess of fragments, which is my portion of the general experience, and play with them, sometimes with the "serious" purpose of understanding the confusion as is the case for me at present, which is comforting; I can amuse myself with the memories of my experiences when they are swept back into the phantasmagoria.

Those with the spirit of seriousness will point out that my position is that of a philosophical aesthete and I accept that. Contemplating the phantasmagoria is attending a spectacle—oh, horrors! The absurd, as it was interpreted by the existential moralist Albert Camus as the human demand for meaningful unity and the failure of the world/reality to respond to that demand positively, is another variant of the tragic sense of life. Yet what if I have become inured to failure, expect it, and even find it amusing? It is a commonplace that many (most? almost all?) people sometimes laugh, indeed, uproariously, over the staging of failure. "It's a fine mess you've gotten us into," Oliver Hardy would often say to Stan Laurel, after some mishap that, of course, Hardy had caused. Do people laugh from a superior position to the comics, in which the former are exempt from the failure, or because they find that they are implicated in it and grasp how ridiculous are their own condition and activities? Some surely laugh at the comics from the safety of their own seriousness, but others laugh at them because they are simultaneously laughing at themselves. If I am always in a mess that I have gotten (myself) into, I have cause to laugh a good deal of the time; the breakdown of meaning(s) is a perpetual joke for someone for whom that breakdown has become normal.

The (serio-)comedy of confusion of necessity infects the present text, which is written from the serio-comic sense of life; it cannot help but be philosophy as a serio-comedy of confusion.

I will confess to the instability of the present discourse/meditation; it is thought-out/articulated by a subject-(position) on the boundary between modernism and postmodernism, infused with various pre-modernisms; and it vacillates among them uncertainly and to some degree with abandon. Is there nothing, for example, outside the text? If so, then all the moves that follow from a subject-position will be made. The reflective review will be interpreted as an "ego-centered discourse." Alternatively, is this text being written by an individual/person/self/ego who is deploying a "home discourse" that has been cleaned up (more and/or less) by philosophical culture? If so, then all of the previously criticized referential terms from modernist philosophy will fill the text. When the term "experience" is used, does it refer to "subjective" experience, to experience of the world beyond myself, or to both confusedly? It is instructive to observe that the term "phantasmagoria" means both the sequences "in the mind" and the sequences "in the world." In the present text, both of those meanings are embraced at once, and often they are confused purposefully or by default. I cannot help the imprecision because I am undecided between the modernist and postmodernist vocabularies, and I am building that undecidability into the text, sometimes using one of those vocabularies by itself, sometimes the other, and sometimes both of them in the same sentence as alternative formulations. The latter move of mixing vocabularies and using marks, such as scare quotes and parentheses, virgules, and dashes, is my preferred one, because it highlights confusion and dispels tragedy in favor of serio-comedy. Yet sometimes I am impelled to be a serious modernist and at others times a playful postmodernist, restraining discourse in the first case and setting it free to proliferate nuances in the second.

Philosophical discourse in the present text is its own (reflected) phantasmagoria, in which intertextuality is rife, whether it is expressly acknowledged allusively or remains tacit. As undecidable, the discourse is suggestive. Pieces of it can be taken up for their uses in other discourses without worry that they have been ripped out of a system and are infected by that system. It is all up for grabs.

The serio-comic/(serio-)comic sense of life is a result of levelling the battering ram of postmodernism unremittingly against the modernist ego's castle, which had already been crumbling from within through the internal subversion of depth psychology, which disclosed the fragility of the ego, and phenomenology, which exploded the unity of the subject into discrete intentionalities. It was not much of a step to rekey decentering as a textual affair and to interpret the ego as the subject-position of ego-centered discourse; yet it was a decisive step, because, although the ego could still proclaim itself as the "radical reality," that declaration-deed became one option among many in the tangles of (inter-)textuality.

Ontological nihilism is a tragedy for a self that holds itself to be a "reality" that is on the way to vanishing when it is no longer able to anchor itself in (some conception of) *reality*. If ontologies are understood as symbolic substitutes for life, then why is not the "ego" symbolic? It surely can be taken as symbolic, but in the moments in which I am intimate with myself, it is felt and judged to be more than just symbolic and I will not surrender that, because it is a real assent. Modernism provides the serious element to the serio-comedy, but it moves within the postmodern comedy. To proclaim oneself to be the "radical reality" expresses a real assent that can only be articulated with self-irony. Riffing on Umberto Eco's account of irony, I might say, "As Ortega would put it, 'my life is the radical reality.'"

Philosophical Autobiography

A reflective review of experience(s) conducted by a conscious center of finite life (a decidedly modernist pursuit) keyed in philosophical discourse (general characteristics) and disciplined by received critical standards cannot help but be

74 Michael A. Weinstein

autobiographical. It is, after all, "my life" that is the source of the subject-matter for my/the reflection.

The fuller statement of Ortega's declaration-deed is: "My life is the radical reality, and all other realities are rooted in it." Ortega makes it clear that he is not adopting a solipsistic position in which his life is the only reality in which all the others are included; he acknowledges a world apart from his "own" experience when he writes: "I am myself and my circumstances." It is his interaction with his circumstances that constitutes, for Ortega, "his" life. His reflection is grounded in phenomenological intentionality, the way in which the interaction between self and circumstances is known to be such.

"My" life, considered as successive reflections on the structure of life is, consequently, a reflection on the general structures of "my life;" that is, it is an exercise in philosophical autobiography, which is a form that prescinds from the details of my circumstances/"existence." The Romanian philosopher, E.M. Cioran (1970), coined the term "philosophical autobiography," which he convinced me is the most accurate understanding of what modern(ist) philosophy is, despite the fact that most modern(ist) philosophers seem to have believed that they were describing, analyzing, and coordinating the frame of things universally or generally, and impersonally, even when the "person" or some kindred term, such as subject, individual, self, or ego, was an important element of their philosophical vocabularies. Cioran shrugged his shoulders at that pretension; he had only his own life to pick apart.

Philosophical autobiography came into its own long before Cioran named the genre. Kierkegaard, Stirner, Nietzsche, Unamuno, Nikos Kazantzakis, and Vasconcelos are some of its self-conscious and forthright practitioners. Others, who might have believed that they were making universal or general truth-claims, also practiced the genre under a rhetorical camouflage. What is one to make of ontological, metaphysical existential-phenomenological, and deconstructive writing of, for example, Husserl, Santayana, Whitehead, Samuel Alexander, Heidegger, Sartre, Ortega, and John Dewey, to mention only a small few of all the many who worked at the margins of ontology and ontological nihilism? Whatever their ambitions, taken together they ended up presenting different takes on the frame of things, as philosophers, taken together, have always done. Their conceptions of the frame of things, presented in "objective" genres/rhetoric are simply philosophical autobiographies, each one marked and suffused by particular sentiments of life.

The serio-comic sense of life as the subjective response to the phantasmagoria's comedy of confusion is simply the latest moment/iteration of the results of my reflective reviews conducted over a half-century, each one an attempt to clarify the structure of the life that I-was-leading/was-leading-me. The successive iterations do not constitute a developmental process, although they are linked to one another; they partake of rupture and continuity.

"My" reflective reviews began in the summer of 1965, when I completed my M.A. in political science, having concentrated on comparative government. At that time, I suffered the first of many intellectual breakdowns; the study of politics, which had absorbed and energized me, suddenly went flat. The idea occurred to me that I should read philosophy, so I went through Morris Cohen's history of American thought and was attracted by his section on Santayana's philosophy, so I picked up Santayana's *Dominations and Powers.*

From the first page, I was astounded by how transparent Santayana's text was for me, so much so that I was able to anticipate the next sentence, sometimes verbatim. I had found a kindred philosophical spirit and I decided immediately to turn away from political science and devote myself to assimilating Santayana's thought.

Santayana's draw on me was the genre in which he wrote—the philosophy of life. As he put it most succinctly: "What will liberty bring to the free man? That is the great question of morals and politics." I took that as the question on which I would work.

Santayana opened to me my first description of the structure of life, formed by the ancient Greek distinction of action and contemplation, which he called, respectively, "vital liberty" and "spiritual freedom," and which he kept strictly separated, creating irresolution and Hegelian "unhappy consciousness."

Then, as I was completing my doctoral dissertation on Santayana's idea(s) of liberty, I was struck with the judgment, as I was crossing Euclid Avenue in Cleveland, Ohio: "I am not Santayana," and my philosophical self came into being.

How was I to "synthesize" the opposition between the desirous and willful vital liberty, and the reflective and more-or-less dispassionate spiritual freedom? It was the 1960s and I found my first answer in the Port Huron Statement of the Students for a Democratic Society: "It is not to have your own way, but to have a way of your own." I embraced "action" and "commitment," and worked out an (idealist, as it turned out) philosophy of "existential humanism," which reconciled self and circumstances in a utopian vision.

In 1972, existential humanism fell apart for me when I began my first sabbatical as a political theory professor, and, walking alone through an empty Lincoln Park in Chicago on a cold autumn day, experienced the eruption of what I immediately called "the beast," endowed with philosophical culture, but stripped of any illusions (as I was then ... and still am) of human unity and fulfillment in "freedom." The beast was an uncivil(ized) savage. He became, on reflection, the "renegade," who bites the hand that feeds him. Unhappy consciousness had again appeared, this time between the socially unassimilable individual and social organization.

It was the time, for me, of Unamuno's agony, laced with the hatred of existence, and so I would have remained, for all I know, had there not been another break, an unplanned plunge into Bergson's "fundamental self" of lived time (*durée*) that blasted the "conventional ego" of (socialized) practicality. The conventional ego was decentered for me then, on a night in 1976, at a party—and my experience became phantasmagoric. It was and remains the most intense and far-reaching experience that I have ever had—I had to acknowledge levels/zones/sectors of experience that were greater than and that outran and grounded my "official" self-definition.

76 Michael A. Weinstein

Since then, there have been more breakdowns, sudden-intense-rupturing experiences, and resulting further iterations; but, for the purposes of providing a context for what I have written so far in the present reflective review, that experience is determinative. It was when I first beheld the phantasmagoria. The surface of orderly social life was rent and shredded and beneath it was not vacancy, but a whirling mass of heterogeneous experiences running the gamut from intellection to unalloyed sensation in disjointed sequences in which world and mind were mixed and blended with each other to the point of being often indistinguishable.

In the years after having experienced the phantasmagoria, I have, in retrospect from my present serio-comic sense of life, undergone/instigated a process of re-civilizing myself in what seem to me to be unconventional terms, that is, devising a way of my own, a "philosophy of life" that initially proclaimed the centric individual and now has decentered that masterful ego (once and for all?). The phantasmagoria has returned, not as a shock but as an ever-present background of all of my more orderly experiences, a guarantee that there will not be, for me, any extra-vital meanings for "my" life that I will entertain. The tragic sense of life was knocked out in/through the re-civilizing process, but not the beast, who has been tamed by the self-irony of the serio-comic sense of life.

Integral Consciousness

The first thought that initiated the process of thinking that has grown into the present reflective review was that of integrality, which is the seed of the mental crystal that describes a structure of life.

In the early hours of an autumn morning in 2012, alone in my home in Indiana, I was struck by the thought that the term "integrity" had been taking up more and more of my reflections. I pushed myself to get up and look up the word in my 1937 edition of the Oxford Universal Dictionary. It was an effort to do so, because I had been letting the word travel through my thoughts as a placeholder and gap filler since the past January, and I was reluctant to specify it, because I thought that doing so might determine any conception of the frame of things in some unwelcome way. By unwelcome, I meant that thematizing "integrity" might lead me to have to acknowledge that a "moral" view had come to play a more important part in my life than had previously been the case.

Giving up on my futile deferral of facing whom I had been becoming, distasteful as that might be, I opened the dictionary and immediately found that the term "integrality" and then "integral" had replaced "integrity" in the forefront of consciousness. Without any idea of how or why I had hit on "integral," I was struck with one of its listed definitions: "A whole consisting of component parts actually (not merely mentally) separable." That use of the word had appeared in 1588 and was now rarely used and obsolete.

Integral Consciousness   77

I quickly realized that I had encountered a concept that would play a key role in my subsequent thinking, and it was part of the discourse on "experience," considered in general, rather than through a moral filter.

For at least a half hour, I kept repeating to myself the words, "a whole with actually separable parts, rather than analytical divisions." That concept connected to a pattern of experiencing that I had been noting in myself throughout 2012, and that I had been discussing with my co-author, who had observed the same pattern in himself. Both of us had been struck by how we had been finding ourselves being absorbed and immersed in our present sequence of experiences, having lost awareness of all the others that might claim our attention, and how, after the sequence had ended, it was quickly relegated to the past, with no over-hang on the next experience, which had drawn our devotion to it.

As I reflected on the connection between the 1588 meaning of "integral" and the experience of being immersed in succeeding discrete "experiences"—each one absorbing attention until the next one came along—I realized that when the pattern of successive immersion was taken as a whole, it was "integral"—the more that experiences set themselves off from each other and lacked the continuity provided by the thought that they were parts of a meaningful life-plan, the more they could be enjoyed/suffered/undergone for themselves, and would be so experienced.

The experience of immersion in sequences of "drops of experience" bears close resemblance to the accounts of the Zen school of momentalism, for which there are only moments of experience, lived presents, as a vitalist might put it. In Zen practice, the point is to eliminate all concerns that are extraneous to the dominant motive or focus of the present moment and to experience it fully. The reason for not immediately assimilating the experience of immersion to Zen is its provenance/genealogy, which seems to proceed from ontological nihilism as an unbidden, unanticipated, unsought, and "spontaneous" result of the latter; it is Zen that is not dependent upon any practice, art, attempt to relieve stress-anxiety-concern, or desire to experience "more fully;" rather, it just appears to happen when the center of consciousness no longer entertains frames of transpersonal meaning to package its life. All the petty meanings that one pursued in the past remain, but they are no longer instrumental to or exemplary of a "master narrative." Thereby the petty narratives lose the significance/importance with which a grand narrative endows them. In that sense, "integral consciousness" is placed under the sign of serio-comedy rather than some form of the "liberation" of life and its experiential fulfillment. Indeed, immersive experiences are often tedious, unpleasant, boring, terrorizing—use any word that specifies aversion. In one of its appearances, living the pattern of immersive experiences (integral consciousness) is another "fine mess" I've gotten (myself) into, and out of which I do not try to find a way.

In contrast to the phantasmagoria, integral consciousness is more-or-less orderly within the sequences constituting each immersive experience; it names the structure of ordinary, everyday life-experience when that experience is not "fringed" by wider sequences that have been composed symbolically into a (relatively) coherent "life"(-plan). The phantasmagoria is a jumble of indecision and indeterminacy/indetermination in which experience is volatilized; integral consciousness shows experience to be sectored off into distinct(ive) activities with their particular meanings, aims, and configurations.

I am eating and I am totally absorbed in its sensory qualities—in the appearance of the food, tasting it, breaking it down, and swallowing it. Then I read an email and I am immersed in it, assimilating the communication, considering how it affects my relation to its subject-matter, for example, a financial concern; and it is as though I had not just eaten—all that is important is some account or other that has to be understood and managed. The feeling-judgments that structure each activity are diverse from the other, requiring different mental and physical operations. They both are, indeed, phases of a whole, and they are related to one another functionally, in the sense that I need money to eat, and that I need to eat to be able to make money; but as experienced immersively and then compared and contrasted to one another, the contrasts overwhelm the continuities. There appears to be a "real separation" between them that cannot be alleviated by making them aspects of an overall system. The subject of eating and the subject of accounting are different "selves," and so it goes for all the many sectors of "experience."

Whitehead said that the central problem of philosophy is "how the many become one," and he attempted a solution of it in his cosmology. The affirmation of ontological nihilism has as a consequence the abandonment of the attempt to solve Whitehead's problem with a symbolic maneuver which would interpret the moving mass of experience as an orderly "cosmos." For integral consciousness, the many remain, irredeemably plural, and any coordination among the elements is in their interactions with one another rather than a plan/pattern that can be known apart or by inference from those extant interactions.

Integral consciousness is, then, one result of the abandonment of the pretensions of modern philosophy, even when those pretensions are attenuated to Camus' unanswered demand for unity, the core of his tragic sense of life. Once one has become convinced that the demand for unity will not be met, then one can broach the question to oneself of whether it is possible, even perhaps desirable to live without that demand and then to surrender oneself to more-or-less disjointed life. Whitehead himself wrote that humans are "ill-construed" beings who are not altogether well-adapted to their environment(s). Integral consciousness is the feeling-judgment (real assent) that there is no way (that I have been able to discover/devise) to think oneself out of Whitehead's conclusion. Life is a sectoral affair in which I enter and leave different "worlds" of experience into which I am temporarily "integrated." I experience a fragmented portion of the moving mass that is itself fragmented.

★★★

The sequence from experience through the phantasmagoria to integral consciousness follows what Santayana called the "order of evidence," which is the exposition of a theme such that the connections between its structuring concepts are presented as intelligibly as the writer can make them. The order here proceeds from the most embracing concept, the indefinite moving mass that includes "me" as the subject of the reflective review; through the phantasmagoria in which (some of) the contents of experience are compresent and confused; to the sectoring off of the contents of experience into more-or-less meaningful sequences of lived presents that are separable from others and are experienced as "really" separate from the others, not only according to their objects, but by their diverse subjective responses. The order records a movement to greater definition. Experience is not even "experienced" by the conscious center, but is an inferential concession to my real assent that I am a fragment of something that "exists" beyond "my" "life-experience." The phantasmagoria is a chaos of content, which is experienced by the conscious center; and integral consciousness is relatively orderly everyday experience, "proximally for the most part," as Heidegger put it. The order of evidence ends with integral consciousness with no attempt to create a closed circle by giving further specification to "experience" that would coordinate the various sectors into a meaningful unity.

Santayana primarily contrasted the order of evidence to the "order of genesis," by which he meant the explanation of phenomena offered by the natural sciences. For him, the phenomenological descriptions of the order of evidence are exercises in "literary psychology," stories of the structures of thinking and how they are connected; that is, modern epistemology, which ends in phenomenology (the "intuition of essence" in the "solipsism of the present moment"), in which he participated without illusion that it provided truth about the world. The scientific statements of the order of genesis gave humans whatever access they had to how the "world" or "nature" worked.

The scientific approach to knowledge will come into play, in part, in succeeding sections of the present reflection, but for now it is left to the side in favor of "literary psychology;" that is, the description of lived experience from a conscious center of (finite) life.

A third order of exposition was identified by Santayana, the "order of discovery," which refers to the temporal sequence in which the concepts making up a thematized reflective review appeared to the conscious center. In the preferred names of the present reflection, the order of discovery is philosophical autobiography undertaken directly rather than as a reconstruction in the order of evidence.

The proximate moments of the order of discovery that led up to the precipitation of integral consciousness show its appearance as a result of a line of thinking that makes that appearance intelligible though not necessary in any sense. It records one way of arriving at the structure of post-ontological experience.

In January, 2012, I was at a conference and was responsible for preparing a document for it. I left the building where the meeting was being held and walked across the street to a cafeteria, got a cup of coffee, and sat down to work. At that time I had not yet become aware of a pronounced tendency for my experience to become immersive, but, but I did expect that I was going to concentrate on my work and was not concerned with my surroundings. I did not resist doing the work and, so, did not become diverted by my surroundings; but instead of settling in with a single focus on writing the document, I had a striking experience in which I was simultaneously very keenly aware of the cafeteria and the life coursing through it, and of the thought-process of writing-the-document in which I was involved.

The experience of writing was distinct from that of presence in the cafeteria, each one coalescing into two compresent sectors of experience that seemed to have no connection with each other. I had no sense of alienation and did not feel disturbed; yet the experience marked itself off for me as significant in the sense of revealing some structure of life that by virtue of its disclosure would change the way that I would experience in the future. A sense of detachment from both experiences became progressively intense so that the preparation of the document became nearly automatic, and the life of the cafeteria became a spectacle that I could not help but observe, but into which I could not enter; both experiences lost importance, yet both of them were "immersive," as I have later come to say, and they were both intensely vivid.

In retrospect, the significance that I attributed to the experience was that it marked a rupture in the "unity" in moments of experience that is provided by a dominant motive/meaning, which clears away present extraneous or adventitious elements. An actual occasion is (nearly) never single-pointed; there is a background to the foreground, and it is that background that came forward to share the foreground in the cafeteria. The life in the cafeteria had no significance for me for-itself; it came forward to relativize the importance of writing the document, taking away the seriousness of the latter (its momentary absoluteness), in the sense of the "spirit of seriousness."

Again in retrospect, considered in terms of the (relatively) coherent "life"(-plan) that I had been constructing for myself at the time, the experience of compresent-split consciousness in the cafeteria leveled the prioritization that ordinarily makes the subordinated aspects of an experience either irrelevant to or, more importantly, functional for the dominant focus. Rather than the writing of the document being an essential activity in my life-plan, "I" became the subject-position of the writing. The experience was, on the one hand, an opening to reprioritization of interests in my personal life-process, and, on the other, the first move to integral consciousness.

After I returned home from the conference, the life-plan in terms of which I was acting began to come apart as the focus of my intellectual life, which at that time was political analysis, lost its attraction and appeal. Nothing else came forward to take its place, leveling all the different kinds of experiences that I had to appear in their distinction and distinctiveness, and their non-ultimaticity. The result was immersive experience, in which meaningful sequences of drops of experience give way to others without concern for how they relate to each other in wider frames of meaning.

Integral Consciousness   **81**

From time to time, I began to experience the breakdown of order and the term "phantasmagoria" entered my philosophical vocabulary. Yet it existed as an unthematized placeholder and cannot be said to have preceded integral consciousness in the order of discovery. More important was a growing sense of the disconnection of clusters of experience, an increasing intensity of all of them, and a simultaneous distancing from them. The serio-comic sense of life had not made its appearance and would not do so until the autumn of 2014; instead, there was an absence of a dominant sense of life registering a period of intellectual transition. Just as Descartes adopted a "provisional morality" to allow him to survive socially his period of philosophical doubt, I let my habitual/accustomed life-practices maintain me.

Through the winter and spring of 2012, I remained intellectually frozen, recalling the experience in the cafeteria frequently, convinced that it had philosophical import, but unable to determine what that was. I had no taste for any intellectual projects and experienced a sense of mild unease, as though philosophy had become a closed book for me. As I let my established practices push my life forward, my experiences became more immersive and less linked meaningfully to one another. With the onset of summer, I began to think that, barring contingencies thrust upon me by the "world," I had entered a time of indefinite duration in which I would simply repeat the same round of life-experience each day marked by the same familiar emotions associated with each sequence. That prospect did not trouble me, because there was nothing to do about its eventuality, since I envisioned no alternatives. I began to increasingly feel that I had set myself up for death, in the sense that my life was not going to change in its structure; the connections among its parts would simply be looser than they had been.

The absence of a sense of life was new, but it was not disquieting; again, there was nothing to do about it. Each distinctive sequence of drops of experience had its own moods, so I did not experience emotional vacancy; I lacked an overall subjective response to life that went along with the lack of any leading intellectual/philosophical project. I felt neutral about life as a "whole;" I no longer framed it in a dramatic form, as I had been doing (without being fully aware of that) since 1966. There had been life before philosophy, I thought, and I could "fall back" to a pre-philosophical position (the thought that there might be a "post-philosophical" position did not occur to me).

On a brilliant hot and sunny day in early July, 2012, I was about to go out and exercise one of my practices, reviewing art-photography exhibits for the Chicago alternative weekly *NewCity*. Seemingly out of nowhere, I was hit by the idea that I had to read Guy Debord's essay on the "*dérive*," which, since the late-1980s, I had told myself that I needed to study, yet had never done so, having felt a resistance to "confronting" it that I could not and did not try to explain to myself. The impulse to read the essay that summer day was irresistible, and I found it on the internet, printed it out, speed-read it, folded it into my back pocket and set off on a six-mile walk to an unfamiliar neighborhood where two

82 Michael A. Weinstein

photography shows were opening. I had launched myself on a *dérive*, which, in retrospect, was the first step toward the serio-comic sense of life.

As I walked west from Lincoln Park, I experienced a flood of ideas. It was neither the confused phantasmagoria nor a disciplined and directed reflection, but something in between those—a variegated sequence of thoughts that were related to ideas and phrases that had stuck in my immediate memory from my speed reading of Debord's essay and my perceptions of my present surroundings. I felt enlivened for the first time since my experience of split consciousness in the cafeteria. I was no longer in a state of neutrality, although I did not yet have words to interpret the infusion of vitality.

For Debord, the *dérive* is both a way of experiencing the public urban world and a method of inquiry into that world that he called "psycho-geography." In a Debordian *dérive*, one visits an unfamiliar neighborhood without any practical purpose to direct one's activities and limit the scope of one's perceptions. Yet the "drifting" does have an aim, which is to experience and record that sense of life of that neighborhood through observations, chance encounters, and fanciful experiences, such as the conceit that one will meet someone at a particular place and time, which, of course, might or might not happen, but adds a component of what Kant called "purposeless purposiveness," the form of aesthetic experience, as he saw it.

In retrospect, it is clear that the *dérive* answered to a desire of which I was not aware to energize my increasingly disparate life-experience without giving that experience a wider meaning. The *dérive* takes oneself out of one's self-preoccupations and into the (social) world as existing for its own sake and indifferent to one's own life. The method of psycho-geography can only be practiced if one is superfluous to the life of the place into which one has entered. One inserts oneself into the life of the place, but not as a participant in the sustenance of that life. The *dérive* is an adventure that is grounded in the freedom of superfluity.

As opposed to the experience of split consciousness (compresence) in the cafeteria, my *dérive* on that July day fused my line of thinking with my perception of my surroundings, because I was thinking about the concept of the *dérive* while I was engaged in one. I realized at the time that I had been taking *dérives* throughout my life since I was in junior high school, going out on walks or bicycle rides by myself to different neighborhoods just to take them in and feel the life in them. Those experiences were usually mixed with reflections on my personal preoccupations, but there were stretches of time when I would give myself over to the "other" life without intervening in it. There had always been the attraction of being present in an everyday "life-world" that was independent of me, a life that went on without concern for me. It was an experience of decentering that gave me a welcome sense of my unimportance that served as a counterpoint to the centricity of "my life" as the "radical reality" that had dominated my consciousness since junior high school and that I had ruthlessly thematized after I took up philosophy in 1966. Now it was emerging from the background into the foreground, and with it came the thrill of adventure.

Through the rest of the summer and into the fall of 2012, the *dérive* replaced split consciousness without being fully thematized. The idea grew on me that the *dérive* did not have to be confined to special experiences that were distinct from the other experiences that constituted my received round of life that continued to repeat itself, not so much monotonously as with expectable familiarity. Why was it not possible to take many if not most of my experiences in the spirit of the *dérive*, as experiences revealing psycho-geographies that I would observe and enjoy as I played my accustomed part in them? I took up the experiment.

Making much of my experience into a *dérive* began to transform my life into play. The activities in which I had been engaged remained as they had been, calling out the same skills and "responsibilities"/commitments, but I performed them with a different sensibility that was characterized most importantly by the feeling-judgment that they were not ultimately important. Not only could they be taken up and set aside with greater abandon than I had allowed previously, but they could be treated more experimentally, as occasions for attempting to make them as pleasurable as possible for as many of those involved in them as were susceptible to enjoying themselves. I began to view those with whom I was in contact less as occupants of social roles than as distinctive and distinct individuals with their own (disjointed) lives, and who had their particular shares in the moving mass of experience to which I responded with what I have later thematized as the serio-comic sense of life, which promotes indulgence towards oneself and others.

★★★

Split (compresent) experience and the distinctively separate sequences of immersive experiences to which it seemed to have led, and the *dérive*, which offered a practical synthesis of them through the adventurous play that attended as many of them as possible, were the concepts out of which integral consciousness emerged. The idea of a whole with real separations provided the form of immersive experiences taken together by the sectoring of experiences into zones, each with its distinctive feelings-judgments. The disjointed round of immersive experiences was everyday life when it had been relieved of transpersonal frames of meaning. There was an indefinite whole in which they all operated, but it was no longer up to me, or indeed possible for me, to unite them symbolically in grand narratives or even in a coherent life-plan. Any of the coordination of heterogeneity that occurred would be accomplished by processes, primarily social/societal, that were beyond my centered experience and my willful control.

The concept of integral consciousness allowed me to interpret compresent/split consciousness as indicative of a structure of (my) life(-experience). In retrospect, I can find no better illustration of a whole with separate parts/phases/processes than compresent/split consciousness, in which the "whole" is an actual occasion (drop of experience, lived present) in which the compresence of separate elements is directly experienced.

Integral consciousness also made sense of the *dérive* with its emphasis on heterogeneous psycho-geographies that were other to my own round of life. Bringing the *dérive* into my everyday life made each of my experiences an adventure that was other to the others rather than a contribution or obstacle to a life-plan; each of my (immersive) experiences took on the character of a visit to a different "neighborhood" with its own psycho-geography. The conclusion of an experience meant that I had left its neighborhood and had moved to another, which was why it seemed as though I might not even have had that experience—it was what it was in-and-for-itself and there was no impulsion for it to linger in short-term memory.

Compresent-split consciousness and the *dérive* organized themselves in my experience-thematization as two poles between which everyday immersive experiences gravitated—analysis and synthesis, dissociation and association, fission and fusion. In the months after integral consciousness emerged as an organizing concept, the phantasmagoria came forward as a compacted, compressive, and rapidly successive experience of the heterogeneity of separate intentionalities before they took on the guise of organization, which is why it preceded the exposition of integral consciousness in the present reflection in its earliest phases when it followed the order of evidence rather than the order of discovery. Reflection on the phantasmagoria began a working back in the order of evidence to the most comprehensive concept of the structure of (post-ontological) life, the notion of "experience" as William James understood that term, as indefinitely defined as possible and proceeding from inferential reference rather than more direct experience or, better, it is the "direct" experience of conceptualizing what is thought not to be directly experienced.

A "philosophy" had taken shape—a description of the structure of "my" life constituted by an interconnected set of terms. It reached its completion in the autumn of 2013 when I realized that my growing subjective-response/sense-of-life associated with the new description of the structure of life was serio-comic. Tragedy is dependent on failed meaning; if there is no demand for or expectation of a meaning for life-experience, one will not suffer a tragic sense of life.

Although the serio-comic sense of life comes last in the order of discovery, as the culmination of the reflective review describing the (present) structure of ("my") life—the yield of the reflective review for philosophy of life/conduct—it precedes integral consciousness in the order of evidence, because it became most prominent as a response to the phantasmagoria, in which rapid succession of the diverse contents of consciousness approaches a jumble of compresence; it is the "directly" experienced breakdown of order. Integral consciousness is relatively orderly; in the order of evidence, it is built up and constructed from a chaos to which one is sometimes privy.

From the perspective of philosophical anthropology, the serio-comic sense of life answers to a "human" condition in which chaos precedes order and the latter is always partial, fragile, provisional, and disjointed. Held relative to the phantasmagoria, integral consciousness is an achievement, as far as order goes for a post-ontological (ontologically nihilistic) consciousness. An alternative to that formulation is to hold integral consciousness relative to a conception of a more perfect/complete order. From that latter perspective, integral consciousness is not an achievement; rather, it marks a failure, defect, or privation. It is just the refusal to deploy the idea of a completed order to judge integral consciousness (unillusioned—not disillusioned with all its resentful connotations—everyday (disjointed) experience(s)) that the view from the phantasmagoria asserts. The affirmation that integral consciousness discloses the structure of life carries with it the judgment that the notion of a (more) completed order is a utopian ideal that serves as a symbolic substitute for life that is adverse to life when it turns upon it to judge it wanting. The judgment that life is not what it could/should/is-supposed-to be is here just another moment in the phantasmagoria, and often a deadly serious one riven by guilt, regret, resentment, obligation, and feelings of inferiority, just to scrape the surface of that emotional cauldron.

Each one has a position, a fragment of the moving mass or experience-at-large. Absent a system that coordinates those fragments into a coherent and intelligible whole, there is no reason to expect that anyone's fragment will or should be internally coherent, that the portion of the portion will fit together reciprocally and functionally to "make sense." There is just too much contingency and accidentality for that, and there is no *prima facie* obligation for one to try to make their portion more coherent. It is just as possible to accept that one is in a mess, and that acknowledgment gives rise to the serio-comic sense of life. There is a point at which it becomes possible "to stop making sense." Holmes, who experienced the Bedlam of Ideals, ended his reflections with the judgment that "we do not know who we are." Santayana insisted that we exist in "circumambient ignorance." For Whitehead, we are ill-construed beings. Our situation takes on a comic cast when we conclude that it cannot be any other way and futility, failure, and frustration evoke laughter at our fallibility rather than some variant or other of anger.

The fact that we desire guarantees that we will be dissatisfied in many particulars and on the whole, but it is possible for (some of) us to find that condition to be ridiculous.

Phenomenology of Mind

The present reflection has been an application of phenomenology of mind aimed at describing the structure of experience, in its most general and framing terms, of a particular "life" grasped by a conscious finite center; it is an exercise in the phenomenology of life-experience.

The word "particularity" is emphasized here. There is no claim made that the structure(s) of life-experience that have been described are universally or even generally relevant to all "lives." Phenomenology of mind as understood here is a

86 Michael A. Weinstein

personal affair; the reflective review of experience is undertaken by a particular individual; it is intended to clarify my "own" experience, which might or might not be representative and, even more to the point, might or might not be useful to other particular "lives" seeking their "own" clarifications. Rather than an argument intended to convince others that they should understand the structure of life as "I" have presented it, the present reflection is an invitation to experience and "organize" life as I do, offering the possibility that the account might point others more precisely in their "own" direction.

It is not clear that the kind of reflection defined here can even be called "philosophy." In one sense, it is closely linked to the philosophical discourses of the past through much of its vocabulary and, more importantly, through the problem that it puts to itself of defining framing concepts of the highest generality. In another sense, however, the present reflective review departs from the philosophical tradition by restricting its initial applicability only to myself, indeed, only to myself at the period and place of my "life" at which I am meditating and writing.

By restricting the claim to applicability so sharply and stringently, I am trying to avoid the excess of what the twentieth-century American philosopher Ralph Barton Perry called the "egocentric predicament," which he concluded had defined modern philosophy. That predicament was built-into the founding of modern philosophy in Descartes' cogito, the starting point in the thinking process itself, from which all other judgments about the structure of being/reality would be derived.

As generations of philosophers who succeeded Descartes undertook the inquiry into conceptions of the "frame of things," the subjectivity of the starting point clung to them. Meanwhile, the natural sciences became modern philosophy's competitor, but, although their practical supremacy was indisputable, they did not produce conceptions of the frame of things; indeed, they renounced the effort to do so, restricting themselves to identifying and theorizing processes within an unspecified frame. Attempts to universalize scientific theories and rekey them as ontologies ended up as monuments to the state of scientific theory in one or another discipline at a particular time. In addition, scientific "worldviews" did not refrain from addressing problems outside the scope of science that had been essential to the philosophical tradition, such as what the best way or correct way of living is; and once those problems had been broached, the egocentric predicament reasserted itself.

By the turn of the twentieth century, the pretensions of modern philosophy had been scaled down to the point that the inward turn to the reflecting ego revealed for Santayana merely a "solipsism of the present moment," in which an "essence" (some discernible appearance) was "intuited." All claims and commentaries beyond the acknowledgment of the event of intentionality were, as Santayana put it with devastating elegance, "literary psychology;" that is, stories about how consciousness came to be what it is according to the orders of evidence and discovery.

It is a short step from literary psychology to the judgment that a reflective review of experience is a personal pursuit articulated in general terms. That pursuit is egocentric, but there is no "predicament" involved in it, because the individual who undertakes and reports the review is not claiming to speak the words of "being" or even of "human experience," which means that there is no call for the report to argue that it expresses "objective" knowledge. The self-clarification will turn out to be more-or-less representative and exemplary, which does not take away from its cogency for those for whom it resonates.

Relieved of pretensions to objectivity, the reflective review is experimental and provisional, subject to change in its conclusions as the individual who undertakes it more precisely names the experiences that suggest framing concepts, undergoes new suggestive/indicative experiences, or makes previously thematized experiences more prominent and moves others to the background, and even reinterprets a previous structure as a whole. The present reflective review records the latter, describing the results of a move decentering a previously affirmed egocentricity to a decentered ego that acknowledges itself as such from an egocentric position confined strictly to the activity of reflective review in "home discourse" generally and here specifically as inquiry into the structure of life-experience.

The move of decentering the ego was not a result of a theoretical reflection aimed at resolving a conceptual contradiction or confusion, but a consequence of a change in lived experience in which it seemed that the last vestiges of the feeling-judgment that I had a coherent "life"(-plan) had vanished. In the absence of an unself-consciously presumed unity, life-experience presented a different structure than it had previous displayed, most importantly, integral consciousness.

The reflective review is carried on with life, yet it places one "above" it, superintending it. In the early 1980s, I experienced a moment in which the words flashed before my consciousness, "I, the whole; above life, a technique." It is only now, at the beginning of 2015, that the second part of that statement-declaration has shown its import-meaning fully: the activity of modern philosophy is simply a move I make, an operation that I perform, a position that I take; as far from an Archimedean point as one can get—simply an incident in life, but the only one that I experience-know that brings me to myself. I am most myself when I am reviewing my memories, sorting them out, and trying to determine their bearings on each other—the contemplative life as I experience it.

As for the first part of the statement, I can no longer affirm my "wholeness." I acknowledge myself as a fragmented fragment of an indefinite and undefined "experience" that extends beyond my ken. I recur to the phantasmagoria, in which the variegated feelings, images, impulses, and ideas that make up my portion of the mostly impersonal whole succeed each other in a rapid-fire motley medley. I find myself in distinct(ive) sequences of drops of experience in which I am immersed as long as they last, only to leave them to become immersed in other sequences, and so on. I conceptualize the phantasmagoria and the succession of immersive experiences as an acknowledged "whole" comprised of separate sectors that display, for me, no unity of meaning. I respond to the structure of life-experience that I have conceptualized with a serio-comic sense of life that judges experience to be a mess, a ridiculous condition in which I am embedded and that at least evokes a smile and in which, when I have sufficient vitality, I revel, until pain, frustration, and failure break me. This disposition that I have cultivated in response to my embeddedness in a situation that lacks overall meaning and can offer intense pleasures one moment and acute suffering the next is the fruit of my reflections on the fragmentary nature of both experience and consciousness itself.

3

EMBEDDEDNESS, SERIO-COMEDY, AND THE THIRD APE

Michael A. Weinstein and Timothy M. Yetman

Embedded Existence *(MW)*

"I" am a fragmented fragment of the moving mass of experience. That is the conclusion about the general structure of experience that I have reached through a reflective review of (my) experience conducted through the phenomenology of mind.

The position of reflective review is on the contemplative side of life. The contemplative position knows itself as being outrun by what is more-than-itself. It contemplates (its) experience as though it were not inside it at the same time that it affirms that it is inside it. The reflective review is a move, a technique—a trick if one will. It is a complication of consciousness, the closest to "transcendence" that "I" get—"above life, a technique."

From my reflective vantage point, I acknowledge experience as a moving mass, I observe the spectacle of the phantasmagoria and respond to it with the serio-comic sense of life, and I find that my experiences have become increasingly immersive and are arrayed in sectors, the collection of which is integral consciousness, in which the sectors are "really" separated from one another rather than abstracted from a system that comprehends the "whole." The reflective review surveys; it remembers, "re"-imagines, analyzes, relates, conceptualizes, and renders judgments on the structure of life. It is an experience that is removed from all the other experiences; the reflective review epitomizes integral consciousness; it is experienced as separate.

The reflective review achieves its "real" separation by virtue of its passivity towards the other experiences that it surveys. It accepts and admits those experiences and lets them appear—it does not care to change anything about them. Contemplation's only struggle is to understand.

The reflective review does not end with experience surveyed; there are also the experiences as they are lived, from the inside of the moving mass, and the phenomenology of mind reaches the last outpost of passivity and projects itself inside, plunging into "existence" and remembering the "active" life itself in order to describe its structure.

Embeddedness (MW)

In the summer of 2014, the day after I had finished writing my first "systematic" thematization of integral consciousness, I was knocked off the perch of reflective review and found myself abruptly inside the moving mass, where I realized immediately that I had always (already) been without being (fully) cognizant of it. I was contemplating the active position and there was nothing passive about it; my being-in-the-world had seized me and phenomenology of mind had morphed into existential-phenomenology.

I was seized by the sense of being radically confined, with no more moves to make and no exit from myself and the world just as they were. I uttered the feeling-judgment, "I am embedded."

Like a stone in a motley walkway, I am a fragment of a larger construction, placed rigidly in relation to the others, surrounded by them and unable to change my position, locked in and tied up. The world penetrates me and works its way through me. I am overwhelmed.

To be embedded means to be a fragmentary part of a whole, yet one that retains its distinction, its separateness. Embeddedness is integral consciousness lived within the concrete particularized world, rather than as the former is cognized in a reflective review of the structure of "my" experience undertaken by a (super-)intending finite center of conscious life. Embeddedness is how I live integral consciousness day by day, inside one or another of its sectors, at this time and place, with this content and no other.

A feeling of oppressiveness came over me that was attended initially by the judgment that I had led this particular life in these particular circumstances, and that I had ended up (and had "always already" been) this fragment of/in the moving mass. The sense of oppression proceeded from my acknowledgment of the obdurate particularity of it all—not of the past, since I felt no regret at all; but by the thought that what was left of the future for me would be framed inescapably and obtrusively by a crushing awareness of particularity. There would be just this and nothing else, a variation on *tedium vitae*.

The "phenomenon" of *embeddedness*, the feeling/being of the "active" life, performs the function that existence (*existenz*) has in existential-phenomenology, undercutting the latter and finding another structure beneath it, the rock bottom so far, for me. It is another step along the path of dispelling illusions about the structure of life, what life is; perhaps it is the last one, at least it seems that way to me, but I cannot know that: the battering ram of (post-)modern(ist) criticism never seems to complete its de(con)struction, its decentering of the "ego." Embeddedness means that the "active" life begins, is grounded, not in passivity, but in the opposite of action, that is, paralysis, not the indecision when one confronts the phantasmagoria, but the global sense of confinement.

The analysis of embeddedness abstracts the distinct and related elements of feeling/being surrounded and of acknowledging the irremediable particularity of everything, both of which combine to produce the oppressive sense of confinement. I imagine myself as a piece of slate embedded in a walkway, realizing that I am always moving in the moving mass, yet I cannot banish the image as determinative of my condition. I am not the same from one moment to the next, but from within each moment I am fixed in place. I am surrounded on all sides, from without and within, and I cannot pull myself out of the moving mass. When I am engaged in reflective review, I am enfolded in the world, squeezed by it, and so it is for every "intentionality" as lived. Just this and nothing else, having become, for now, just this "summed-up-self-in-process," as the American philosopher of the mid-twentieth century, Justus Buchler, put it.

The sense of being surrounded and penetrated, permeated by the world, is a feeling-judgment; it is a full and comprehensive experience (of radical intranscendence). I feel/have-been cornered by life. The next moment of the analysis is to understand that I am surrounded by particularity and that I am *particular*. The world is (just) what it is and I am just "who" I am *in* the world, here and now. That, not "my life," is the "radical reality." Nothing that I do, nothing that I think will change my embeddedness in the moving mass. The world is so much bigger than I am that it overwhelms me. I am like the "coral-insect" that Holmes imagined, unaware that it is part of a process of making a reef. I do know that I am part of making something—most proximately "society"—but the shifting product has, for me, no determinable meaning—no more meaning than a coral reef that is a "collective" product that is just there and has more or less effect on the "eco-system" in which it is embedded.

It is inescapable for me that the experience of feeling/being embedded is "serious." There seems to be nothing "comic" about being trapped in particularized existence. It is attended by an uncomfortable squirming feeling. It is a collapse, and there is only a squirming that knows itself to be futile. Yet I begin to smile. The passage from the reflective review to embeddedness is quite similar to slipping on a banana peel—I was always on the ground anyway and any pretensions that I might have had were vain in the face of the world, ridiculous.

Existence *(MW)*

Existence precedes essence, but embeddedness precedes existence.

(Post-)modern(ist) criticism is another name for the Euro-romance, which is the tragic story of the dashing of the hopeful dreams of satisfying meaning that successively fall under the former's battering ram until it seems to end in ontological nihilism.

Considering (post-)modern(ist) philosophy in retrospect, it appears as a double movement with a "constructive" side in which one conception of the frame of things after another is created and then is de(con)structed by showing that there are alternative conceptions to it that cannot be defeated "rationally" or (more importantly) sentimentally, and that its claims cannot be vindicated by life as it is lived rather than imagined.

The subject(s) of philosophy collectively have enacted the Sisyphean myth, placing forward symbolic substitutes for life and then tearing them to shreds, and in some cases (Kant comes to mind) the same thinker has gutted his own creation. I will not play that game; ontological nihilism renders it impossible. The paralysis of embeddedness appears when confronting what is left after the transcendence of meaning over life is no longer entertained and, as a result, the latter is no longer covered and veiled by a tapestry of ideas.

The paralysis of embeddedness only lasts so long. As long as one is still alive, vitality will assert itself and the organism will make a move in one direction or another, caught up in the movement of the moving mass and adding one's contribution to the propulsion, doing something that is often attended by ideas about what one is doing and why. One is launched into the "active" life, for better and worse—it does not matter.

Existentialism names the final chapter of the Euro-romance, when only the bare and unadorned structure of the active life remains—projection, propulsion itself. The existentialists were on the brink of confronting embeddedness and, indeed, touched it without staying with the experience long enough to grasp its implications. Heidegger's comprehensive intentionality of being-in-the-world, Sartre's being-in-situation, and Ortega's "I am myself and my circumstances" all acknowledge that the individual is surrounded, but they persist in putting the "ego"/self/subject in a position outside the world/situation/circumstances, determining how that ego "comports" itself towards its surroundings.

The existentialists might have remembered that they were once infants, who live embeddedness. Heidegger put it precisely: the individual is thrown into the world, literally expelled from the womb. Heidegger then went on to say that the individual then "catches" himself and so begins self-propulsion, which becomes so pervasive that it can be mistaken for the very structure of life. Yet think of the newly minted infant, a helpless, squirming lump of flesh, caught in the toils of its surroundings, able to thrash around when irritated or when pleasured ebullient, but incapable of projecting a "plan" for the future or of trying to put it into effect if it happened to generate one. Embeddedness can be understood as a return to infantile dependency (and vulnerability) only now with cognizance of the condition. It is always possible at each of life's stages to return to that condition. The nervous system, indeed, becomes more organized, language allows the mind to define itself and its surroundings, and, most decisively for the existentialists, there is an intentionality towards the future that gets filled with ideas of what might be (desired or feared) and what should or should not be. Those ideas of futurity are the stuff of propulsive projection-action. They can and do collapse.

Human beings "hurl" themselves into the future, says Sartre. "Man makes himself." "He" does not (necessarily) conform to some "essence." Existence precedes essence, and so it does; the experience of embeddedness does not cancel the experience of projection-propulsion, but (merely) decenters it. "Existence," as understood by the existentialists, is a phase of the (experienced) life-process, which, when it is abstracted from the life-process and made its "essence"—the "essence" of suspense—occludes embeddedness.

It is, indeed, another humbling blow of the (post-)modern(ist) battering ram to reduce the self to sheer propulsive projection without "essential" content. After all the moments of the Euro-romance have been ticked off, I am left with those (seemingly ceaselessly) recurrent instants in which I am suspended on the knife's edge of some immersive experience, seemingly undetermined, on the brink of propelling myself. I am most myself when I am "nothing," that is, in suspense, in a realm of ideas called "possibilities."

The infant (presumably) does not entertain possibilities. The existentialists wielded the battering ram, but they still played the Euro-Game; they still had the possibility card to play. Possibility takes me out of the sense that I am embedded; I have ideas of what is not-yet, and those ideas give me a sense that there is "play," that I am not boxed in, that I stand above my surroundings as an actor. It can get to the point that I entertain the conceit that I am self-determining, even as I acknowledge that I am being-in-situation.

"Existence" is intoxicating. I can make the declaration-deed that "my life is the radical reality," and mean it because I (think that I) have possibilities of my "own;" I can (and will) consult "my" interests, whatever those might be. No one and no text can tell me who I am, and I will not deny, not only that I think that way at the time, but that I actually take that position. At that moment, I am as far from infancy as I can be; I have achieved Sartre's "age of reason," having taken charge of my life (for the time being). Onto-theology, as Derrida calls symbolic substitutes for life, might have been blown away by ontological nihilism, but "useless passion" that I am, I feel-judge that I am empowered by *my* possibilities—hopes and fears, desires and aversions. When self-propulsion grows into its "positive mode," it is (captured by the term) *self-determination*. I have a "better judgment" and I am prepared to (try to) exercise it.

At the zenith of "existence," I am *confident*, not in my ability to carry through my projects to "success" (contingency lurks around every corner), but in my judgments; I have the "courage of my convictions." It all can be overturned in a snap and a flash, and I will even predict that I will slip, but while the experience lasts, it perfects the position of the active life. It is the form of maximum vitality.

Existence, as I have interpreted it in the present reflection, is (just) a moment in the life-process, but it is as much a life-structure-defining experience as embeddedness; indeed, it is the latter's "opposite" in the terms of a more-or-less standard Hegelian dialectic from the *Phenomenology of Mind*, the second moment that "negates" embeddedness. The passivity of embeddedness is not sustainable, not because of any ideas, but by virtue of the life-process, which is on the move along with the moving mass. When that propulsive movement has been linguistically organized and socially disciplined, it takes on the general structure that has been described by the existential-phenomenologists as "existence." It is an illusion that I am my "own," except at the moments when I am.

Embedded Existence *(MW)*

For every moment in which I find myself to "be" the radical reality, there are uncounted thousands in which I am immersed in some particular activity as an operator doing something particular. I am not overwhelmed by my surroundings to the point that I am paralyzed by my confinement in them, and I am not centered within them in a condition of undetermined suspension on the brink of making a commitment to "do" something. I am ordinarily doing something, either having been swept up into an ongoing activity without having made a self-conscious commitment, or having made such a commitment and now caught in it, following it up.

Embedded existence describes life as I live it, "proximally and for the most part." It is the "sublation" of the opposition between embeddedness and existence, in which one is down-to-earth again, but now as a moving part of the moving mass with more-or-less initiative/impulsion of one's "own." I make some directed effort enmeshed in some concatenation of particulars.

I am always "acting"/operating within some sector of experience and, while I am immersed in that experience (actual occasion), I am a particular self/subject (-"position") that is more-or-less appropriate to the activity in which I am engaged in/with these particular circumstances. Embedded existence on the whole is fragmented in accordance with integral consciousness. I am, for example, making love and I am the lover of this particular Other; I am driving this car on this road at this time of day in these weather and road conditions, and I am the driver.

As an operator, I am part of an activity-complex, in which my circumstances are more-or-less organized temporally around the achievement of some result or other. I cannot and do not want to fool myself that I am somehow in charge of what is happening, although—as long as I stick to regularized experiences in relatively safe places and times—I will ordinarily be able to make a substantial contribution to the result, which will have a high probability of being what I thought I wanted/expected it to be when I became immersed in the activity. Such routine (safe) experiences are the privilege/curse of a relatively ordered life in which the society (with its regularized activities) and the cultural and non-human environment(s) in which I am embedded have a more-or-less predictable rhythm in which I am implicated and involved, a round of life. If my own psycho-organic rhythms are more-or-less synchronized with those of the society-environment, I might begin to think that I am the "master of my fate" and the "captain of my soul," but if I have any (dubious) claim to those titles, I only have them on loan from society, and I had better stay within the limits that have been prescribed for me on pain of being dislocated. The operator is in no way the "radical reality;" the latter, in the present reflection/meditation, being reserved for the moving mass of experience, which I co-constitute with everything else that is not-me.

It is ego-philosophy that has died in/for me through the experiences that began in the winter of 2012 and that I am now thematizing in an attempt to discern a new/altered structure of (my) life. The collapsing slide into embeddedness killed it. The feeling-judgment that I am embedded did not appear as the result of a philosophical reflection on the limitations of ego-philosophy; it was a comprehensive acknowledgment of my condition that was not subject to debate, it was what John Henry Newman called a "real assent." Only retrospectively, on reflection, does it become clear that I have been engaged in destroying/dispelling the pretensions of the "self." As Sartre noted in his philosophical autobiography, *Words*, he had spent a lifetime trying to rid himself of the (idea of) God; I can now say something similar, only, in my case, it is not God, but (the vanity of) (my-)self that I have been squeezing into a corner and successively diminishing. To repeat, I was not aware of what I was doing, but, in the summer of 2014, I snapped, slipped, and collapsed into the "world" on the same level as the circumstances/situation, a conscious circumstance, to put it paradoxically.

Existentialism seemed to be so ruthlessly, uncompromisingly true to my experience when I first encountered it in high school in the 1950s, reading Sartre's *Nausea* and Camus' *The Stranger* in the school's library. The more my sense of marginality and disillusionment came back to me from their pages, the stronger and more inflated my ego became. Such is what will happen to a healthy teenager who exposes himself to philosophies of bitter struggle; vitality will overcome despair and despondency, and absurdity will become a badge of the honor of (believing that one is) drinking life to the dregs and emerging intoxicated doubtlessly, but not debilitated. To be ego-centered felt good and real, and, until now, I have remained that teenager in that respect, and so I still remain, but now with a heavy dose of irony, that powerful anti-intoxicant. The teenager, as I experienced that type, is defiant; the old man looks back on the teenager and laughs indulgently.

From the swamp of embeddedness, the formulations of the existentialists present themselves as ludicrous reversals of the "truth of life." "I am myself and my circumstances." That formulation obviously makes circumstances relative to myself, with the ego presiding over it all, ready to pounce and make a commitment. For the feeling-judgment of embeddedness, "I" am relative to circumstances. "I am an appendage of my circumstances." I am, proximally and for the most part, a succession of operators in activity-complexes.

That most resolute of ego-philosophers, Max Stirner, to whom I have incessantly recurred since I read his *The Ego and its Own* in the 1960s, as a redoubt, uttered the declaration-deed, "I am my own," that is, I take charge of my life and consult my (own) interests. That is what manhood means, the "age of (un) reason." Stirner added judiciously that he was only qualified to speak about the mature, unillusioned/adult individual, and that he had nothing to say about the old man, of whom he had no direct experience. Having "achieved" old age and having previously thematized my "active" life in terms of ego-philosophy, I can venture to fill in the blank that Stirner left.

As embedded existence, the ego has not been abolished; I remain Stirner's "creative nothing" who pops up from time to time and has the experience of self-direction. What has changed is that I have not made those moments in which I am my "own" definitive of who I "am." When I slipped and collapsed, I suffered the injury of being decentered and swamped. In many ways nothing has changed. I still get up in the morning and live through a day, mounting projects, trying to carry them through, desiring and fearing, loving what I find to be loveable and despising what I find to be despicable. What has changed is that feeling-being embedded has made it impossible for me to take myself and what I do with unadulterated seriousness. "My" projects are simply phases of the movement of the moving mass. I mount my projects, others mount theirs. They mesh and/or clash, and their shifting results are parts of the moving mass. The effects of my "doings" go as far as they go, and on the whole they go nowhere, so far as I can tell, in terms of contributing to any wider meaning. My doings are self-referential and parts of an undefined "experience." All projects and possibilities are embedded in all the rest. Projects are always already intranscendent; they are initiatives that interact with others in the social world and with more environing processes in the "world"-at-large. They are fragmentary.

★★★

As embedded existence, I acknowledge myself to be a fragment of an undefined "whole," the movement of which has no discernible direction, no meaning of its own to which my life is subject or to which I (can) contribute or thwart.

That judgment is implicit in ontological nihilism and leaves ("ontic") experience as full as it ever was, untouched by the rejection of meaning on a (purely symbolic) ontological level. Initially, as I have already recounted in the present meditation, embeddedness is attended (for me) by a sense of strict confinement. That condition/feeling is countered by the (experience of) existence in which my consciousness appears to me as unconfined—free from determination. When I leave the suspension that sometimes precedes active involvement, I carry through some commitment or am swept into some (directed) process. When I am "doing" something I do not revert to the passivity of embeddedness but retain some of the play of possibility that characterizes existence; that is, I have some discretion within the activity in which I am engaged, and I make my own

Embeddedness, Serio-comedy, the Third Ape **97**

contribution (positive or negative) to that activity by virtue of more-or-less disciplin(iz)ed and enculturated self-propulsion. There is a profusion of meanings in and across my doings, even though there is no (discernible) meaning to all of them.

The absence of overall meaning can be taken as either a loss or a liberation. In the first case, post-ontological existence asks: is that all there is, an absurd round that keeps going on? *Tedium vitae* sets in, along with a sense of "spiritual" suffocation. In the second case, embedded existence responds: "Yet there is so much going on, more than I can comprehend and, I acknowledge, can imagine. The absence of meaning-at-large does not affect my enjoyment, for example, of preparing and eating a meal, unless the (Camusian) absurd puts me in a despondent mood, casting a cloud over my vital responses and making them seem to be (in)vain." I become enlivened and can breathe again.

When I adopt the comprehensive intentionality of experienced existence as a milieu in which I act, rather than as a prison, I become capable of joy. It is not that experience all of a sudden becomes enrapturing, but that desires and their fulfillment sometimes appear in it. That recognition is enough to prompt me to want to keep living, even at the moments, which continue to recur, of helpless and abject embeddedness. Without that recognition, I would surely be contemplating suicide, as Camus did, even if I was incapable of taking my life because my self-propulsion stayed my hand. As long as I have vital promptings to get me going or even entertain the judgment that I might have vital promptings in the future, suicide does not enter into my prospection. I cannot take suicide seriously as an option at present, not because I feel obligated to keep living or have figured out some justification for living, but because I have too much vitality. When my vitality has been depleted beyond a certain point, I expect that I will entertain what Simmel called "rational suicide"—the balance of pain over pleasure will have just become too great. As Unamuno put it, he had no arguments to give against someone who was at "the bottom of the abyss" and committed suicide. At the moment, embeddedness is not squeezing me into self-inflicted death.

At the decisive point, towards the middle, of *The Ego and its Own*, Stirner writes that he has up until then been writing as a "ragamuffin" who had stripped himself of the garb of "spooks" (illusions, idealism, regulative meanings), but that henceforth he would write as his "own," in charge of his judgments (if nothing else). I have recounted a similar process just now, although one that is far more modest than was Stirner's.

I emerge to myself, as the analogue to Stirner's "own," which he also called the "unique one" and which I would prefer to call simply particular, as a fragment of a fragment of a fragment: the "ego" is a fragment of conscious life, which is a fragment of the organism's psycho-physical life-process, which is a fragment of the moving mass of experience. As embedded/fragmentary existence in an apparently purposeless experience, the judgment impresses itself on me that, unlike Stirner, I am not important to myself. I am thrown into the world as a throw-away that has a measure of self-propulsion that has prevented me from acknowledging through and through, from top to bottom, that I am, as Sartre put it, superfluous, unimportant.

Rather than my "own," I am merely more-or-less self-propelled. As self-propulsion is experienced by conscious psycho-physical life, it is attended by the "will," to persist in existence, as Benedict de Spinoza put it, that is, to protect itself from immediate threats through "fight or flight." That the urge to survive physically or even, as Freud had it, to die in one's own time is definitive of human nature is another ridiculous symbolic meaning from which some people appear to draw comfort who think of themselves as realists when they are pathetic last-standers for meaning. People are ceaselessly finding ways to kill off themselves and each other, sometimes slowly and sometimes more-or-less rapidly. The phenomenology of mind does not discover a survival instinct that determines the doings of life-over-time; instead, I note that when I am presented with an immediate threat, I (almost all of the time) become immersed in trying to eliminate or avoid it. That is as far as it goes. Sometimes I throw myself away and burn tissue on activities that I know endanger me, and sometimes I do that out of perversity, but sometimes out of a devil-may-care desire, the inability to stand up to social pressure, fear, the vestiges of obligation, a surge of altruism, or devotion-love. Were I actually motivated by a will to survive over time, I would not live as I do, but I would bend every effort to the futile project of protecting myself, making that project my sole pre-occupation, which is impossible for me, because I am far too multifarious and multi-valent for that, and my observation shows me that the same holds true for most, if not all, the other people with whom I come in contact.

Survival has been thrown at me by many people and by myself as the last redoubt of ego-philosophy, once (rational) self-interest has gone by the boards. (What, after all, does self-interest end up meaning but a usually empty pretext attached to explain/justify anything that I have happened to do?) Embedded existence persists as long as it does at the whim of the world, which includes most proximately "my" body-psyche. A fragment of a fragment of a fragment contains within itself, not a microcosm of reality like a Leibnizian monad, but a swath of experience presented in one of its modes as a phantasmagoria, a Bedlam of Ideals. My "life" has as much order as circumstances, primarily society, have allowed it to have, and social discipline constructs simplifications of experience that always leave out, without expunging them, contents that remain in the phantasmagoria, ready to erupt, bidden or unbidden.

The first response of embedded existence under the sign of liberation is a sense of overall relaxation. I am a self-propelled element of a mess and there is nothing that I can do about it, so why not enjoy what I am capable of enjoying about it and shrug my shoulders about the rest? Why not love whom I love? I cannot help but do that anyway. That is my way; there are other ways. Without the transcendence of projects, anything goes and there is plenty to go around, pleasure and torture, and everything between.

The Serio-Comic Sense of Existence (MW)

As embedded existence, life falls apart into pieces, philosophical reflection being one of them. I might have once thought that those fragments were or could be organized into a meaningful pattern, on the whole or at-large, originally, and later for my particular life-over-time. I am no longer capable of taking that project seriously, of finding or constructing a general or personal order of things. I am deconstructed and decentered. The "unity" that I achieve in home discourse directed to reflective review, a transient position in the life-process, is what remains of the ego after it has been dispossessed of the power to execute a life-plan. The practical ego is always compromised in terms of its self-definition, whatever that might be. The contemplative ego is unscathed, though chastened, and it retains the power to construct a "subjective response" to the mess in which I have been swamped and, through self-propulsion, continue to muck around.

The (self-)determination of a subjective response to one's/my life, undertaken in a reflective review, is the last redoubt of ego-philosophy, the last move that I can make in which I have the sense that I am "free" and that I can have some effect on how my life is conducted. I can try to make it so that the subjective response that I have constructed carries over into my involvement in the other sectors of integral consciousness, into the sequences of immersive experiences that I undergo, into my "active" life.

For an ontological consciousness, the subjective response follows intelligibly from an account of the "meaning of being," a description of the world on the whole. Post-ontological consciousness, having eschewed symbolic substitutes for life, has no idea of what reality is and, therefore, cannot derive a subjective response from such an idea. What response the reflective ego makes is at its discretion, which means that there are many responses that it could make, and, perhaps, it need not make a preferred response at all, but, instead, let its feeling-judgment of (its) life float free to change as each immersive experience comes up.

There is an appeal to renouncing the determination of a subjective response. I am in a mess studded with meanings bound to desires and fears that are temporarily stilled by their fulfillment or frustration, their realization or avoidance. Why do I need a response to the moving mess of a mass, especially when it does not appear to have any intelligible direction?

Why not let the ego let go of any lasting determinations? There is a (particular) round of life into which I have fallen, and I can just as well let it persist, as long as it does, (self-)propelled by its (disciplined) automaticity, giving me its accustomed prompts that I am "programmed" to follow. Circumstances will change, provoking me to take initiatives so that my (self-)propulsion will be capable of going on. As my circumstances and responses to them change, my moods will follow along, and I will have as many senses of life as I have distinctive moods. I will not try to use reflective review to determine and standardize a sense of life. I will renounce having a coherent personality, but will, instead, cultivate a tolerance of my unresolvable and irreconcilable diversity. My experience will be as vivid or monotonous as it happens to be, there will be passion and indifference, love and hate, action and abjection. I will make as much effort to increase the extent of the experiences that I feel-judge to be valuable/pleasurable as I am prompted to at that particular time. Sometimes I will try to preserve myself and then I will throw myself away. I will undertake "projects" and then I will put them aside. I will not be anhedonic on the whole; I will be devoted to loved ones and I will keep my own counsel. I will abolish a qualitative self and will still be a conscious center of self-propulsion who is capable at some times of recognizing an identity across memories of experiences in reflective review. When I wake up from a sleep, I will say, "here I am again," as I always implicitly have done, as long as I continue to do so. My identity will be the self-recognizing memory that "I" am the one who had the experience that I am remembering at some moment or another.

I have no "theoretical" objection to reducing myself to bare, sporadic self-recognition through memory. What objection could I have? I am recording my feeling-judgments at the present time, and I have no others. The subjective response, sense of life, is a throw away, and I can get rid of it.

Yet I cannot escape the feeling-judgment that I am interpreting (my) life through the construction of serio-comedy. Is it time to abandon that construction as a scaffolding that had been supporting my reflective review until the latter reached the point at which the support no longer performs a function?

I remind myself that serio-comedy puts a comical situation in a serious form. There is nothing problematic about saying that "philosophy" is a "serious" form, at least it has always been taken that way, and I know that I am not laughing at the moment, although a smile is sporadically flickering across my lips impelled by the faint sense of the ridiculous. The issue is whether embedded existence can "properly" be called a comical situation or whether it is just as well to leave the former to be undetermined subjectively.

The question posed here is similar to the one that exercised Camus in "The Myth of Sisyphus:" how does/should one comport oneself towards the absurd? The difference between Camus' account and that of the present reflection is that the former was pained by the lack of a response from the world to his "demand" for unitary meaning, which led him to ennoble the effort to persist in pushing the stone up the hill each day, only to see it roll down again, knowing that the ritual would be repeated each day that he lived, the core of the "absurd life;" whereas I find no nobility in continuing to muck around in the mess that I feel-judge embedded existence to be.

The nerve of the absurd has been cut for me; I have no desire for the unity of meaning, that desire having become, for me, ridiculous. Rather than acknowledge the absurdity of the "human" desire for meaning, as Camus did, I find the desire itself to be absurd. Its pretension, when contemplated, is the source of a smile; yet that smile is gratuitous, because the problem of meaning is meaningless

Embeddedness, Serio-comedy, the Third Ape **101**

for me in the sense that I am indifferent to it and have no stake in whether or not it is resolved.

Bereft of nostalgia for meaning, I contemplate what is left without it with that same faint sense of the ridiculous, now directed at embedded existence itself, which I construct as a *serio*-comedy. I could take my life, but I presently have too much vitality (self-propulsion) to do so. I could withdraw into meditative quietism. That does not appeal to me, so it ends up not to be a live option. I do what I have come to be doing, as this particular "summed-up [bundle of selves]-in-process." I am a fragment of a fragment of a fragment. The comedy comes in when I am tempted to think of myself as anything else. It is a stabilizer, a reminder that I am simply an element of the moving mass that has come to know itself as such, involved in thousands of pretensions that fall into each other and back upon themselves. Those pretensions, mine and others, are *serious* when they are present and ridiculous when they are not, which makes them ridiculous on the whole, yet I only live "on the whole" in reflective review.

★★★

I would like to carry through the faint sense of ridiculousness into all of the immersive experience of embedded existence, but that is not, for me, possible. There is too much "negativity" for that. There will be many times when dire anticipations fill my consciousness and the feelings of being on the cusp of panic consume me, instigated by thoughts that I will not be able to perform my round of life. There will be many other times when I will learn that all my best efforts to do something that I judge to be worthwhile have failed, and I will feel crushed. There will be still other times when I will be crestfallen because I have been undone by acting on desires that I later repudiate because they have eventuated in undesired results. There will be, at the end, times in which I simply suffer too much pain and discomfort to smile, and I will not try to force a smile when it does not come unbidden. I will feel that most corrosive of emotions, self-pity.

How ridiculous of me to feel self-pity. Being in the experience of reflective review at the present moment, I contemplate my descents into self-pity, which I am now not feeling, but only remembering, with the faint smile. So what? Who cares? That is the way it is. I also have ecstatic experiences. There will be times, the best times, when I set off on an adventure with eager anticipation and overflowing vitality, enlivened just because I do not know what will eventuate; when I am making love; when I am having a burst of insights; when I am immersed in pleasurable activities; when I am immersed in reflective review and I relish my memories. Life is a torture chamber and a pleasure palace.

It is not that the torture chamber is tragic and the pleasure palace comic; the serio-comic sense of life contemplates them both at once and renders its feeling-judgment on the "whole." I smile because I have slipped and collapsed yet again, and, for the moment, I have picked myself up again. I expect that I will continue to do so, and, for me, there will be nothing else. I will continue to do what I do, whatever that might be, until I cannot do it anymore. There were never any worlds to conquer; there is only more of the culture jungle where I live among the other restless monkeys. Most of them have been-convinced/convinced-themselves that they are dwelling in a world that they imagine, and they act more-or-less accordingly, causing more trouble for themselves and, of course, others than they would have, had they simply acknowledged that they are embedded existence.

That thought evokes another smile; most of those with whom I share the world temporarily are self-deceived buffoons. So be it. I have no contempt for them; I was the same and, for all I know and probably, I still am. Just because I judge them to be self-deceived does not mean that I do not enjoy the company of many of them and sympathize (on their terms) with them as they enact the serio-comedy of embedded existence, a comedy of confusion, in which they are lost in a fog of symbols thinking that they know where they are going.

It is a crazy mixed-up mess that we are in.

A Philosophical Primatology (A View of Homo Pseudosapiens Panisco-Troglodytes) *(TY)*

We can more completely thematize embedded phantasmagoric existence from a serio-comic point of view as the form in which one experiences the actual context of life "proximally and for the most part" by means of an exercise in the Schelerian practice of "philosophical anthropology." In this section, we will expand on the above description of experience from the first-hand point of view to provide a more comprehensive accounting of the concrete experience of life as a fragment of a fragment in its larger, actual, cultural milieu. We will avail ourselves of the theoretical distance provided by ontological nihilism and the refusal of anthropocentrism, which is merely universalized egocentrism, that the phenomenology of mind demands/employs. Focusing on certain crucial characteristics we human beings appear to share with the two species of ape closest to us—chimpanzees and bonobos, it may be instructive to turn momentarily away from the intimacy of immediacy and its thematization to the discourse of formal theoretical thinking, and perform an experimental "philosophical primatology." Such an undertaking will merely be an example of radical phenomenology of mind writ large in action, one that seeks to thematize its object ("we" humans) in radically, purely descriptive terms, resulting in a(nother) (particular, partial) picture of who we are as a species based strictly on observation and in no way on ontological or other preconceptions or presuppositions.

Mind as a Possibly Illegal Alien *(TY)*

When one looks at the human species from a proper distance in the context of what science would refer to as its natural environment—*viz.*, as one species of organic life among others on the planet, it is easy to wonder at what occasioned the deepening of our unique kind of mindedness. This uniquely dimensional mindedness of ours has brought into existence exceedingly elaborate systems of shared consciousness in which we now as a global culture have become so deeply ensconced, that it would seem we have nearly forgotten actuality as an appreciably meaningful thing.

There are plenty of perfectly natural factors that can be brought into the speculative discussion on our origins, and specifically, on what led to the advent of our kind of mindedness. As a natural phenomenon human consciousness is so strange that it might even seem to have (or might as well have) had extraterrestrial origins or the involvement of some such extraordinary factor in its advent on earth. It is certainly true that we are unique entities, but in its rendering of who we humans are, the phenomenology of mind distinguishes between the Euro-romantic assumption of human ontological exceptionalism and mere factical peculiarity. On the other hand, when we consider the specificity of our peculiarity—our having been endowed with such a robust mental life, it is no wonder that we humans have always had some notion of a transcendent power that is at work here.

This sense of the alienness of human consciousness is given expression in Kant's "Conjectural Beginnings of Human History."[1] Kant essentially concurs with the biblical assessment that the coming into existence of "reason" (by which he refers to human consciousness) constitutes an act of "violence against nature." It is an expression of confusion in the face of the unforeseeable and inexplicable occasion of our emergence as the minded apes that we are.

When Kant claims that it is our *fault* that we are human, he is merely describing us as constitutionally faulty beings. Such an observation merely locates a factual malfunction. In his (albeit half-handed) attempt to move beyond the religious thinking from which comes the concept of original sin, Kant substitutes simple observation for moral judgment and assumes human free will as an unquestioned given, but does not determine culpability for the act of violence against the natural order that our mindedness constitutes. We are here simply the occasion for the coming into being of the categories of good and evil.

Our present phenomenological discourse carries itself out in a space beyond the knowledge of or concern for good and evil, in the non-epoch of ontological nihilism. Once it is acknowledged as the defining "theme" of actuality, ontological nihilism immediately attenuates the traditional landmark-providing conceit of developmental history, and we are in a position calling for a kind of wisdom for which we seem unprepared. When the myth of transcendence is shattered, we recognize ourselves as occupying the untimely moment in which there is no longer any meaningfulness to concepts like original sin and free will. We on that account can no longer in good faith search for causes, teleologies, responsible parties, etc., and thus must abandon the question, "why?" After taking to heart the lessons of Nietzsche and Dostoevsky, we acknowledge our being deprived of the (secondarily) satisfying scenario of being able to blame either ourselves or God for the (speculatively imagined) event in virtue of which we came to be what we are. At the same time, we remain intrinsically maladaptive, faulty beings. We are forced to reckon with our faultiness without recourse to justice. It is a "crime" without a perpetrator.

In keeping with conclusions we arrived at in Chapter 1, Kant's text suggests that the very existence of human consciousness as we know it on earth is a "black swan" event. As mind undermines, or deals a devastating blow to the ideal of justice, it does the same to science's claim to supremacy and exclusivity among ways of knowing and understanding things, because it violates the paradigmatic principles that Western reason has proposed as *necessarily* explanatory of all natural processes and phenomena.

The one tradition of approaching the world that promised the eventual resolution of all mysteries via its mind-regime came up as short as any other when it took itself on as an object. Radicalized phenomenology of mind eschews the aims of comprehensive delimitation and illumination—the rendering transparent of all things—and other fantasies of the Western will-to-truth as impediments by which science has rendered itself relatively ineffectual in the face of the question, among others, regarding what mind itself is.

Phenomenology of mind, as we understand it, is able to tolerate, in a Deweyan spirit, exceptions and outliers, and most significantly, remaining questions, without feeling compelled to throw out all of the plainly reasonable accounts of the world that science has provided us with. The revelation that truth-as-comprehensive-delimitation is strictly fantastic has in the contemporary situation become the great casualty from which Western ontologism will never recover. In the resultant post-ontological present, science has been demoted to just another in the endless array of narratological genres through which human mind has given and continues to give, testimony to its search for/creation of meaning, and science enjoys neither privileged nor second class status among the accounts provided by faith, myth, common sense, and other "irrational" ways in which mind "finds" meaning in the world. This is a function of the absolute relativization of everything in the imaginarium-fragmentorium that is today's culture.

The quest for ontological explanations (metaphysics) and evidentiary origins (science) of the human mind are will o' the wisp-seeking futilities. When undertaken in earnest as a serious, literalist pursuit, such an endeavor merely manifests an impulse to, as Freud might say, return imaginatively to the event of a conceptual trauma (i.e., a finding that deeply challenges one's preconceptions, in this case, the event of human mindedness) in an impossible attempt to "get ahead of it," to retroactively prepare for it, as it were. Clearly this is in every sense impossible. Kant plainly demonstrates that it is a question beyond the power of reason to make sense of.

Mind, it would seem, demands that we understand it on other terms. Such terms do not proscribe using descriptive language that is not bound to, or by, the terms of a (Kantian) metaphysics that itself is anthropocentric, built as it is around the assumption that the nature of the human mind itself provides the organizing principles according to which everything (including mind itself) must be made sense of. The inadequacy of Kantianism therefore spurs us away from literalism and objectivism to the realm of the figurative. Hence, I propose that we can still arrive at a (working) phenomenological description (one among many possible others) of our unique form of human consciousness that substantially, if only (always) in part, illuminates it, by the adoption of the following figurative scientific myth: it would appear (it might as well be true) that we humans are the result of the cross-breeding of chimpanzees and bonobos.

Such a myth functions as a kind of metaphorical characterization which, in lieu of the misguided, impossible Euro-romantic aim of objective comprehension, may actually get us closer to an accurate understanding of who/what we are. The primatological view that we are taking here has much to offer that mere Kantian speculation does not. "Straying" into the figurative does not, on the present view, take us further from truth, but instead gives us powerful, palpable images that illuminate the human experience obliquely, images that can be of some use if we but relinquish the impossible goal of total conceptual and/or empirical determination and delimitation.

De Profundis Clamavi (TY)

The human-as-bonobo-chimpanzee-hybrid concept, to which I will return to flesh out imminently, is an image that arose among my ruminations on the nature of human consciousness and the strangeness of (our human) mind around 2006–2008. It emerged specifically as a product of some stock-taking I had undertaken in the context of what might appropriately be referred to as a "mid-life crisis." I had come to a point where the stresses of life, the loss of a significant professional contract, the questioning of major life choices that I had made, and, most importantly, an intensification of the feeling of abject inadequacy that we all face at times, rendered me paralyzed at virtually every level of vitality.

In 2008, I experienced an acute case of anxiety, the climax of a psychic fever that would clear up the indolent infection of vital stagnation I was suffering from. In the midst of this experience, I realized that at a deeply affective level, I had not yet fully extricated myself from the suggestive power of idealism (either secular or religious—they are the same poison under either label) and its Janus face, abjection. I had internalized both sides of this coin from the Western thought-and-value system in which I was raised, and it unconsciously dominated my deepest sensibilities. In response to this unbearable state of despairing abjection, whose terms allow for no vitality, I resolved to fight for my proverbial life, to free myself from the crippling power of what Wilhelm Stekel called the "anagogic" valence of psychic life, another word for what Freud described as the "super-ego."

My (abjected) self-image wasn't truly my own. None of my images were. I had until that point failed to rise to the task of grasping the meaning(lessness) of my life in terms I developed entirely from out of my own resources. By introjecting a foreign sensibility into my thought and feeling (as we all do), I had been unwittingly taking the easy route of Ghazālian slavish conformism, passing off the dirty job of evaluating my life, myself, and my "worth" onto a readily available stand-in: the time-tested value schemes of Western thinking, specifically, the institutions of guilt, self-hatred, and other vitality-sapping mechanisms that Nietzsche described in his damning critique of Western Morality.

At that point in 2008, I was still perfectly exemplifying what in Chapter 1 I referred to as the human tendency to shrink away from evaluatively confronting one's life and formulating a subjective response to it without emotional and intellectual recourse to traditional ontological and axiological conventions. Servile conformism will kill you, either literally, if you are a serious enough thinker (it can't be sustained—one cannot lie to oneself forever), or imaginatively, if you are less so inclined.

As in the case of Al-Ghazālī, I found that the task of escaping from the confines of a thought system that had been essential in enabling me to spiral into a state of total abjection, was monumental. I was already a nihilist intellectually, so I was not prepared to take—I was incapable of taking—any kind of easy path back into the comfortable traps of mind and out of the situation. It required weathering the storm of taking the practice of rigorous intellectual doubt to the far more difficult level of a comprehensive embracement of nihilism, to see if there was something left for me after the radical questioning of meaning at *every* level of life. It is difficult to describe the experience of working toward vitality from a state of its near total absence. Fear and despair are laughing at your every pathetic effort all the way, and, by definition, one finds at every turn no reason whatsoever to continue the work.

De Altus Clamavi (TY)

Everything changed for me when I eventually found my way out of the intellectual and affective desert of despair. I found that my heart and mind, "enabled" by the traditional thought-and-value conventions I had internalized had simply duped me into feeling impossibly worthless. Standing above myself and seeing this now, I was able to embrace nihilism as a positive, absolute state of freedom, rather than the disaster that I had initially endured it as, and which it was mistaken for by the West in its late modern Euro-romantic travails. I found that all my previous feelings of guilt and inadequacy had no basis except in the realm of ideas—particularly those of my culture, none of which I came up with on my own, but learned through socialization.

With this insight, I had a Stirnerian "aha" moment wherein my perspective on everything human changed forever. I saw myself and all of my kind (humans) as suffering tremendously under the psychological burden of the ideas that reigned in their heads, and that the "second life" of the psyche was not merely fascinating and uniquely human, but was also a force to be reckoned with, one that could be

Embeddedness, Serio-comedy, the Third Ape 107

as devastating as it was strange. If there is an apex of the serious side of serio-comedy in this reflection, it is here. As Freud recognized, our mental life-world is unfortunately not limited to the comforting escapism of denial in wishful thinking, but, via the moralism that is part and parcel of all significant cultures/mind-views, the life of the mind can be a self-torture chamber of perfectionism and idealism. Outside that chamber and looking back into it, I saw that we humans are just animals like all the others, with the gigantic and crucial difference that we dwell so deeply in the world of mind, and as often as otherwise, therein participate in the cultivation and sustaining of our own suffering. It is for this reason—the prospect of psychological emancipation from a mode of slavish conformism that was conducive, even if not exclusively so, to my own vital diminution, and not mere wonder and curiosity—that I came to see that there is immense practical value in cutting through the webs of illusion and delusion that we minded human fools weave for ourselves, individually and collectively.

Having gained this perspective when I turned my gaze to myself, I found that I had been no different. Pure nihilism, pure relativism, is the result of the putting into perspective of the human addiction to meaning as a comedic (ridiculous) habit of mind. When all meaning is lost, and one is left still standing, the world, society, and most importantly *oneself* take on an entirely new aspect. An absolute seriousness with regard to *anything* is no longer possible from this position.

The anthropologizing (not anthropocentrizing), ontologically nihilistic attitude was essential to my own overcoming of my sense of inadequacy. It amounted to a "de-potentiation of thoughts," a ripping back of the curtain behind which the phantom of thought's feared-but-actually-non-existent "omnipotence" hides. One of its most essential revelations is pure actuality. The embracement of pure actuality crucially involves dispensing with the ontological and metaphysical pictures that we inherit from tradition. These pictures become forceful when we "personalize" (introject) them just enough to give them the "feel" of being integral to our own "sense" of self and our world (cf. Althusser). The complete casting aside of the metaphysical coincides with the liberation from axiology. The embracement of pure actuality allows one to divest utterly from the self-defeating moral idealism with which our received narratives are infected. In order to extricate oneself from the powerful clutches of idealism, in which I had myself dwelt for decades (even despite being a hard-core Nietzschean and therefore, of course, not being aware of it!) one must accept that one is only human and that that in itself is not necessarily a crime. This is only possible with a total embracement of brute actuality. Why had I felt so worthless for simply being who/what I am? I considered that, for example, insects and cats had no such dilemma, and that this problem appeared not only to be uniquely human, but a genuine, essential malfunction in our nature. Embracing my strictly actual self coincided with forgiving myself for my humanness. From out of self-forgiveness eventually came universal forgiveness.

When one sees oneself and others as curiosities rather than potential sources of hope or disappointment, one has transcended, even if only momentarily, the poisonous realm of morality understood from a Nietzschean perspective as a revolt against actuality in its apotheosis of the ideal. One becomes capable of living and thinking (at least part-time) beyond the categories of good and evil. In this vein, the attitude of universal forgiveness is part and parcel of, or the affective corollary to, the intellectual act of granting freedom to worldly phenomena (Heidegger's *Gelassenheit*) that is at the heart of the practice/attitude of ontologically nihilistic phenomenology of mind. Universal forgiveness is not a moral or ethical act of acceptance and understanding in response to a transgression; it is rather an always-operative practical technique of the mind putting its own operations and works into a perspective that transcends both the negative and positive valences of the conditional mood that undergirds all valuation. It is the overcoming of the force of the mind-phantasms of good and evil. Together with the rejection of metaphysics, axiological transcendence leaves us with pure, simple, (absolute) value-neutral actuality and nothing else.

Universal forgiveness came for me first as a mechanism by which I fortified myself for intellectual and emotional survival, but it also became clear to me that it is a *sine qua non* of radical phenomenology because it places one utterly outside the distorting attitudes of any and all idealisms. Forgiveness robs mind-regimes of their expropriating "omnipotence" over us and is necessary not only for sustaining personal vitality, but for the execution of any kind of useful inquiry. Occupying the standpoint of such an attitude, one is enabled to stand above the fray of strife that generally so plagues our care-burdened human existence and exclaim that one is ecstatic in *both* the intellectual sense (at the remove required for phenomenology) and in the affective sense: one is capable of receptivity to what I call the "immanent glories" of the actual world.

Essential to the inculcation of the attitude of universal forgiveness (one that englobes and defuses the power of both axiology and ontology) for me was the work of one of the most magnanimous thinkers I have encountered: Georg Groddeck.

Groddeck's thought, laid out in his major work, *The Book of the It*, is another precursor to the radically distanced phenomenology of mind that we have been seeking to flesh out in these pages. Groddeck's primary thesis is that, with the apotheosis of our collective intellect, and its complement, our collective *conscience*, we have lost sight of ourselves as animals who are, as we have been saying throughout this work, not so fundamentally different than any other species. Taking the Freudian concept of the "id" and running with it, he hypothesized, with reference to clinical example after example, that the idea of free will is at best overestimated, and more than likely nothing more than sheer wishful thinking born of idealism.

Groddeck suggested that what Freud referred to as the "ego" or the "self" as traditionally conceived, was little more than an abstraction. In order to

Embeddedness, Serio-comedy, the Third Ape **109**

understand the human being, he maintained, the habit of seeing ourselves as entities capable of freely determining who we are, even what we do, must be abandoned in the face of its apparent near impossibility at the empirical level. In a similar spirit to that of Stirner, Groddeck suggests that our Western idealized, impossible self-image as ahistorical, free rational agents is not only a principal impediment to understanding ourselves, but more importantly, the cause of our greatest suffering. Accordingly, again like Stirner, Groddeck called on us to adopt an immanentizing, practical view of ourselves as entities who are primarily *media* rather than agents, entities whose behavior and attitudes are the products of often inscrutable, and always multifarious, forces we will never fully understand. It is a delicious irony that many of these very same un- or anti-humanistic conclusions regarding the illusory nature of free will that the long-ago "discredited" psycho-analytical likes of Groddeck came to a hundred years ago are now being "confirmed" by latter-day neuroscience.

Groddeck's claim that human agency is largely illusory is yet another formulation of the pre-classical tragic wisdom that holds that we will never understand ourselves unless we humble ourselves before actual forces that appear to be beyond our complete understanding or control. In the case of Groddeck and Psychoanalysis more generally, the most significant forces under consideration are simply internal, rather than external to the individual minded human animal. Groddeck offers a deeply critical perspective on the experience of being human that can be personally liberating because it fundamentally questions the Euro-romantic myth/apotheosis of subjective agency, founded on the mistaken understanding of freedom that is central to that thinking, which conduced to the anthropocentrism that has misled that tradition's approach to virtually all philosophical questions. Because he was a proto-radical phenomenologist of mind, Groddeck underscored the *mystery* of human mental life, but did not promote any kind of naturalistic *mysticism*. He is the most humane anti-humanist one will encounter.

For purposes of the present work, Groddeck's work serves as another example of an approach that emphasizes the often deep disconnect between who we are and how we behave on the one hand, and the narratives we maintain about ourselves on the other. The Groddeckian view of human mental life is yet another example of post-ontological inquiry that can be used to understand and confront oneself actually, transcending the seductive power of the stories one tells oneself about oneself. The adoption of this kind of phenomenological approach to one's own person is a *necessary condition* for its being applied *outside* of oneself.

This is the logic behind not only Groddeck's, but also Freud's focus on the individual human psychic life as the starting point for any inquiry concerning the human animal more generally conceived. If you think you are looking directly at yourself or your world, but are in fact seeing it through borrowed lenses, your entire approach, your every perception, what you notice, what you don't notice, will be infected or affected by all the immediate and enduring psycho-dramas that set the stage of your current mind's viewpoint. Although you may be fascinated, horrified, or entertained, you will get nowhere in terms of understanding what you think you are looking at. The Althusserian understanding of the power of ideology applies in equal measure when the interpellating voices that command our attention and loyalty come from within as when they come from without. You can be expropriated by a voice from your own individual ideo-identity drama in just the same way as by the "call" of ideology that comes from the other.

The human tendency toward dramatism and the mediation of actuality via narratives, whether they be self-generated, borrowed from culture, or some combination of the two, is rooted in the deep psycho-affective desire for ultimate meaning. One is able to distance oneself from the power of these narratives after one drags oneself out of the stifling quagmire of ultimate despair born of the loss of all metaphysical and axiological landmarks in the experience of nihilism. This applies to both individuals and cultures. While I utterly eschew retrospective justifications of suffering that are so often put up after struggles ("what doesn't kill you makes you stronger," or "it all happened for a reason"), I cannot but affirm the course of my life and my resolve to see through to the end the experience of negative nihilism that brings despair. The process resulted for me in a world that was (almost) nothing but a gift: the freedom of "positive" nihilism.

A newly found perspective on the human world came for me with the overcoming of the sense of devastation in the face of my "failed" life as (mis)understood via my internalization of our culture's deeply ingrained moralism that my reading of Groddeck helped me to accomplish. It left me in the strange but glorious no-place where the human search for transcendent meaning becomes deeply ridiculous. This leant an entirely new aspect to the human world when I turned to consider it. From outside the deep tension and emotion of the drama, the outsider—the totally divested neutral nihilist—looks at the human world of family romances, politics, culture wars, etc., and sees nothing but human apes behaving the way human apes do, *viz.*, living their material lives under the powerful sway of the affectively charged ideas that dominate their thoughts. I looked back on all my former practices of self-abjection and saw that by escaping completely from the conditional realm of the ideal, one finds the rich cornucopia of the actual.

Perhaps the thinker who most contributed to the coalescence of my de-abjected perspectival distance from human dramatism, generally, is Max Stirner, who offered at the level of political and cultural analysis, a complement to what Groddeck did at the psychological and biological level. In *The Ego and its Own*, Stirner offers a criticism of the life of Western mind unique in the literature, to my knowledge.

Engaging with the leading intellectual figures of his day in debates at the zenith of the Euro-romance, Stirner rose above it all and allowed the development of a picture in his thinking of the human world as a gigantic "madhouse" populated by a host of animated inmates. On the surface, these inmates appear to be merely going about the daily business of practical life, but they are more accurately described as engaging a haunted dance of ambivalent fascination and horror with the "spooks" that are their idea(l)s. This is where the phantasmagoria takes on a more than merely personal, occasional significance: the phantasmagoric fragmentorium-as-haunted-madhouse can function as a power that has very real effects on *how* we undergo or enjoy our slice of the moving mass of experience embedded in a human world that is dominated by the ideal/ideational. It is only with the benefit of a radically critical reflective review of mind broadly conceived (shared mind) that takes stock not only of one's own mind, but that of the culture/society in which one finds oneself, that we are capable of holding the suggestive power that our thoughts can have over us at bay. It doesn't matter whether you are "positively" deluded into believing that your life or endeavors have meaning, or whether you are "negatively" convinced that you will never be the person you "ought" to be: in both cases you are living under the sway of an idea. There is certainly little if any freedom here.

The humans Stirner described are difficult at a basic level to distinguish from the primitives that Freud discusses in *Totem and Taboo*, who, far from "free thinkers" at the height of so-called civilization, conduct themselves and their every activity under the sway of magical thinking, enslaved to the "omnipotence of thoughts." Stirner noted with the calm detachment of one who sought to truly think for himself that the "freedom of mind" that the Euro-romance fancied itself to have arrived at was an illusion on a par with any that had preceded it. "Freedom of mind" was not, as Stirner saw it, something exercised *by* individuals, but was rather something that exercised *itself on and through* them, that "possessed" them. In this sense, shared mind is understood as the agency itself and individual minds its media; in an expression anticipating Baudrillard, it has broken free of the individuals who collectively brought it into existence, going "orbital" into an independent existence, complete with its own efficacy as a causal force. This is precisely in keeping with the present work's understanding of shared mind as a consequential power whose nature has been largely unseen in our Western literature.

The Primatological View *(TY)*

I have always been fascinated by the other great apes in a casual way, most likely for the fact that they can present us with another example of what Freud referred to as the "uncanny:" something familiar and foreign at once. The Freudian sense of the uncanny is disturbing because it is a visceral assault on our system of identities and differences—the conceptual foundations on the basis of which we understand our world, and more proximately, ourselves. It is as compelling as it is alarming. When approached from the vantage point of ontologically denuded actuality that shows itself via radicalized phenomenology, this sense of alarm that is usually occasioned by the experience of the uncanny is absent. To be a phenomenologist of mind operating under the principle of ontological nihilism is to be at once at home with oneself and one's kind, and alien to these also; one is, to echo Kristeva's title, a "stranger to oneself," but finds that this is no cause for concern.

In 2009, having become acclimated to living in a more or less permanent state of phenomenological distance toward the world and myself, and continuing to practice philosophy as a vital activity, my interactions with others took on an unavoidably anthropological cast. I engaged others intellectually and emotionally at the practical level, but there was a new, extra dimension of insight into everything human that was essentially Stirnerian in its serio-comic detachment. This experience produced in me a revised notion of the experience of the uncanny. Although devoid of the terror that is usually associated with that concept, interactions with other human beings nevertheless become exceedingly strange in the sense that one is interacting with individual selves—friends, colleagues, even intimates—while seeing them as curious beings who live principally through and under the sway of their received ideas, generally with no conscious idea that they are doing so.

This experience is not, so far as I have lived it, one in which one "looks down" condescendingly upon others as one who is free from such humanness. Rather, this experience is only possible when one has the same distanced perspective on *one's own* thought and behavior. Eventually, I started to experience interactions with others during the course of which I saw the behaviors displayed by *both* myself and them as ridiculous, predictable, idiotic, or hilarious, charming, etc. If you can't reflect on the specifics of one of your own interactions and plainly see how you have manifested your humanness in much the same way, then you cannot have this exquisite, but strange experience when interacting with others. A consistent discipline of keeping in mind one's own curious humanness is essential to the freedom that makes such an experience possible, and it is entirely beyond moralism and its attendant judgmentalism.

Inebriated with this new phenomenologico-anthropological perspective of mine, I ran across an article about the differences between chimpanzees and bonobos. The separation of these apes into two different species was, it is supposed, the result of two halves of their common ancestors having found themselves on either side of the Congo river within the last two million years or so. The two populations, divided by something so simple as a river, evolved into (or already were?) profoundly different apes. I had only become aware relatively recently of the existence of bonobos, but I had found the differences between the latter and chimpanzees fascinating. Revisiting the matter from a newly acquired radically phenomenological perspective, I was struck bluntly with the insight that the characteristics that distinguish the two *Pan* species from each other were *both* core characteristic of us humans. We are at one moment angry, and the next moment we are kissing and making up; we are fiercely competitive and also capable of patient and effective cooperation. We are lustful and loving, but also full of murderous rage. We are at once chimpanzees and bonobos.

deWaal's Bipolar Ape, or Apes as People *(TY)*

After my anthropo-primatological understanding of human beings as characterized by a strange combination of chimpanzee- and bonobo-esque qualities had had some time to coalesce in my mind, I found it so exquisite and compelling that I wondered whether or not anyone else had come to such a radical conclusion. I did an internet search for "humans as chimpanzee-bonobo hybrid" and to my delight, I discovered that Emory University primatologist Frans deWaal had already conceived human beings in that very image in his 2004 book *Our Inner Ape*. I read this and several other of deWaal's popular works, which enhanced my appreciation for the fact that contemplating the apes—especially the two species most closely related to us—is qualitatively different than studying something like insects or physics. They are our kin, and they have much to tell us about ourselves.

Despite my excitement at having found that someone had come to the same anthropological conclusion as myself, I found my own take on the shared natures of humans and these other apes to be more empirically and phenomenologically sound than deWaal's. deWaal looks at the other apes and sees proto-humans—much like Rousseau's noble savages, to be precise. deWaal is a humanist; in his popular works he has argued that morality is a naturally occurring, evolutionarily adaptive phenomenon, and is not a strictly artificial human institution. He bases this conclusion on years of observations of behaviors among apes that manifest what primatologists refer to as their "pro-social," "empathic," and even "altruistic" tendencies. He cites the widespread presence of these behaviors among all apes as part of a general rejection of the Hobbesian idea that human moral traditions and political institutions are not only artificial (and therefore strictly human), but that without these, humans would be at each other's throats in the free-for-all of the hypothetical "state of nature." While recognizing that this is a very summary look at deWaal's ideas, the bottom line is that his cultivation of the idea of a trans-species moral naturalism is deeply entangled in the Euro-romantic idealism of modern Western thinking. deWaal's take on all the apes, including us human beings, is a Rousseauvian romantic one. He looks at the other apes and sees (idealized) humans, and his conclusions are therefore colored by a kind of second-order anthropo-centrism whereby human ideal qualities (that we and other apes have "naturally good" tendencies) are imputed to other primates. The subtitle of one of his books makes this clear: he is "in search of humanism among the primates."

With all due respect to deWaal, I find it methodologically suspect, from both a scientific and a phenomenological point of view to look out upon the world of primates in search of anything other than data (namely, the ideal of naturalistic morality). The theoretical thematization (i.e., that of moral naturalism) is supposed to come *after* the data is collected, not the reverse. deWaal's thesis of moral naturalism is a difficult one to support. Morality, as we understand and practice it, is a complicated, sophisticated cultural phenomenon; its demonstration would require that we have access to more evidence than simple behaviors, no matter how deeply they impress us. One does not, as deWaal claims to do, "find" morality *itself* among the data; all one can observe are behaviors that can be classified as evidence weighing against the veracity of the (Hobbesian) "veneer theory" hypothesis that rigidly self-serving behaviors are the rule and altruism the rare exception. Approaching primatology from a humanist angle is, it seems to me, something of a basic methodological error. How can one freely encounter anything if one is already attuned to it in a very specific way?

My own reflections on the similarities between us humans and the *Pan* apes were the product of a thought-process fundamentally different than deWaal's. Although we were both seeking to understand human beings in a new way, my own was rooted in an ontological nihilism that calls for the rigorous rejection of *all* axiological idealizations and ontological presuppositions. When I compare human beings with their kin, rather than seeing us all as moral actors who happen to be animals, I see all three species as (de-idealized) animals, some of whom happen to live in the world of their minds as much or more so than in actuality than do others, noting that this mind-dwelling tendency of our own has had a long history of severing us from actuality because it nearly always, consciously or not, informs the views of actuality that we form when we look at anything in the world.

There is, however, a crucial point of convergence between my own and deWaal's perspectives, which holds the key to the philosophical-primatological view of humans that I have been working under in these pages: his notion that we are "bipolar" apes. In the unsatisfyingly summary final chapter of *Our Inner Ape*, deWaal introduces this concept. Although one could make a convincing case that at a certain level, the hyper-minded human is by virtue of that very fact, a pathological being, neither myself nor deWaal (as far as I can tell) use the expression "bipolar" to refer to the clinical psychological notion of bipolar disorder in proposing this thought, but we are simply making a description of humans as beings who share some of the most significant and contradictory traits displayed by chimpanzees and bonobos.

Most crucially, from the point of view of the present discourse, the notion of bipolarity sets the stage for the more fulsome understanding of ourselves as deeply conflicted, multifarious, and confused entities. While no species is as simple as a standard biology textbook account may suggest, there is much on which to base the provisional claim that we humans are perhaps the most dramatically unsimple of all. We are not special because of our rationality, nor our brain size or any other such quality; rather, we are uniquely "bipolar" (or even "multipolar") apes because we are constitutionally both joined by, and torn between, powerful tendencies manifested severally in the *Pan* apes, but in this case, these tendencies occur all at once in a single species.

A Revised Diagnosis of Bipolarity, or People-as-Apes *(TY)*

To summarize my own take on the bipolarity thesis in distinction from deWaal's, I maintain that *Homo sapiens* is an ape extremely alike to the two *Pan* species, but

Embeddedness, Serio-comedy, the Third Ape 115

with a life lived simultaneously in dual realms (the actual and the ideational/imaginary). Especially after the advent of writing and subsequent communications systems, this deep mindedness has made possible the immense efflorescence of that "second world" of imagination in shared mind, or culture, that is such a significant part of the human experience, and which, from all appearances, is a comparatively insignificant element in the experience of the *Pan* apes.

Much of our discussion in this text has focused on the notion that we (at least Western) bonobo-chimpanzees have overvalued the world of the ideational, the imaginary, and this could lead us to underappreciate the actual, practical similarities between us and the *Pan* apes. Our received understanding of what makes us different from the other species has been distorted by the nature of the very human mind that, from our anthropocentrically myopic perspective, has traditionally understood us as not merely different, but more "highly evolved" than the other two ape species. To this I say that the human capacity for extreme intelligence does not necessarily imply superiority: we are neither inferior nor superior, just more complicated. If the Darwinian notion of "fitness" is to be operative, then we might be called *inferior*: while our intelligence may have taken us out of the "incommodious" state of nature, that very intelligence has since brought to us a seemingly never-ending series of new, artificial hardships. It is the strangest thing: a blind intelligence, an incomplete intelligence, one that appears to be missing some key component for it to be realized properly, and without which, much malfunction has resulted.

We humans misrecognize both ourselves and our two closest relatives based on the overvaluation of rationality that has tainted the worldview of Western culture from its very beginnings. This self-misrecognition is rooted in idealism, which undergirds the Western tradition of anthropo-narcissism. Our tendency to experience the world in a way so thoroughly mediated by our idealizing imaginations, ironically deprives us of an accurate view of either of the three ape species under consideration. If we put aside momentarily, or demote in significance, the question of our distinction (our different/more abundant mindedness vis à vis the two *Pan* species), especially when we note that nearly always, "distinction" in this case has become confused with "superiority," we can focus on the more *actual* (i.e., affective, social, sexual, etc.) commonalities that appear to exist between us and chimps and bonobos, rather than *ideal* differences.

Our deepened mindedness is the source of all the works of human culture, and also of all the existential illnesses that are native to human experience—our restless, ill-construed, never-satisfied, care-burdened, occupation-seeking natures, swooning with an insufferable freedom. All of this may or may not have been *caused* by the concurrence of chimpanzoid and bonoboid traits in a single, separate animal. Anyway, it *accompanies* that concurrence, and that is enough evidence in my estimation of the deep truth of the primatological-philosophical myth of the human-as-chimp-bonobo hybrid.

We can even bring the myth a significant step closer to standard scientific rigor and away from the figurative by merely calling humans the third of a close family of great apes, of which the two *Pan* species are part, and with whom it should not be surprising to find that we share any of a number of traits. In our case, it happened that we manifested both the loving, lustful, indulgent, and receptive qualities of bonobos, as well as the guarded, militant, scheming, and violent qualities of chimpanzees.

Understanding Our Phantasmagoric Selves *(TY)*

The present discussion is an example of Schelerian philosophical anthropology, which takes the Nietzschean appreciation for distance as a necessary condition for the possibility of any kind of proper understanding to a new level in the study of mind. The "removed, but embedded observer" position from which philosophical anthropology is carried out is essential to the idea of phenomenology of mind that we have been cultivating here. It is the same thing.

To subject one's own kind (one's own "native" cultural mind-view) to unillusioned scrutiny and analysis, is neither easy nor simple. It requires something Althusser thought impossible: a sensibility that lies outside of all of our existing sensibilities. This sensibility (or sensibility-lessness) is phenomenological philosophical anthropology conducted from the point of view of ontological nihilism. As a variant of phenomenology of mind, philosophical anthropology endeavors to bring to bear the mind-as-critical-faculty on the mind-as-realm-of-experience and the mind-as-weaver-of-and-believer-in-stories, putting under free consideration our own personal idiosyncratic world-and-self-pictures together with all other such pictures.

It may not be possible to achieve the requisite distance from one's own personal dramas to make possible a reliable, "objective" perspective of oneself in real time, but a fundamentally different perspective can be acquired on both self and world over time when one cultivates sufficient distance from all the received exclusivist perspectival claims of mind that have been generated, so that one is able relatively soon to laugh or wonder at oneself, one's thoughts, one's behaviors, etc. Especially with the benefit of time (retrospection in reflective review), this serio-comic, ecstatic sense of oneself as a strange and curious animal is possible at least for brief moments.

The level of restraint and imaginative freedom required for the specific phenomenological practice of philosophical anthropology is even ostensibly greater than it is for the primatologist studying our primatological kin. The other apes remain (morphologically and behaviorally) distant and distinct enough to give us false confidence in the idea that our study of them has nothing to do with us, but is simply a product of giving scientific wonder and curiosity free rein. This is not immediately the case when looking at ourselves. The closer we get to "home," the more our mind hides from itself by telling itself, and believing, its own lies.

When one makes human beings one's analytical concern, one needs to see through all of those lies at a certain level, and to approach one's own kind as at once a total stranger and an intimate. The insight one can gain from intimate familiarity is obvious and easy: if one is one of them, then one knows them. It is quite another thing (assuming one is, and continues to be, sane, of course) to maintain the perspective brought by that intimacy while at the same time directing one's enquiring gaze onto those among whom one has been "born and raised," and in a Kantian move, act "as if" one had no identification with them. Familiarity without identification.

In order to be able to view things phenomenologically, one must have divested and disenthralled oneself from one's dramatic panoply of preoccupations, dispositions, sensibilities, fears, and hopes, whether these be idiosyncratic to oneself or part of one's larger culture. For human beings, this is perhaps the tallest order conceivable because, like it or not, regardless of all of its privileges and distinctions, one of the conditions that comes with those unique features is the fact that human mind is always eluding itself. The benefit of seeing the deep similarities between us humans and the other great apes phenomenologically is that the sense of curiosity one feels when looking at them can be more easily transposed onto ourselves.

The comedic side of serio-comedy is part and parcel of this perspective on distance, or maneuver of distancing, at the heart of anthropological phenomenology of mind. It enables one to laugh at oneself not (just) tragico-sarcastically, but (also) in the same detached way that inspires amusement and intrigue when one watches a moth as it circles the candle. It is to dwell in the split consciousness of one simultaneously undergoing life in all its awesome incomprehensibility, dreadful unseemliness, and wondrously vast multifariousness, while thoughtfully observing the whole (experience) at the same time (including a thoughtful observation of myself observing). I am the moth (watching the moth (myself)).

The challenge of philosophical anthropology, or phenomenology of mind, is to break through the successive layers of resistance to self-awareness that mind, in its inherent modesty, tends to take refuge in. This is the Stirnerian irony—we need mind in order to break free of mind—not to "restore" it to its mythologically inflated "proper" place, but to simply make it available for use in the demythologized, practical service of life. In order from the particular to the more general, these resistances occur at different levels. First there is the level of sub-individuality: there are multiple agencies within me, each with its own story, and each of which wants more or less to assert its priority according to my mood, or to take center stage in my person. Next, there is the individual (the ego), with his or her socially, economically, and politically contextualized struggle for significance. Then onto the larger groups such as family, nation, species, etc., among which there is no dearth of examples of self-assertion. Each potentially resistant narratological agency on its surface offers only stories (lies) by which it defends itself from what, as we discussed above, it perceives as threats to its unique meaning. This meaning, in the province of mind, is functionally equivalent to its very being.

Mind is in a sense the anti- or unwilling phenomenon: starting with my own, it takes every opportunity it can find to disallow, augment, confound, or distort the picture we seek to form of it, to send us after wild geese, red herrings, or anything else, rather than show itself "as it is."

There are no final answers, but if we retain a basic sense of the nuance given to experience when we refuse to discard a figurative sensibility in our rendering of mind descriptively, there are many possible spot-on ways of rendering the tendencies, products, and traditions of human mind as well as the behaviors empirically demonstrated in the historical record. The notion of humans as hybrid chimpanzee-bonobos, or as the third ape of the *Homo-Pan* clan is less a theory than a metaphor or allegory, but one which, I believe, is a critical component of the larger phenomenology of mind as we have presented it here.

It is my contention that this trans-species figuring provides a picture of who we are as a species that can stand alone, but can also be considered alongside any theological, philosophical, or scientific descriptive forerunner or follow-up. It is a provisional idea put forth in response to Scheler's still valid claim in *Man's Place in Nature* that we as yet have no satisfactory image of ourselves as human beings. The endeavor of cultivating, in thought, an image of who/what we are, furthermore, involves developing a description of the precise, actual psycho-sociocultural context in which we today live the pendular swing of life between the poles of pure embeddedness in the moving phantasmagoric mass of experience and the more removed mode of reflective review in which we find the moment's precise rendering of the relationship between memory, life, and thought.

The Adaptivity of Maladaptivity: The Human Brilliant Idiot *(TY)*

We humans, to repeat the Whiteheadian description, are ill construed. All we have been doing in this discussion has been giving this ill-construal more precise imaging. The history of Western thought is one great response to our sense of puzzlement in the face of being teased with what would appear to be transparent access to the truth, only to find that it is always withheld in some way. Despite this most generalized statement about the relationship of our mind to the world it finds itself in, most everything that we need to concern ourselves with in the world of nature has fairly reasonably been made sense of. This is not the case with the *part* of nature that is human *mind*. The "why" or explanation for the advent of human mind has eluded science as much as it has theology and philosophy.

Mind presents us not with a proper object, but with a recalcitrance that exceeds our prevailing notions of how things work. Not only the unique and extraordinary occurrence of human mind, but what appears as its misplacedness and maladaptivity is left unexplained by any of our knowledge traditions. This

Embeddedness, Serio-comedy, the Third Ape **119**

unfinished Western struggle to understand has been going on from the pre-Socratics through the present. All of our thought-regimes address and give testimony to the mystery of who/what we are, often emphasizing the inexplicability and maladaptivity factors. Further support for the notion that something seems objectively amiss with us human beings is supplied without exception by the great non-western thought-and-value systems of Daoism, Buddhism, Hinduism, and Islam. For the West, from the concept of fatality in the Athenian tragic tradition, to the concept of original sin, and all the way to existentialism, achieving its most honest expression in Dostoevsky's Grand Inquisitor, there are no shortage of testimonials to the idea that we humans appear to be the product of a bungling of epic, and for us, deeply consequential, proportions.

As such, the human would call for "correction" as Dostoevsky figured it. Not only suffering itself, but what would appear as the patently cruel way in which the suffering is made more acute by its inexplicability, its incommensurability with reason, is at the heart of Dostoevsky's message in that much considered and quoted passage from the *Brothers Karamazov*. The story itself might be referred to as an understandable, if ultimately not sanctionable, revenge fantasy in which we humans enjoy an epic turning of the tables in throwing the threat of the *poena talionis* back in God's face, and we do so with the pathological relish of a broken, maddened torturer. This image only reinforces the idea that we are maladaptive. The Grand Inquisitor's bilious hate, something to which every human can relate at some level, is exemplary of the chimp ("ape-shit") strain in us.

Other examples of descriptions of our ill-construed nature can be found in Kant, who described us as "crooked trees," and in Kierkegaard, who called for the cultivation of faith as a "new organ" that our original constitution lacks, and which alone is capable of making "right" the disaster of human consciousness.

Human maladaptivity, incidentally, can be seen as a glaring exception to, if not an underminer of, the theory of evolution. The rise to incomprehensibly disproportional terrestrial domination that the human species has achieved has come about in contravention of the notion of the survival of the fittest. "Fitness" not only implies strength or superiority, but also something that is *fitting, viz.*, predictable and appropriate to a situation. With the hypertrophied mind that we enjoy/suffer, we humans do not "fit" into the picture of the world proposed by modern biology. We are outliers on account of our extraordinariness as well as our ill-construed, maladaptive nature. How can something so at odds with itself have happened? Our occurrence as a species calls for a revision, or at least a putting into perspective, of strict Darwinism.

Frans deWaal playfully invokes the notion of our maladaptive nature, our contradictory simultaneous possession of unimaginable intelligence and profound lack of an innate understanding of what to do with that intelligence, by making reference to the "Darwin awards," which highlight examples of individuals' astonishing stupidity. One could attribute that sense of astonishment to the disconnect evidenced in certain specific examples of human behavior between the relatively high bar that our intelligence has set in general and its failure to manifest itself consistently. The Mike Judge film "Idiocracy" is an example of this sense of astonishment at human stupidity, especially as it can manifest itself in mass society settings. Nevertheless, seeing our stupidity as a failing rather than a simple fact is only a function of an idealism that has arisen in the Euro-romance; it is part and parcel of a fundamental misunderstanding of ourselves as something closer to gods than to animals. If we but discard this idealized picture, we are left with our empirical selves: brilliant idiots.

Having articulated our newfound conceptualization of human beings as a kind of minded ape whose inexpungible animality has always belied and undermined the misconceptions it maintains about itself and its world, we proceed in the next chapter to an "applied" phenomenology of human nature and experience through a thoroughly serio-comic look at today's world of culture. Our approach will be one that highlights the ongoing social and political consequences of the dissolution of modern Euro-romantic discourse, fleshing out the ways in which the latter's pursuit of a unified, objective truth has been utterly shattered into a cacophonous array of fundamentally discrete and irremediably irreconcilable perspectives in today's technologically mediated social world.

Note

1 In *Kant, Political Writings*.

4

WELCOME TO THE FRAGMENTORIUM! IT'S RIDICULOUS!

Michael A. Weinstein and Timothy M. Yetman

(MW)

Everything about the socio-political-economic-cultural "world" is breaking up into jagged pieces that don't fit together into any (semi-)coherent pattern, moving and morphing, abrading each other, penetrating each other, linking with each other, and crushing each other. Taken together, the fragments aren't moving in any discernible direction. There is more signifying going on than ever and less significance, indeed, no significance on the whole. Always prone to make a mess whenever it thinks that it is making an "advance," the bonobo-chimpanzee (BC) has finally gotten itself into a kerfuffle from which it cannot extricate itself.

The BC collective/world-historical mind got *overloaded* in the "globalized" twenty-first century, so much so that any attempt to characterize it by any meaning or purpose is *ridiculous*. There's no wiggle room for any (collective) "actor" to mount a "successful" project. It will crash into and get entangled in some other actors' incompatible plan, and the results will be truncated, compromised, and (often) the reverse of what anyone had prevised. Yet the BCs keep pretending that their particular fragments bear the *truth*, that they are the agents of world history, that their values are somehow more real and their interests somehow more legitimate than those of the other fragments.

BCs are constitutively *brilliant idiots*. No doubt, they have been brilliant in creating "globalization." It is quite wondrous to contemplate how they began as small bands whose members couldn't distinguish themselves in their assessments of their nature from other groups of animals, and have ended in over-populating the earth and linking themselves with each other through communications and transportation technologies. Brilliant! Then they can't manage what they have wrought. Idiots!

It's not a matter that they might (probably will) destroy themselves. It is now clear that they were never going anywhere to begin with, so it is no loss if they happen to kill each other off or, if they don't die out, use themselves as a platform for some successor bio-technological entity (cyborg). The point is that they have proven themselves to be *idiots* in their own terms. They seem to have to take themselves seriously in direct proportion to the obvious emptiness of their pretentions. There is no way to rescue the BCs from the mess into which they've gotten themselves. What would rescuing an ill-construed being mean anyway?

Once I acknowledge the world as fragmentorium, I am left with some options for disposing myself towards the public situation, towards the world that is primarily revealed to me through the mediascape. I can exist practically in my little portion of the moving mass and pay as little attention as possible to the rest unless it disturbs my "everyday life" too much to ignore, which happens with more or less frequency. I can take the time-honored and timeworn path of withdrawal into some form of the contemplative life, removing myself from the "world" in advance of death. I cannot try to live in terms of an overall meaning to my life, since I have made myself incapable of believing in or committing myself to any such meaning; yet I can pretend to be directed by one (I can *simulate* a life of meaning). I have no objection to anyone opting for any of the foregoing alternatives—after all, how could I? Yet I don't opt for any of them.

I am a privatist who is fascinated by what the Chicago modernist art photographer Mark Ballogg calls "the parade of clowns." As he points out, everyone in that parade is a clown, so there is no "normative character" in the comedy. If you laugh at the clowns, you laugh at yourself, too. I join that parade as a participant-observer, embedded in it, allowing myself to become passionate about some part of it when I am moved to do so, but never so much that I surrender my indifference to it. I am in the world *and of it*, but I am not committed to it. The BCs exist to entertain me and to amuse me, and I will do my part in the monkey-mind show by constructing it as the BC serio-comedy, and maybe amusing some of the other BCs.

I am a fragment of a fragment of a fragment embedded in the fragmentorium. I have been writing up to now purposefully maintaining an ambiguity. Yes, I have declared myself to be a BC like all the others, yet I have also written as though I was separate from them, reflecting on them clinically. That ambiguity is the result of the reflective review that constitutes the phenomenology of mind. The "concept" of the fragmentorium is the outcome of a reflective review of the present "world-historical moment," gleaned from the mediascape, which is the access that I have to the public situation, supplemented by the observations that I have in my round of "everyday life," my interpretation of which has been infected by significations from the mediascape. That is not to say that the fragmentorium is merely the figment of an imaginary, except in the sense that all BCs' experience partakes of some imaginary as soon as some comment is made about it. In reflecting on representation and reflection, I cannot help but turn myself into some kind of *alien*.

Yet make no mistake—I am not alienated in the sense of experiencing myself as some kind of stranger in a strange land. I am a BC with the complication of being aware of myself as such because I have opted to deploy the (scientific) myth that the so-called "human" is the third primate, the "bi-polar animal," as primatologist Frans deWaal calls "us."

Acknowledgment of the fragmentorium involves the "problem" (strictly a problem of exposition) that there is no aspect of it from which it is most intelligible to begin an account of it, develop that account, and complete that account in a "meaningful" way. An account of the fragmentorium could just as well begin and/or end anywhere. Open up a newspaper, turn on the television, or get on the worldwide web, and you are communing with a fragment of the fragmentorium. You will find out what some BCs are doing, thinking, and feeling, and you can be sure of one thing—that they are part of the disarrayed parade of clowns, actors in a comedy of confusion, the more so if they believe that they are engaged in serious business.

If there is no intelligible path through the fragmentorium, then an account of it is still possible as a series of probes guided by the whim of the fragment of a fragment of a fragment "who" undertakes it. It will neither be possible to determine in advance what topics will be addressed nor the mood in which they will be addressed. What will eventuate will depend on how I feel on the day when I am taking up my pen. There will be no attempt to maintain a uniform sensibility throughout the encounter with the fragments. The fragmentorium is the "worldly" counterpart of the phantasmagoria, and I will remain close to both of them.

This particular privatist, ME/me, has a problem writing about the public situation/fragmentorium. When I survey the mediated phantasmagoria, I prefer a daily newspaper because I have no say in what I read and see, and I can spend as much time as I like with each article/fragment, savoring it, going back over it, bending every effort to comprehend the text, as though it was part of a philosophical treatise. I do not experience, nor am I able to summon sufficient passion to put down words for others whom I don't know to read.

It's a ridiculous predicament; I am ridiculous for undertaking to produce a general description of "our" times when I am convinced that it doesn't matter. The sticking point is that I have become convinced that the BCs have gotten themselves into a mess from which they cannot extricate themselves; they have produced too much diversity for them to coordinate, so they are set up perpetually to attempt to set the world right according to their different and divergent lights, and, as a consequence, are set up for failure.

I have set myself up for failure! The serio-comic smile crosses my lips. I have set myself a textbook Sisyphean task—to go out each day to fulfill the self-imposed mandate to lift some fragment of public experience into a comedic register when I have no ideal to which to compare its (tawdry) "reality."

Failed (Serio-)Comedy #1: Crash in Practice (7/6/15) *(MW)*

What could be a better start? I sit down in Dunkin' Donuts on Clark and Belden in Chicago, where I am scratching out this writing, and what should be piping through its sound system, but the great hair metal band Poison's classic ballad, "Every Rose has its Thorn," sung so plaintively by pretty-boy Brett Michaels. The title says it all, no need for further lyrics or commentary.

What, I think, about a plant with countless thorns and no flowers, perhaps because the flowers dried up long ago and have turned to dust spread somewhere or other, "dust over the city," as Hegel put it commenting on all the imaginaries that were discarded in the movement of the world-(historical)-process.

Brett Michaels is gone, replaced by a string of ads—they go by too fast and indistinctly for me to grasp, much less remember them. My initial reverie has been broken by the intrusion of the pop-radio phantasmagoria, which is a requirement for doing this writing; it keeps me *honest*!

When I left my apartment this morning, I took along with my writing pad, an article from the July 4 *Chicago Tribune* about an incident that occurred at Daytona International Speedway the day before during a practice session for NASCAR's Coke Zero 400 race. Out of the more than 200 newspaper and magazine articles that I read over the past week, that is the only one that excited enough passion (albeit almost none) to motivate me to take it with me. The piece, from the Associated Press, is headlined "Busch blames Keselowski for multicar crash."

Why did that article excite me more than any other during a week when negotiations between international lenders and Greece collapsed over the latter's defaulted debt to the former (the first time a Western country had so defaulted!), when an agreement between Iran and its Great Power adversaries over the former's nuclear program hung in the balance (US President Barack Obama threatened to "walk away" if Iran didn't come to heel), and, among many other noteworthy events, master promoter Donald Trump, now a contender for the Republican Party nomination for President, let loose a load of bile against illegal Mexican immigrants, accusing them of being rapists and drug dealers, setting off a dither among the other thirteen contenders (an unprecedented number!), some of whom, seeking the "Hispanic vote," repudiated "The Donald," while others, seeking the nativist vote, either kept their mouths shut or cheered Trump's ballsy candor?

Having formulated the foregoing question, I see that I don't have to answer it. Just recounting the "big stories" of the past week has started me laughing. Take the Greek debt crisis. Here's the narrative: A bunch of shameless, reckless, deluded, or all three, financial predators shell out money to a country they know is a deadbeat, and then turn the screws on the mark, who then thumbs his nose at the big boys, flirting with a "Grexit" from the Euro, which would be *unprecedented*. Na, na, na, na, NAH! It's a *game of chicken*, and maybe both sides won't let up on the throttle and they'll CRASH!

I leave it to you to construct (serio-)comic "narratives" for the Iranian nukes imbroglio and the Donald-is-a-*contender* farce.

It took that little excursus to let me overcome Nietzsche's "spirit of gravity," which I thought I couldn't do (good-bye Sisyphus), and, as a consequence, to see why I was intrigued (slightly at the time and now with relish) by the crash at Daytona: *I love "Bad Brad" Keselowski.*

Here's what happened. During practice, Bad Brad bumped Kyle Busch from the rear, sending the latter up the track where he was hit by Greg Biffle, whereupon Busch and Biffle gathered Martin Truex Jr., Denny Hamlin, and Carl Edwards into the mess, ruining all their cars (and making them go to back-ups for the Coke Zero 400), whereas Bad Brad escaped unscathed. All the aforementioned drivers are among the elite Sprint Cup Drivers. You can be sure that the victims of the misadventure were *not amused*!

Busch blamed Bad Brad for the calamity, arguing that, although bumping is a normal part of NASCAR racing, it shouldn't be done in a practice when "you don't need to be up a guy's left rear." At the same time, Busch scotched any thought that he was looking to start a feud: "I've also been in the same boat and caused [accidents] before."

I like it that Bad Brad's at it again. During the 2014 season he had angered the other elite drivers so much by what they had judged to be his over-aggressive/reckless driving that some of them physically assaulted him and all of them, except for his Penske teammate Joey Logano, ganged up on him, maligning him as an immature wimp. After the guild masters had asserted themselves against him, Bad Brad quieted down. He even launched a media charm offensive, cultivating a cheeky affability and winning the oohs and ahs of TV racing commentators. He seemed to be fully disciplined and domesticated in the 2015 season, up until now. He has recurrently tried to curb his penchant for driving on the edge, but has eventually given the effort up, because, as he says, he can't drive at his best unless he presses the envelope. I can breathe a sigh of relief; it looks like Bad Brad is through (for the moment) with knuckling under to the guild.

As for Kyle Busch, another driver known for competing aggressively, I marvel at his measured response. It looks like NASCAR, the team owners, and most of all, the guild is determined to avoid driver feuds, which have been absent from the 2015 season. Can you imagine? If you want to find *civility* in the fragmentorium, look to NASCAR! If you want to find a perfumed crap heap, look to the European Union.

Failed (Serio-)Comedy #2: Mash-Up/Crash-Up (7/7/15) *(MW)*

The Coke Zero 400 was run late on Sunday night, July 5, after a more than three-hour rain delay. Dale Earnhardt Jr. had the dominant car and won the race. Good for Junior! The son of *The Intimidator*, Dale Earnhardt Sr., Junior is, by virtue of his father's fame, consistently voted by fans as NASCAR's most popular driver. I've always had trouble with that. Don't get me wrong; I like Junior as a public personality, but is it possible that the reason I like him is the same as why others do? I doubt it.

I like Junior because, unlike his macho-man father, he's an unabashed child (in his own mind), an extraordinarily humble, self-effacing, and self-doubting one. A money machine, hawking merch and suffocated by product endorsements, his latest TV ad for Nationwide Insurance has him recounting all the wonderful people who have made him an elite driver. Most appealing to me is that Junior is a manic-depressive, with an emphasis on the second of the pair. When things aren't going well for him, all of his perceived inadequacies in relation to The Intimidator surface, his doubts about having been dragooned into being a race-car driver emerge, and he falls into a blue funk. In contrast, when he has a success, he is bursting and beaming (most of all *relieved*), but that moment never lasts very long. Life is Sisyphean for a manic-depressive. Junior evokes protective tenderness in me. Maybe he does the same for others. We want to lift him up when he's down, and we dote over his joy when he makes it to Victory Lane. That weasel! He turns a "grown man" (*really*)—me—into his *mother*.

How can I let myself feel that way? Junior took away more than $300,000 from Daytona, and has bagged more than $3,500,000 so far in the 2015 season, not to mention the merch and the endorsements, and his park in North Carolina. Who is Junior? I'll never meet him; I'm not doing anything to do so. All I have is the snippets of him that I grab from the mediascape. I have the impression that when he appears on TV right before races that he is not fully scripted, that he cannot altogether control himself. Feel contempt for me if you like (I'm setting myself up for it); Junior is attractive to me because I have judged that he can't control (fully) his "presentation of self."

No other driver in "NASCAR Nation" has his own (sub-)nation *Junior Nation!* He is the (figurehead?) president/emperor—the perpetual (brooding) boy-king, the very epitome of the *brilliant idiot*, in this case some (fabricated?) *innocent!* Here I thought that I liked Junior for my own special reasons and now I realize that I've been sucked in in the same way as every other citizen/subject of Junior Nation.

It's ridiculous! Am I having fun yet? Yes.

I had intended to write about the crash that happened in the last lap of the Coke Zero 400 and then mash it up with some other news of the day, commenting on some conglomeration of fragments; but I got seduced by the Junior persona. Here's how it happened: Junior, sailing to victory, claims to have been watching the mayhem through his rear-view mirror, preoccupied by hopes that no one got hurt (too badly). For the moment, I had put myself in his place as a device for imagining the crash. So, let's do it.

Behind Junior, the other drivers were in the last-lap mad scramble for position that is supposed to happen at Daytona, a super-speedway, an ultra-fast track. Kevin Harvick bumped Denny Hamlin, setting off a "chain reaction" in which Austin Dillon's car lifted off the ground and hurtled into a catch fence, shaking him up and injuring some fans. (The Intimidator had died in a similar incident at Daytona, leaving Junior with no choice but to honor his father's legacy by taking the wheel. To embellish the storyline even further, Dillon was driving the

Welcome to the Fragmentorium! 127

Number Three car, *The Intimidator's number!* Hype-memories are made of this! "Sweet, sweet the memories you gave to me." Stop it! Stop the associations!)

Dillon was not a happy driver. He told the press that speeds at the ultra-fast tracks should be lowered so that cars would not transform into erratic missiles. Dripping with irony(?), he expressed hopes that the fans had enjoyed the excitement, but made it clear that the drivers (at least him) had not.

Mash it up! Greece is about to crash out of the Eurozone, bumped by the EU. It's going too fast, says Greece. At least give us an extension on our loans, if not a "haircut" that forgives some of them. Slow the race down! Slow down, says The Donald. Cheesh! I can see that Univision would sever their ties to my Miss Universe "pageant," but NASCAR? (Yes, NASCAR has repudiated The Donald; its "diversity initiative" includes running a series in Mexico and an effort to recruit Mexican and Mexican-American drivers.) I wish it would slow down says each of the participants in the Iran nuke negotiations, but how many of our so-called self-imposed deadlines can we extend? (There's something to be said for an interminable extension.) The present Miss Universe is from Colombia and she has expressed her disapproval of The Donald's slurs against Mexican immigrant rapists, druggies, and lately, bearers of infectious diseases. The Donald is not amused and accuses Miss Universe of hypocrisy for not giving up her crown. She will not do so. Why should she? It's like telling someone to honor the niceties of classical liberal civil disobedience—if you want to break a law to protest injustice, you should let yourself be arrested. If you disagree with the guy who owns the beauty pageant you won, you should give up the crown. It's ridiculous! What does one thing have to do with the other?

The Donald is trying to extricate himself from the hole he dug for himself. He admits that there are some good Mexicans and now blames the Mexican government for dumping its human waste products across the border. Maybe the Mexicans and their government like it, but The Donald doesn't. What will he think of next? The Donald is getting bumped on all sides and he's going sideways; he's about to go ballistic, as Macy's has decided to drop his signature line of clothes and accessories. Wait! He's still a contender for the Republican Presidential nomination, and recent polls show him running second only to Jeb Bush, the establishment favorite. He's getting publicity. He's got a lot of money (*more personal wealth than anyone who has ever run for president!*). Above all, he's amusing me. That thing about the Mexican government dumping human refuse is just the kind of outlandish claim that I would like to be shameless or stupid enough to make myself, but I can't (yet), so I'll let The Donald do it for me.

It takes all kinds. The Donald is the anti-Junior. The latter is bonobo-dominant (although I don't know about his sex life) and the former appears to be as close to a chimp as you can get (whether he has a sex life at all is in question). There is some kind of structured comparative cultural-personality analysis to be made here. We can begin with the fact that Junior and The Donald are both celebrities *with their own lines of merch!* You can take it from there.

(Failed(?)) Serio-Comedy #3: Legacy Mania (7/8/15) (MW)

There's no telling what the BCs will say next. Before I get to my point, if there turns out to be one in the mash-up/crash-up that I fondly contemplate writing today, you (regrettably, from my point of view) need a "back story." A couple of weeks ago a brooding white kid named Dylan Roof went to a prayer meeting at an African-American church in Charleston, South Carolina, hung around "participating" for a while and then shot the place up, killing nine of the faithful after they had welcomed him into the fold. He is reported to have admitted later that he had second thoughts about executing his plan, because the congregants had treated him so well, but he overcame his compunctions because he was convinced that alien races are taking over America, was appalled that nobody was doing anything about it, and figured that he would (seemingly with some reluctance) have to be the one to take action (no one else would!). So much for that.

Roof's idiotic attempt at direct action sparked a clamor to remove the Confederate battle flag from the grounds of the state capitol because the kid had posed with it for some photos that he had posted on the internet, breaking new ground in the emerging genre of the self(ie)-portrait. Thereupon the forces in favor of keeping the good old "Stars and Bars" where it was, mobilized, another example of the zombie supporters of the "Old South" trying to pull a Lazarus. The South Carolina legislature had to approve the removal of the flag and, but for three dissenters, the state's senate did so. It was a great day for the New South, especially its conservative Republican Indian-American female governor. Do you need any more proof that the "Rebels" are the *undead*?

None of the foregoing, of course, is relevant to the point that I think I'm trying to make; it's just context, which BCs seem to need to convince themselves that they're "rooted" or some such. Boring!

To get to the "point," one of the three dissenters against getting rid of the flag plaintively warned that if (white?) South Carolinians failed to honor their forebears, there was a good chance that future generations of South Carolinians would not honor the present generation. Duh!

It seems like a swarm of tourists (an honorable term used advisedly—*what are they?*), scads more than ever (all the lonely people, *we know where they belong*), are making a bee-line for Hollywood's Walk of Fame where they are gushing out honey-money that has attracted the flies of the marketplace, that is, tour-bus and tour-van operators in unprecedented numbers, clogging the street and spilling over onto the sidewalk where they wave their handbills and hawk their tickets. Now, in a scene out of a slapstick comedy, they are trying to seize sections of pavement for themselves and crowd out their competitors, setting off shoving matches with each other. Double Duh!

Hey *Southern Man*, white-boy, South Carolinian heritage monger, *nobody cares about you except you and your little fragment*. Forget about future generations, as I write and you read, the present generation is feasting on the *heritage of stars*. Say

Welcome to the Fragmentorium! 129

what you want *old* Southern Man, the best you can do is shoot up a prayer meeting. You can only fantasize about a horde of tour-bus and tour-van operators jostling for position in front of the state capitol vying to sell tickets for trips around Civil War heritage sights. Give up! You can't beat Hollywood. Go back home and put "Birth of a Nation" on continuous loop.

We need to arrange an encounter between the imaginary hordes of infectiously diseased, raping, and drug-dealing/taking Mexican immigrant refuse in The Donald's brain and those tourist-dolts filing on to vans and buses to get a hit of celebrity-heritage-history. Mash them up and throw in some Old-South zombies sporting Stars-and-Bars shirts like I saw in a news photo. As the guest of honor and Grand Marshal, we can have Prime Minister Alexis Tsipras of Greece, who was captured, in another photo, emerging from the meeting he had with the EU Bigwigs—where they told him he had five days to knuckle under on pain of being dumped from the Eurozone—with a demented-moronic-boyish smile on his face and a jaunty step. We need The Donald to set up a reality show in which the Hollywood tour-van-and-bus operators are pitted against each other in shoving matches like Sumo wrestlers—"Banging Heads for 'Tourist' Bucks." Hell is being on a van with a global menagerie of Simulacrum Gawkers, "smelling good," looking clean, and decked out in fashionable leisure outfits; conducted by a transgender woman who has just come out of a shoving match with a rival (militantly male repressed transgender woman) tour-van operator. The Donald could clothe them in the remainders of his ill-fated signature fashion line. Everyone gets dabbed with The Donald's cologne. Why is it that from Christine Jorgenson onwards, it's "biological" men who get it into their heads that they're "really" women trapped in alien bodies? What's wrong with male BCs? Valerie Solanas had it right back in the day in her SCUM (Society of Cut Up Men) Manifesto where she proposed that men be eliminated, the high point of feminism that has not been achieved again since then. Why doesn't Greece just stop pretending it might pay its debts and simply start printing drachmas? Meanwhile make the drachma the official currency of Hollywood. Maybe Tsipras looked so elated because he was dreaming of drachmas. So am I.

All this obsessive disingenuous/ingenuous worrying about "*legacy*," which has become a buzz word in the summer of 2015, *is ridiculous!* My apologies, I can do no better than Jean Baudrillard when I contemplate it. What does it mean to worry about *legacy* in the *fragmentorium*? It's a Baudrillardian *deterrence machine* masking the judgment that whatever will be remembered (and almost nothing will, even though everything might be archived) will be entertained as an *imaginary*, just as it is on *the walk of fame*. My "legacy," which I can say in advance *will not* exist, would be something that *I was not if by some miracle I had one*. In any case, in the fragmentorium each putative "legacy" is lost among all the proliferation of others, checked, nullified, and swamped by them; rendered *insignificant*.

How touching it is to buy into the pious magic that if I honor the memory of my forebears and glorify it, my successors will do the same for me in turn. BCs were aptly diagnosed by Schopenhauer as being cursed with the need to feel that they are significant; they have to count for others in order to count for themselves. Christianity solves the problem by making everyone count for God. That makes a lot more sense than believing that presently unborn BCs will care about what I did. A certain measure of desperation seems to go along with the fragmentorium.

(Maybe) Failed Serio-Comedy #4: Mash-up *Legacy* Breakdown (7/13/15) *(MW)*

It's ridiculous: legacy obsession.

I can't get it out of my mind. *Okay,* I'll say it: If everyone is striving mightily (of course, they're not, but...) to leave their *own legacy,* who will be left to contemplate those legacies? There needs to be a profession of specialists in appreciating the legacies left by the other BCs. The legacy of the appreciator of legacies will be to be remembered by other legacy appreciators as a noteworthy legacy appreciator. The legacy appreciators will be the high priests of the legacy-seeking society.

Yes—the legacy-seeking society. That is the macro-socio-cultural theory of the summer of 2015. Theory still exists in the fragmentorium; it is transitory and its foundational concepts are the *memes of the moment.*

Have no doubt about it, the master name of *legacy* will be dethroned soon enough and will be stale and nauseating by the time that anyone has the chance to read the present writing. Some other meme for meditation will have presented itself, capable of provoking the most profoundly amusing existential anxieties. There's nothing I can do; I have to entertain the meme of the moment and inflate it into the very theme of "our" present (now recently or remotely past) world-historical moment. It is, with a bow to Hegel, a moment of the phenomenology of mind, *my* moment grafted on my mind from the mediascape, *now.*

Josh Gad is *anxious.* At least that's what the comic seems to be communicating in an interview that he gave to *Chicago Tribune* serio-comic workplace columnist Rex W. Huppke. Gad was talking about his relationship with the more famous comic, Billy Crystal, who was also in on the interview and who stars with Gad on the TV show, "The Comedians," based on a postmodern meta-move in which they play themselves making a "fictional" comedy. I haven't seen it and I don't want to, and I've only mentioned it to provide the back story. *Boring!* It should also be noted that Huppke's column on the encounter appears to be intentionally *serious.* We are expected to believe—at least it appears so—that Gad is *serious.* This is a serious column about a serious man who happens to be a comedian in a comedy about comedians written by a serio-comic journalist.

Huppke focuses his column on Gad, who is 34 years old and is in the early stages of an existential mid-life crisis. Woody Allen he is *not,* or at least he doesn't seem to be. Gad tells Huppke: "I'm at a point in my own life where I'm trying to define my own legacy. I'm trying to make the right choices [what could that

Welcome to the Fragmentorium! 131

mean?] and along the way I screw up a lot [don't we all?]." Then we cut to the core of the agony: "I'm chasing dreams [he probably should say 'shadows'] faster than I can keep up with what the reality of all that means."

I find myself incapable of adding any commentary to what Gad has said; it stands as a presumably unintended parody of existential-historical angst in the fragmentorium. What's worse is that I suspect that Huppke seems to take Gad at his word and so seriously because Huppke is suffering from the same condition.

Why is Gad framing his mid-life crisis in his struggle to define his "own legacy?" It doesn't seem to be obvious that someone would articulate the quest for the "meaning of life" in those terms. If one is so committed to deriving "meaning" out of society, one could content oneself with worrying about how high they might rise in whatever hierarchy in which they happened to be embedded. Alternatively they might question the importance of social meaning in comparison with what else might satisfy them more. What about helping others right now? What about reconciling oneself to the vanity of it all? How about trying to check off the items on one's "bucket list?" But, *no*. Gad's quest is to define what his legacy is supposed to be, what he will leave to others whom he will never be able to know and who won't care about him, except (at most and unlikely) as a construct. *Ridiculous!*

It gets worse. Gad reports that Crystal has been just the mentor that he needed, the older comedian (67) having told him to "*slow down*" (emphasis added). Crystal has "already achieved a legacy, one that's of an iconic nature," and he somehow has shown Gad a "sort of worldly, relaxed, almost peaceful view of what it is to be in pursuit of that legacy." But Crystal is already an *icon* and Gad is *not*—that's Gad's problem. How can Crystal's example calm Gad down? Don't expect BCs to make sense when they make the mistake (as it seems they must) of pro-blematizing the "meaning of life."

Gad's comfort, such as it is, seems to come from Crystal's having reflected on his present situation and having said: "What am I going to do, retire?" Gad reports having been "blown away" by that remark: "To look at that guy and you literally can't have accomplished more in comedy than he has, and this guy doesn't feel like he's done. It never ends. You never stop wanting to do more." Again, I find it impossible to do other than let the parody of existentialism stand. *It never ends* (at least, presumably, until one dies; does "legacy" even matter to Gad by this point in the conversation?).

For Gad, Crystal provides the example of an older comedian who hasn't gotten sick (yet) of being a comedian. That's what Gad thinks, but I can imagine that Crystal meant something else. I'll give my imagined Crystal some lines:

"Icon, Shmycon. Legacy, Shmeggegassy. I'm done and I know it. I've seen the best and I've seen the worst, and the thing about it is that I can't figure out what else to do with the time that's left to me but to keep doing what I already know how to do, even though I know all too well how far that goes—not very far. I'll admit that it's fun (sometimes); I wouldn't do it otherwise. But that's all it is. And as for you, Gad, you brilliant neurotic excusably (because you're young) narcissistic and self-deluded *idiot*, maybe someday you'll realize that you don't get a legacy—for the nothing that it is worth—by chasing a legacy. You get one, and it won't mean anything to you when you get it, because you'll see that no one else cares and you also won't by that time, by doing what you've learned to do. You'd better try to enjoy what you're doing; that's the best way I know to get people to tolerate you, which is more than you can expect. I'm not still in this game because there are new worlds to conquer, but because I don't know what else to do. *Get real, Nigga*."

That is *my* Billy Crystal. "He" probably has nothing to do with who the "real" Billy Crystal is misrecognized by himself; the signifier "Billy Crystal" exists in the present text as a foil for Josh Gad as he was represented by Rex W. Huppke—a fragment of a fragment of a fragment of a fragment ...

Gad got bitten by the legacy bug and, comedian that he is, (inadvertently) demonstrated the absurdity of the legacy quest. "Legacy" is the deterrence-machine absurdity of the moment, another instance of locking the mind's door after the meanings have gotten out irretrievably into the fragmentorium.

Failed Serio-Comedy #5: Anything and Everything (7/27/15) *(MW)*

Anything can be amusing, as long as you're already amused ... by (your) life itself.

Just form your lips into the serio-comic smile, loosely closed lips slightly upturned, breathe deeply and easily, and feel a quiet mirth overtake you. Then say to yourself: "*It's ridiculous!*" Imagine yourself spreading out your arms, palms facing outwards, hands slightly cupped, your body relaxed, in a gesture that signifies: "What can I do? (nothing) This is the way it is. *What the hell can I do about it? (Nothing) Who cares?* (not me)."

At this point the associations should come, the thoughts that occur in the serio-comic mood. Anything will do, but the writer in me, conditioned by repetition over decades, tells me that I am supposed to address something significant. What a curse! Worse, I am supposed to have some idea of what I am going to write about that significant theme and even devise an at least rough outline of the important points that I have committed myself to make.

Understandably, I can't convince myself that there's anything significant about Kyle Busch's winning yesterday's Sprint Cup Jeff Kyle 400 at the fabled Indianapolis Motor Speedway (Brickyard!); yet that is the only fragment from the mediascape that sticks to my fly-paper mind, the others, like the big political story of the day—Turkey and the USA collaborating against the Caliphate of the Islamic State—grazing against the glue and then flitting away.

I can't get the image of Busch's Toyota outdistancing Joey Leguizano's Ford at the end of the race out of my mind. How, I think, is it possible that Kyle has won four of the last five Sprint Cup races after he had been sidelined for the first eleven of the season following a track accident in which he broke his right foot and his left leg? Talk about comebacks! Allow for the fact that Gibbs Racing, for which Busch drives, has been having a strong season; there's something amazing about Busch's recent performance, especially considering the presence of other competitive organizations, teams, and drivers; and the inherent contingencies of racing.

Could it be that Busch went into motivational overdrive in order to prove to himself and everyone else that he still had the right stuff? That was how the driver and now NBC Sports Network commentator Jeff Burton explained Busch's success. I won't dispute Burton, at least in part, yet I think there is more to it. It might also be the case that all the painful effort that Busch had to expend to make himself fit to race again made him physically stronger and made him wiser than he was before. Before the accident, Busch often veered to the cocky side. I sense a change in him now, a recognition of his fragility that has humbled him and as a result, made him *confident* of his *actual* (considerable) powers. Watch out for Kyle Busch! He knows he can be broken and it doesn't scare him; indeed, it gives him a big edge over drivers who have naïve and self-deceived confidence, and those who have been damaged and have not been able to overcome the impulse to be cautious.

Come to think of it, *I do dispute Burton.* Busch might well have become *too strong* to have to prove himself, to himself or anyone else. Might I dare to imagine that The Donald might shed his self-deluded naïve confidence and take up humbled confidence, a bombastic demagogic wise man!?! He would say the same kinds of things that he has been, yet he would say them with a *hint of gravitas.* Then let the Republican establishment, the commentariat, and the chattering classes try to run him off the ranch; a smidgeon of *gravitas* would make The Donald unassailable. He'd just have to raise an eyebrow now and then, let a sweet ironic smile flicker across his lips momentarily, and relax for a second into a worldly-wise "there is a time for every purpose under heaven" attitude; and call Senator Lindsey Graham an idiot and give out his cell phone number. Lindsey Graham and the other presumptive Republican nominees are the idiots that The Donald calls them, (brilliant) idiots. The longer he muscles himself into the spotlights, the more fun. The Donald won't let the Republican candidates get away with bloviating about being against *Big Guvammint* when they are *parasites* off it.

It's a delicious spectacle to observe The Donald savaging the Republican establishment and the chattering classes when all the latter can do is feign schoolmarmish shock and disapproval of his *incivility* and *irresponsibility.* They are convinced that his current popularity will be short-lived, a summer bubble that will burst when the electorate emerges from the silly season and realizes—as it *must*—that it needs leaders of experience, substance, and "responsibility." They can't match The Donald's snark-on-steroids. Yes, Senator John McCain, says The Donald, might be a war hero, but he got captured and it's obviously preferable not to get captured. The Donald's scythe cuts everyone down to size. He's shameless, which is just what is needed to dispel the cloud of smarm.

Listen up, *peaceniks*, The Donald is your man! He has a notorious aversion to the military, having deferred his way out of it in his youth. He's not a warrior. (It's time to castrate all warriors.) He says he is and he really is a *dealmaker*. He practices the Kim Jong Un rhetorical diplomacy of outrageous threat and intimidation. McCain was tortured by the North Koreans (or was it some other "north" country in Asia?); The Donald *imitates* them. Listen up, *postmodernists*, The Donald is your man! He's into hotels. He's a *"reality"* TV impresario.

Think of what The Donald could do if he, by some absolutely happy stroke of luck, was elected President. He could make a deal with the Islamic State to open up for adventure tours to the Caliphate. The Donald would build the hotels and the tourists would flock to witness beheadings in real time. They would be able to contemplate at their leisure rotting dead heads—not shrunken heads, a poor substitute—on poles in town squares. Tell me it wouldn't be a unique experience; you couldn't see it anywhere else in the world—only in the Caliphate. Entertainments would also include stonings and *autos da fé*, and don't forget a day at the slave market.

The opportunities for study abroad are breathtaking. Imagine a semester in Mosul learning Shari'a law as it should be practiced. The Donald could make it all happen. All he has to do is to add a drop of *gravitas* to his presentation, just as Kyle Busch has.

Failed Serio-Comedy #6: Gluttonous Media Overdose (7/28/15)
(MW)

Let me state at the outset (you can't stop me!) that I don't know much about what I'm intending to write about today. For example, I'm sure you'll all give me credit for knowing that there's a group of people called the "Kardashians" who are celebrities and have one or more TV programs; yet, that's about all I know about them, because I've somewhat studiously avoided knowing about them, because something about the tone of the snippets about them that impact my monkey mind revolts it, like I'm being aversively conditioned by *stimulus Kardashiana*.

Be that as it may, the Kardashians are part of the back story (*boring!*) for the point that I may eventually get to. I have an inkling that the Kardashians might be related to a person named alternatively or successively Bruce/Caitlyn Jenner, who I seem to recall as Bruce, famous athlete, I think, from decades ago, who now has "their" own TV show spinning off from the Kardashians' that addresses Jenner's transition from a gendered male to a gendered female.

I have slumped down in my seat at Dunkin' Donuts, exhaling a sigh of relief; I have completed the back story. (I refuse to call Jenner Bruce or Caitlyn; I call them B.C. Jenner—bonobo-chimpanzee Jenner, how convenient.)

Who cares!? (a lot of people seem to, yet I don't). I'm interested in a "think piece" by *Time Magazine* media "critic" James Poniewozik in the August 3, 2015 issue on B.C. Jenner (Caitlyn or Cait to J.P.) whom he considers to be a "remarkable woman living among the mundane" (the last a reference to living *among the Kardashians*). Ridiculous as that might sound—and simply thinking of the signifier "Kardashians" makes me laugh and retch simultaneously—J.P. gets worse, reaching the nadir of confusion (the height of serio-comedy) in the last sentence of his piece: "But as reality shows—however edited and self-consciously presented—they can send a message of *authenticity* (emphasis added) that people like Caitlyn … are real (whatever anyone says [!])."

What's going on in that *ridiculous* sentence? Taking the "high-(culture) ground," J.P. has inaugurated the new paradigm to replace postmodernism. Yes B.C. is a *construct* ("edited and self-consciously presented"), therefore, J.P. is *hip*; yet B.C. exudes *"authenticity,"* therefore, J.P. is *also a sentimentalist.* "Reality" *shines through the construct.* Jacques Derrida spent his thinking life trying to banish *nostalgia* and then in just one sentence, J.P. reinstalls it in the very "heart" of the simulacrum—back to the '60s structuralism becomes the *last Puritanism*; henceforth, we can have it both ways and every other. *We are in the age of the mashup*—just join together any signifiers and make your "point." J.P. is the quintessential brilliant *idiot.*

J.P. is all serious; he needs some snark. One of his sentences has stuck to my flypaper mind and I can't rip it off (I don't want to) because it is "genuine" cultural theory and I'm a sucker for that. J.P. writes that B.C. has been "trying to close the decades-old gap between her self-image and her self-presentation." Despite his blathering about "authenticity" (I am not doubting that he is "serious" about his sentimentalism), J.P. can fire off the *pomo* vocabulary with the best of the *hipsters*: notice he does not say that B.C. has been striving to bring self-presentation into synch with the real self, deep self (essentialist) *soul-the real me*; J. P. says that B.C. has been trying to square *self-image* and self-presentation, both of which are *constructs* (or are they?). As Derrida would say, J.P.'s "text" is *undecidable.* Maybe B.C.'s femininity is an emanation of a B.C. *primordial self.* That wouldn't be *hip!* (So J.P. doesn't write anything of the sort.) Yet if B.C.'s femininity is simply a construct, their identity could be reconstructed. (You can see the advantage of essentialism if you want to take your identity seriously—*(please) don't take my identity away from me* (even if I have to admit it's just a construct in order to remain cultural-theoretically correct).)

Give J.P. credit for framing B.C.'s "struggle" as one of reconciling the Hegelian "unhappy consciousness" between *image* and *representation.* B.C. is playing a monkey (phenomenology of) mind game. I can only speculate, because I have no plans to query J.P., that all he was trying to do was hash out a think piece, and that he hit upon structuring it around a storyline (that impulse is hard-wired into the commentariat) of the struggle to overcome what threatened to become a *tragic* conflict. Poor B.C.! The *self-image* of a woman with a "man's" body, trapped by backward social attitudes and having to project a *public image* at odds with their *self-image*. Yet, wait a second, isn't it normal for celebrities to *enjoy* (?) such a split? Let me suspend disbelief. It's a bit of an effort, but it's gotten the tears welling up in my eyes. Oh, B.C., B.C.—all those agonizing years wanting to be ... who you *are* (no, that can't be) ... taken by others to be who you *imagine* yourself to be (yes, that's a better formulation, though it probably doesn't serve J.P.'s narrative purpose of telling an inspiring story of a struggle with a happy ending). J.P. is just another brilliant idiot—brilliant for (I'm convinced inadvertently) taking the step beyond post-structuralism into anything goes in(to) the text, and an idiot for writing yet another tiresome riff on the Euro-romance, in this case a made-for TV think-piece on a TV comedy structured by serio-comedy.

I'll put a stop to this ridiculous reflection. The silly-season summer of 2015 preoccupation with dignifying "transgender" people (who form their very own fragmentorium) is just a half-and-halfer compromise formation camouflaging a *radical* "insight." I summon Sigmund Freud to the scene. The BC is capable of *any* "gender identity." Do you want sex-gender freedom? Don't add yet another identity to the mix of politically-correct "types;" just give everyone a chance to be *everything*.

Bisexuality won't do it; we have to have pansexuality. The truly *"remarkable"* BC "living among the mundane" is the *pansexual*. Who will dare to occupy the ultimate territory, that is, the *whole* territory? I'll shave my legs in the morning, save the hair in a bowl in my bathroom, put on seductive shorts, etc. and venture forth into the streets, swishing and stripping, whereupon I will return home, paste my hair back on my legs, exchange my shorts for grungy shorts and saunter out again, ready to play cock of the walk—and that's only the beginning. Unamuno's "tragic sense of life" drove him to want to be "myself and everyone else." That was logically impossible and he knew it. I can be *everyone* else only if I am ready to give up on myself, and I am quite ready to do so. Bring on the Kardashians!

Hey, J.P., what did you want to be in college, when growing up? Yes, I know, you wanted to be a discursive alchemist transforming popcult into the golden words of a cultural-critical theory story! It won't work—all you can get is *smarm*. You need a dollop of *snark* and I'm here to give it to you.

A Crash of Civilization(s) *(TY)*

It would appear that, when Al Qaida attacked the US on 9/11 under the leadership of Osama Bin Laden, the organization had some semblance of strategic insight into the nature of their enemy. Per the statements released on video after the attacks, it was ostensibly carried out as a tactical act of war in service of the relatively straightforward strategic aim of repelling from the Islamic world an intruder whom they perceived to pose a threat to the material (and therefore, cultural) security of their way of life.

The sequence of responses by the American-led Western world to the 9/11 attacks would support this hypothesis. They have predominantly had enduringly

Welcome to the Fragmentorium! **137**

relatively negative, destabilizing outcomes, most of which run counter to both immediate and long-term strategic interests of the West broadly and the US specifically. From the trademark Euro-romantic point of view of rational analysis, nearly everything the West has done in the wake of 9/11—when effectual at all—has served the anti-Western purposes of the now-dead Bin Laden in ways he likely would never have dared believe possible. The spending of upwards of a trillion dollars on the wars, the most consequential one of which had nothing to do with the 9/11 attacks, the multi-pointed destabilization of the Middle East and now parts of North Africa, the establishing of a domestic police-state-in-waiting which consistently demonstrates its ineffectuality regarding its purported *raison d'être* (counterterrorism), and the spying on the high-ranking officials of one's closest allies, would all be seen as positive developments from the point of view of any enemy. If the United States had done nothing more than take up George W. Bush's advice and simply returned to the shopping malls, the actual outcomes would have been far better.

The invasion of Iraq in 2003 and the Ashley Madison scandal of 2015 are examples of what can happen in the absence of the practical wisdom that would suggest that, from the point of view of a strictly strategic, non-moral assessment, "paying it backward" (the Iraq war specifically) is poisonous to the entity who indulges himself in it despite himself. US policy post-9/11 has also served as a confirmation of the Buddhist thesis that evil suffered and/or perpetrated in the present is never guaranteed not to issue in baleful effects into the future. Evil is understood here as nothing more than the occurrence of actions taken in the throes of expropriating passion, whether chimpanzoid (Iraq) or bonoboid (Ashley Madison), which can plant the seed of future sorrow as well. Everything about the current 2016 US election media circus further confirms this theory of the undeadness of the West, and it is symptomatized perfectly by the Trump candidacy. When the last thing a public wants is contact with actuality, these are the kind of things that happen. We may be undead, but we sure are live ones!

Islamic extremism may or may not have lately become less organized, more myopic, and less of a real material threat to "our way of life" than it has since 2001. From what I have seen, I wouldn't attribute the lack of a major attack to anything but disorganization, a lack of resources, and short-sightedness on the part of groups like ISIS. As soon as they get their hands on a nuke, they will surely demonstrate the restraint of a computer program in using it. For my part, I would warn them against using such a weapon, because its use would end their war, and they would be left with the feeling of tedium vitae and would likely have to go find a new enemy, which may not be all that easy at that point. If they but cultivate a little patience, they won't have to wait too long for the West to destroy itself (or will they?).

Enough about the dying West. One might also ask, how different, how "alive" and "well" is the rhetorically austere culture being pushed by radical Islamic jihadists? Perhaps there is another reason why the agents of radical Islamist terrorism have failed to regroup; it seems they have now become distracted by and enamored of the medium through which they broadcast their propaganda. The spectacle of the precipitous material and political collapse of the West is only *one* of a host of things they are spending their time watching on their computer screens. Consider the fact that it is likely, in keeping with the deeply insecure embarrassment to masculinity that extreme Salafi interpretations of Shari'a represent, under which extremist jihadi groups like ISIS operate, that the only people allowed access to computers in the radical Islamic world are *men*. If I had to guess, I'd say that it's likely these men are most certainly spending at least *some* of their time ogling pictures of women on the internet whose hair and faces they can actually see. This is entirely speculative, and a gross understatement, all at once. "If" it is true, however, then, they, too are undead.

On this view, analogously to the events depicted in George R.R. Martin's *Game of Thrones*, we are mistaken when we see the contemporary world as framed by a struggle between two living cultures, the West and Islam. It is instead a war between (spiritual) *death*, embodied in global high-tech mediation, and *all* of the living, whether Western, Middle-Eastern, African, East Asian, Christian, Islamic, or Secularist. The technology-based global media culture, if it persists on anything like its present trajectory, will eventually kill Islamic culture like it killed Western culture, like it kills all organic cultures.

The morality police in Iran and Saudi Arabia are renewing their efforts to enforce modesty on women in response to the latter's recently emergent practice of posting pictures that show their hair on Instagram and other such media. The dilemma facing liberal-minded women living under rigid Islamic theocratic regimes, as far as I can tell, is a choice between two diametrically opposed, but equally morbid worlds: hyper-modesty or hyper-exhibitionism. It is a choice between the oppressive world of Salafi Islamic patriarchy, and the fast-paced, high-tech world of Western globalized who-really-gives-a-fuck-for-anything media culture. Neither is a flattering testimony to human greatness. So now Muslim women are demonstrating that the unlikely implementation of Western-style gender-equality "reforms" in Islamic societies will probably result in the Muslim world being flooded with selfies of celebrity- or attention-seeking people just like in the West. I have read that the Lebanese reality TV show "The Sisters" has steadily risen in popularity since its first airing. Is this the face of liberation? The dream of a chance to be a reality TV star?

Zarathustra Returns to an Even Motlier Cow to Post an Imaginary Blog (5–15–15) *(TY)*

I find it intriguing and hilarious that the people involved in the presently growing tradition of puerile, provincial, insipid Islam-bashing—people completely removed geographically and culturally from the hearts of Islamic culture—are becoming increasingly more grotesque manifestations of the buffoonish cartoon

Welcome to the Fragmentorium! 139

caricatures that they draw. Don't get me wrong, Islam is every bit as ridiculous as Western secularism, but I'm doing my best to be as egalitarian as I can force myself to be when it comes to making note of, and looking into the causes of, human stupidity in whatever form it presents itself. Although it's none of your business, I'll do you the courtesy of informing you that I'm only addressing these Western "free thinkers" because *they* have just now stirred me from my thoughts with their excruciating caterwauling. Talk to me tomorrow and we will see what new thing has caught my attention. Perhaps it will be the idiotic holy warriors with whom the cartoonists imagine they are engaging, or maybe the American Evangelical Christians who have not lost their romantic masochistic ardor for the idea of being persecuted. Who knows?

I never gave much consideration to the art of political cartoonistry, but once I trained my attention on the dipshits that are drawing pictures of the Prophet Mohammed, inciting nothing but unhelpful thoughts and feelings on either side of the "debate," it became clear that I had been laboring under an anachronistic, false, image of what that tradition stood for. If I paid any attention to cartoonistry at all, I saw it as a step, albeit, infinitesimal, above the vapid fray of today's regnant culture. I saw cartoonists (at least slightly) more as wise-waxers than provocateurs, which in my view was kind of already quaint, anyway. Within the confines of their own little media culture, they valiantly sacrificed the sublimity-loving part of our romance with artistry to keep us mindful of the bottom on which we all ultimately rest. They did us the courtesy of installing a proverbial air freshener in the incurably stale room of today's public discourse—at least in our minds.

The European cartoonists who keep drawing Mohammed have either lost sight of, or never were part of that tradition, which, I own, was actually a figment of my own fantasies. Regardless of my own notions, the fact of the matter is that the artistico-journalistic tradition of cartoonistry has allowed its avant-garde to show a face that demonstrates its own, and Europe in general's, lostness.

It is actually—without irony—being suggested by many that these artists/journalists, are doing *nothing more* than giving voice to the notion that *all* ideas should be allowed to be expressed, and that the only forum for such a sharing of ideas is the so-called "open society" that is the norm in the West. For my part, I *haven't seen an idea shared in years*. Whatever is going on on these computer and cell phone screens does not conform to my notion of what it means to share ideas, but that's just my opinion.

While this valorization of "free expression" is being presented as though it were a positive expression of strength and vital plenitude, it appears from my perspective to be little more than a self-absorbed, defensive lashing out. It is but another example of the latter-day tendency to transvaluate victimization into synonymy with heroism. This is another manifestation of the lostness I just made mention of above. In response to being materially victimized, Western journalists have recently staged what I will here rename the "Memorial Charlie Hebdo

Invitation to Hate" forum (in which artists from all over were invited to draw the Prophet Mohammed).

This forum, of course, drew comers, created a security risk, and further aggravated tensions between Muslims and the West. (Duh!?!?) I find no openness in the new tradition of anti-Islamic media that thinks it is standing up for the free exchange of ideas. Mockers must have a sense of humor: they should be able to take a mocking if they're going to dish one out. In the words of an old friend of mine: "if you're not having fun, you're failing." This goes for comedians first and foremost. There's something that just makes no sense to me about a humorist without a sense of humor ...

To the Charlie Hebdos of the world: *you idiots are supposed to be the wise ones who enjoy the privilege of mocking people!* You are the ones who are supposed to keep not just the Bin Ladens and Baghdadis, but also the Geert Wilders and Pim Fortuyns of the world *honest*, not to act as free airwave providers for voices of stupidity like the US media does with The Donald. Once love is out of the picture, mockery is *ridicule*; ridicule is practiced by the very weakest and least wise of us. Your enlightened (light-hearted) mockery-turned benighted (heavy-hearted) ridicule has consequently become just another part of the shit-pit that you are now only pretending to try to rise above.

My beloved imaginary readers, let me quickly say, Je ne suis *pas* Charlie, any more than je suis Osama or Abu Bakr. I find it unfortunate that Islamic jihadists are wretched, small-minded cretins (this exceedingly apt appellation will offend them even more when they consider its etymology), but they make no pretense to being anything else. In the West, you enjoy the privilege of hailing from a tradition that ostensibly devoted itself to cultivating ideas. In the post-idea era of global virtual media, no one cares about *anything at all* except taking one's opportunity to partake in the universal practice of crying into the wilderness and bullying others for doing the same thing. The Charlie Hebdo-style demonstrations of free speech are really just hifalutin' versions of twitter wars. Contemporary public culture proves that all Western progress, promised or actual, is utterly eradicable and rescindable.

I also should say that I'm having all atheists shot—or rather burned. I say this mostly jokingly because I saw a gentleman by the name of Lawrence Krauss "debating" a young Islamic scholar on Youtube the other day and what struck me was none of the content of the "conversation," but its spirit. I was downright shocked at how far below the level of the floor Dr. Krauss started, eventually melting completely out of sight. In the end there was nothing left of him but a faint mumbling, whining sound that made no sense. How hard can it be to argue successfully against a simplistic provincial religious doctrine? Panic and vitriol are the hallmarks of latter-day evangelists for (the memory of) Reason. They are *petit* inquisitors. Say what you will of the *Grand* Inquisitor: he was one cool customer by comparison.

Insecure bullies are not qualified to be humorists (what *are* they qualified for?); they only mock pusillanimously (lovelessly). They bring us all down toward the

Welcome to the Fragmentorium! 141

bottom and their humor becomes one of a different, unintended, sort (they become the joke themselves). They don't understand how to mock magnanimously, which is the only way the not-to-be-taken-lightly privilege of mockery can be carried out without causing problems (fucking *duh!*).

Magnanimity is now only a personal (no longer a social, or cultural) possibility (I suspect that was always the case—a self-reward for those who expect nothing). Its absence on the public stage may be of more consequence than we are ready to think: mocking even only slightly pusillanimously may have unintended consequences. We live in a world of half-wits. Most of them are shockingly content with their shitty lot. Enough of them aren't. Some with astoundingly good lots have appallingly bad attitudes. European cartoonists: you may be a step or two above most of them, but why encourage them? Enter Pamela Geller. Don't you see, European secularist wise men, that when you go petty, you may be inviting a bunch of idiotic thugs you may not have wanted to be on center stage with (witness The Donald). These are the kind of dumb thugs who are just getting started when you finally say "Whoa … okay, okay, I was only [kind of] joking?" (Frankenstein!). You can't go "play American" and not expect to have at least a small crowd of idiots misinterpret your "grand gesture" celebrating free expression as an invitation to a fun, family-friendly hate-off.

The privilege of mockery has recently tanked in value on the global cultural stock market. I nevertheless hereby and until further notice revoke from all imagination- and heart-less fools the privilege of mockery—it's reserved strictly for *lovers* forthwith (wisdom is *love*, not intelligence). In fact, until such time as you demonstrate that you have gotten some perspective, you have forfeited the right to say another word. It didn't have to be this way, and that's a fact, but one far less relevant than the fact that it *is* this way. I'm going to go ahead and say it: *Fuck your stupid speech. It sounds like shit smells.* It's not that I particularly care *what* you are saying, it's *the way that you're insisting on saying it* that is as seemingly ineffectual as it is irritating. From my point of view, strictly analytically speaking, all you seem to be doing is maintaining and aggrandizing the perceived *gravitas* of your juvenile, historyless, witless enemy, who merely apes past anti-semitic Euro-traditions of degradedness by shooting up Kosher markets; you're performing an "own-goal" in direct opposition to your avowed cause simply by letting them know your goat's been gotten. If no other criticism should move you, this should.

Your behavior suggests that you are not merely in a panic because your world-picture has been thrown into the trash pile of history like every other preceding world-picture (which is why I (being myself a fool) find it curious that you were so surprised when it happened with your own). Perhaps it is because you yourself have had doubts about its reality, its reliability, in your heart of hearts. Respectfully go sit in the corner and think hard about your actions and your attitude, pumpkins. Or not.

With no real concern for how any of you choose to actually conduct yourselves, I will continue my fantastic rant and unilaterally proclaim to the void of the fragmentorium, in celebration, the inauguration of a new, absolutely non-binding, draconian statutory regime criminalizing *insipidity*. In theory. This new regime will replace tired old fear-based regimes such as the terror war, drug war, "broken windows" policing, and other such farces. I have a million more outstanding policy replacement proposals in my bag of tricks, should anyone be interested.

In the process of attempting to come up with a way to describe the world to which I have returned after rolling around in my grave for over a hundred years, I find that I am not putting in much of a good word. Of course there is evidence that there are still traces of vitality, intelligence, and magnanimity in the human world, but they are all no longer headline-worthy today.

Wait … *I just heard a PROPHET speak.* His name is Willie Nelson. This prophet said (I paraphrase): "… it's not what goes *into* your mouth [e.g., presumably smoke] that's important, *it's what comes out of it*" (my italics, I think). This is a gracious rejection of the new social trend exalting, celebrating, and banalizing benighted audacity. Hail Willie. He makes a person think for a few seconds that we don't live in a hopeless human-all-too-human shit-show for which there is no more ridiculous precedent.

Most of what I have been saying is in response to the general "feel" of global virtual media culture, which has normalized the attitude of entitlement and willful ignorance, and about that, I am feeling speechless. *Hateful idiots have colonized our ears.* I find it interesting that we can close our eyes, but we have been ill-equipped, in one among a litany of other ways, by the fact that we have not been endowed with earlids. It is on the basis of this oversight of Nature or God, or no one, that I am forced to implement this new statutory regime regarding the things that come out of mouths. Don't worry, speech will remain protected as much as it has ever been. In name only.

The new statutory paradigm simply makes *cretinous barrel-bottomry* a punishable offense. Under the new regime, you can say whatever you want, but if you're a hateful pock of infectious human morbidity, you will be found to be in violation. It will be considered a grievously aggravating factor if you conduct yourself as such with no discernible material or psychological cause to do so.

You've had plenty of time to get it out of your system. That was part of your (being afforded the extraordinarily luxury of a) pre-trial. I went back up to the top of the mountain and waited and (of course) you didn't shut your mouths. Practicality and your behavior have re-educated me. Your dramatism belongs on the *literal* stage, not in the context from which that stage was meant to be a cathartic respite. I know as well as anyone that growing pains *really* hurt, but it's time to *graduate now*, pumpkins. Or not.

In the interest of egalitarianism, I must proclaim that I hate the Nazis and the Inquisition as much as, but in different ways than, I do ISIS and Pam Geller. All that matters is that they are all pod-sharing-peas of human depravity. So I say presently to the likes of Baghdadi, Geller, etc.: *You, too, shut your idiotic pie-holes.*

Welcome to the Fragmentorium! **143**

I'd truly rather be burned alive or beheaded on video than hear any of your voices. No more cretins within a quarter mile of a microphone or a firearm.

Oh, I forgot that firearms don't matter as much as microphones (especially for the sustainability of ISIS, which lives off the internet as much as The Donald does), and that the new microphone is televisual and internet media. The rules governing today's media include a prurience clause requiring that when the most unseemly of us give vocal or practical expressions of their sickness, all outlets are required to show the images, and talk about them *ad nauseam*. This indicates that the primary function of the media is to be the amplifier that broadcasts a message that would appear to anyone with a semblance of wisdom to be one of embarrassment concerning this species. Too bad this hypothetical statute is just a fantasy and nothing of any of this will ever change. In the meantime, I am returning to my much more comfortable grave. Enjoy the show!

Don't Tread on "My" Identity: Imaginary Victim Culture *(TY)*

I now return to face the fragmentorium from the point of view of my "real" identity, without the Kierkegaardian coyness involved in assuming the pseudonymous imaginary voice of a Nietzschean editorialist.

The latter-day profusion of lists of "politically incorrect" things that are frowned upon in contemporary public discourse is not rooted in the concern for offending some*one*, but rather in the concern to avoid stepping on a *sensibility theoretically occupiable by anyone*—not any actual individual, but a sensibility. They are protections against threats to categories of people, not actual individuals. The social identities we inhabit are, to say the least, borrowed, and like all identities, the ones available to us in the given moment in which we find ourselves are completely accidents of history and chance.

The chickens of Western chauvinism have come home to roost and we are now suffering a most ridiculous form of penance. We Westerners still want to dominate the world but we now want to do it with a perfectly clear conscience. Our (self-imposed) punishment is a condemnation to a (virtual) social world that interestingly enough resembles one of those (actual) poultry "farms" of today. In these, the birds are confined to a cubicle roughly equivalent to the size of the individual, and, despite the fact that there is no *actual* contact between individuals, there is no room to maneuver without causing a stir, and no way to cull the crowd to make room for any kind of fresh air. We're being factory farmed by ideas.

Our allocation of a higher value to relatively generic ways of thinking about ourselves ("identities"), of "knowing" ourselves as who we "are," than to the particular, idiosyncratic, concrete person each one of us is themselves at any given juncture, is confirmation that Kantianism is both alive and dead. It is alive in the sense that the generic is that on which we place ultimate value. It is dead in the sense that the prospects for a cosmopolitan enlightened civilization are at best dismal. The fact that a person has intrinsic value only in virtue of their non-particularity, in the sense that identities are not limited to manifestation in one individual at one moment, gives a far greater breadth of application to this proliferation of proscriptions of potential offense.

When we look at the socio-politico-cultural landscape in contemporary early twenty-first-century America (as it manifests itself via media), we see the total divorce of things traditionally bound to or at least associated with other things. *Everything is interchangeable*—everything has equal value and no value at all (except drama-value), just as the postmodernists say. All that matters is that you *have*, or occupy, an identity—*any* identity—what the substance of that identity consists in is immaterial—and even less important (absolutely irrelevant) is the concrete, actual, idiosyncratic individual occupying it. The real outliers are no longer those who hew to "marginal" identities, but those who eschew altogether the game of identity-acquisition, maintenance, defense, and celebration. Needless to say, those who do not derive a sense of the meaningfulness of their life from the above-mentioned game cannot be heard, if they speak at all, over the din of Trump-tweets, trending internet shaming videos on Youtube, and all the other inane digital noises that constitute the material of our latter day digital Forum.

You say there's a war on women? Well, what about the war on Christmas? You say there's racism? Well, what about reverse racism and the scapegoating of the police for all of society's problems? You say transgenders should be protected under the constitution? Well, what about freedom of religion? Blah! Blah! Blah!

The principal lesson of postmodernism is that the functional exchangeability, neutralization, and nullification of all identities in late modernity has undermined each one's specific unicity and hence, its viability. It seems we Western bonobo-chimpanzees are forever doomed to the habit of surpassing our reflexive concepts with our behaviors. At this rate, we will never catch up with ourselves. Look at the present manifestations of the American left and right in the 2016 election season. On the left you have a new push to sanitize expression, particularly, and not coincidentally, on virtual media (televisual and internet social media), a push on two fronts. On the one hand there is the sappy, post-racial, post-gender, post-(fill in the identity blank) feel-good front consisting of relatively naïve but newly sophisticated, slightly frontal-cortically immature students and administrators at colleges and universities. These Pollyannas manifest the socio-political durability of tissue paper. On the other front you have the hardcore liberal intellectual elite: bitter, cynical, often fascistic digital demagogues who have zero tolerance for the benightedness of the broad mass of Americans, whom the former despise precisely for *their* intolerance.

Who can blame either of them? How can you blame a generation who came up outside of history altogether for lacking perspective? From whence or whom is it supposed that they were to have gotten the perspective in question to begin with? Boomers and Gen-X-ers who (generally rightly) dismiss the often incom-prehensibly naïve rising chorus of millennial whiners must take their share of the blame—they were the ones who bred and created millennial culture to begin with—*and then blamed it on their children*. *They* (the pre-millennials) were the ones who insisted that all their children wear helmets on their bikes, who refused to give them the physical or ideological leeway to figure out how to navigate life on their own, who gave all of them participation trophies, and taught them constructive techniques of conflict resolution, and at the same time installed computers in their children's rooms as soon as they were available. Where would this inapt causal regression end? Whose fault is it that we are where we are now? We are always just arriving at the scene late enough never to have had a chance to do anything in the first place.

I can't blame the liberal chatterers for their contempt for the so-called "real" America—it's a crazy mixed up mess, and I don't forget it. Because the liberal elite, like the university students, are nothing but voices crying out in the digital wilderness, they seem to think they have no choice but to be hipsters and adopt the race-to-the-bottom rhetorical approach that rules in contemporary "discourse:" an all-out imaginary (not actual) war footing. Raging and hurting fragments. Where are all the ataractic voices? Holding their peace—at least in public, it would seem. The Dalai Lama is a refugee, and is just another faint and quaint fragment in the fragmentorium. To the extent that he gets any press coverage, he is just a reminder that wisdom is a joke in today's world. Those like the Dalai Lama, who remain relatively reticent and keep their mouths shut (or at least keep their voices down), are quixotic and irrelevant. The ones keeping the fragmentorium "alive" and interesting are the ones who know nothing of restraint. Each voice occupies his or her own distinct, fiercely guarded, and specific sensibility-bubble (fragmentary virtual life-world) from among whom one could draw essentially an infinity of different examples, from dismissive, defensive atheists behaving like inquisitors to so-called "Bernie or Bust" hard-liners who behave like the redneck Trump rally-goers they hate, etc.

Concurrently with the infinite proliferation of voices in the digital wilderness that we see on the left, we see also the return of the militia movement on the right (as seen, of course, on the internet), whose latest moment in the light of media significance was the recent occupation of an Oregon wildlife refuge by a group of rednecks led by Ammon Bundy, the scion of a newly emergent dynasty in the virtual militia movement, established by the latter's father, Cliven Bundy. Hilariously, this right-wing mirror image of the "Occupy Wall St." movement a few years earlier will undoubtedly have just about as little impact on policy as did the latter. When frustrated with unjust, threatening, anti-American institutions like the scheming, oppressive federal government or the heartless, kleptocratic economic elite, apparently the thing to do is go camping in a public place where camping is technically not allowed, and to stream video of it from your smartphone.

Because social and cultural events and processes occur solely via mediation, whether in the form of the cable news outlets, talk radio, blogs, or social media, most everyone is safe from anything actually happening to them. Their lifestyles have not changed much, a fact in direct conflict with the narratives being woven by both the left and the right, which share the common theme that their way of life, their identities, even their very existences, are under all-out attack in the contemporary social and political world. One of Ammon Bundy's thuggy side-kicks stated that they are hoping to inspire a broad movement of armed resistance against a government that has become tyrannical on a level comparable with that of Hitler's Germany. Though they have real guns and ammunition, being armed with guns is of infinitely less importance than being armed with an internet connection.

Even if they had substantial numbers and massive weaponry, I guarantee that the moment they got word that play-time was going to be forcibly ended, they would fold like the Iraqi army did in Mosul in 2015 when a small but determined ISIS contingent arrived. The reason why they would do so would not be cowardice but confusion, because the actual forum in which they are operating is not at all material but strictly imaginary and rhetorical. They would be baffled by the intrusion of reality into their virtual resistance game.

Commentators have lately expressed concern that the government is legitimizing the militia group by letting them alone, citing as a motive for restraint bad memories of the standoff in Waco in the 1990s. Ignoring them is actually the most brilliant approach authorities could possibly have taken because it constitutes an implicit recognition that these are just "boys being boys," who want to have a little harmless fun, but in a serious way, as it were, and beyond that, they *don't really count*. Notwithstanding the often-noted institutional racism in American law enforcement, on the basis of which it is most likely correctly assumed that a very different approach was taken to these white armed protesters than was taken to the black armed protesters raging around the same time in the streets of Ferguson, Missouri when another one of the countless white police officers involved in the death of unarmed black men walked free. My sense is that the Black Lives Matter protesters are a little more of a threat, if for no other reason than that their struggle has at least some connection to *actual*, not strictly imaginary, suffering, as in the case with the Bundy Posse out West.

The biggest threat the Bundy Boys will face is probably going to be the outraged birdwatchers who will more likely than anyone else run them out in defense of the sacred rights of certain species of wildlife. Just like the faith-hating "friendly" atheists who are sick of their world being run by idiots, the right wing militia in Oregon is first and foremost servicing an imaginary narrative about their own impending extinction in the face of *everything* else in the buzzing world of mediated human life.

In lieu of actual engagement, there is an endless verbal melee between actors and groups that involves no real contact between its ostensible mortal adversaries. The absolute real distance between interlocutors on an internet forum frees normal interactions from the trace of humanness that takes the decontextualized amplitude of road rage to another level altogether. Cyberbullying is another name for the tone of our entire virtual public exchange, not just among teenagers on

Facebook. It is fascinating to observe people suffering from real, excruciating feelings as they look upon a phosphorescing pane of plastic a foot or so in front of their faces. Simply fascinating. What would an observing alien possessed of the same capacities as us humans, but without the drama and vanity, make of us? We created all of this and it has trapped us. Internet culture warriors don't realize (duh!) that the exaggerated power to hurt feelings that virtual mediation gives to words applies apparently to themselves as much as they hope it does to their "enemies." It's so bafflingly irrational it's comical. It's a virtual reenactment of the tragic *lex talionis*, made even more sustainable because it has no real context, and it therefore has *no real consequences*.

The tactics used in right-wing actions like those led by Bundy are reminiscent of classically leftist actions of the '60s such as those taken by the SDS and the Black Panther Party but the circumstances couldn't be more different. The location in which their occupation is taking place is geographically in the middle of nowhere. Where would this "movement" be without the internet? The same place as was the now moribund "Occupy" movement and the Arab revolutionaries in their virtual fulgurations: nowhere.

Meanwhile, the left is busy trying to limit the rights of those who would speak their minds lest they "microaggress." The thing connecting all contemporary culture war campaigns is the realm from which their motivations arise. Now, *all* grievances come solely from the purely imaginary realm of ideology and identity. In the absence of real, material hardships, Americans fabricate their grievances using materials from the part of the world most central to their concerns: the imaginarium. Even in the relatively few cases where virtual cultural militancy arises from real hardships or concerns, it is *public recognition* and *normative legitimacy* that they are seeking above all else. That recognition need not depend on relatively rare windfalls like the passing of laws or Supreme Court decisions, because legitimacy can be acquired by "crowd sourcing" rhetorical engagement on a mass virtual scale. One of the most convenient aspects of this system is the fact that it is of no significance whatsoever whether this engagement comes in the form of glowing affirmations or vitriolic excoriations, because either way, *any* engagement increases virtual legitimacy. This is our new virtual hyperdemocracy. Solving the actual purported problems that are the ostensible reasons for the involvements to begin with would put an end to the priceless prospect of continuing to participate in this game indefinitely. This may be what Baudrillard means when he hyperbolically claims that the "real is dead." It's not that there is no such thing as reality any more, it's just that it no longer has anything like the value that imaginative significance in the mind-world of the fragmentorium has. How do you measure your value? By how many twitter followers you have.

This does not mean that the psychological grievances arising from one's being deprived of normative recognition in the fragmentorium-imaginarium are not felt as strongly or taken as seriously as traditional, actual motivations—it's just that now *perceived* grievances are all that matter: no one can argue with me about my feelings! One of the results of this is that it is nearly impossible to anticipate all the potential ways in which one's words or actions might aggrieve someone else. Virtualized public intercourse is a carnival of practical triviality and normative solemnity. The fact that it takes place outside of actuality allows us to service the militant chimp aspect of our nature, simply skip the boring, messy process of real engagement, risk, and their consequences, and go directly to the dramatic. Safely. Because, as part chimpanzee, it appears that we love fighting itself more than anything actual over which one might have assumed that rational people would be willing to take a principled stand. We have finally reached the original goal of the Euro-romance: to live exclusively in the realm of the narrative, outside actuality altogether. The requirement of an alibi has passed into desuetude. The right is asserting its right not to have their *ideas*, which, like those on the left, *have become synonymous with their identities*, impugned or taken away from them, *not* their land or their homes and families, as is the experience of the Syrians. There is no organicity or autochthony to the fulgurations of concerns voiced in the fragmentorium. Most of the Malheur Wildlife Refuge occupiers, once again, are *carpetbaggers*. Participants in the Bundy-led occupation are at once integral players in the virtual sphere and interlopers in the practical sphere.

Actual, physical location is irrelevant in the fragmentorium. They are all, on the left and right, living in a phantom world where action rationally based on real material conditions has little or no meaning. For latter-day bonobo-chimpanzees, there is nothing of consequence outside the fragmentorium-imaginarium (the shared mind-world) of simulation.

Civilization is Mono(mania)culture *(TY)*

Civilization, when considered at a distance, in strictly *a posteriori* terms, is not entirely dissimilar to cancer. Like the latter, it appears to be a kind of anomalous, independent, patterned growth that is at once native and alien to, the host from which it arises. Civilization is of the earth, but has its own independent life, and certainly its own agenda. Because it appears to answer to no other logic than infinite self-replication and expansion, it seems that, like a cancerous growth, it is in the end unsustainable for both itself and its host. This observation is in no way normative: there is as little point in getting outraged at human beings for being the brilliant idiots who created a civilization that they lost control of as there is in getting angry at cancer when it strikes. Civilization, at least in its Western-dominated instantiation, appears to be on the path to self-destruction, and it looks like it's going to take the rest of terrestrial life down with it.

At the moment, civilization has conduced to the unprecedented and clearly anomalous runaway proliferation of one of the perhaps trillions of life forms the earth has generated over the eons. It is impossible to say for sure whether the same thing would have occurred had Western civilization not been the dominant

Welcome to the Fragmentorium! 149

one. I suspect those other tribes, given the chance, would probably have come up with their own brand of train wreck, but it is pointless to speculate.

The terrestrial autoimmunological problem of civilization in its present form seems to have originated in the shift away from the more "primitive" scenario in which tribes were more concerned with *destroying* their enemies than conquering and co-opting them into their own ways of life. What started with the Macedonians and achieved escape velocity with the Romans, was the specific logic of the West's emerging culture, which supercharged civilization as such by *economizing* everything. Sure, their military and political leaders certainly undertook conquest and expansion at least partly for such old fashioned aneconomical reasons as the pursuit of glory and power for its own sake, but, unlike the Mongols, for example, once established, Roman civilization sought for the first time to reap and preserve the fruits of their conquests, to build *value(s)*. Civilization, on this view, is not a one-off, but a going concern.

According to the testimony of literature and histories, the pre-golden age Greeks (and all other early-, pre- or "un"-civilized groups) were more Battaillean in their warfare, as in most aspects of their living. They did not yet undertake to make *building* their principal endeavor. We are living with the legacy of the idea that, once the sword has done its initial work, the pen takes over and creates something *much harder to be rid of*: culture, and the creation of culture is what the West, it seems to me, has done more successfully than any other civilization.

War and its incessant threat of return keeps a check on both the physical and imaginative overgrowth of the human species, especially in its old-fashioned form, in which threats were not simply contained, but enemy societies were annihilated when defeated. It is what was most likely for millennia humankind's way of maintaining itself in a sustainable balance with the world. War is a disease, one that recurrently plagues humankind, but, as horrific as it is, it has been remarkably ineffectual in exterminating the human species. Civilization, on the other hand, trumps war in the measure of its totally con-/destructive potential and aim. By the latter duality, I refer to the fact that the logic of civilization is unchecked growth, non-stop building, in equal measure materially and conceptually. No one, it seems, can argue with the idea of building, of creating. It is both sublime and an indication of commodious life. It is deceptive in this way, because when one takes the long view, never-ending *con*-struction leads to what appears to be the imminent *de*-struction of the planet and, with it, the very apes who will have constructed their way out of existence. Once civilization gets its unlikely foothold by circumventing the terrestrial immune response that things like plagues and wars and such used to constitute, at least in the form it took in the West, it is like a cancer on the track to metastasis. What intervention is there to remedy this situation? I hear Heidegger mumbling in the background. Something about God.

It would appear that the formula for the success of civilization is similar to that of our latter-day agricultural practices, i.e., the most successful civilizations are monocultures. Human bonobo-chimpanzees are Ghazālian slavish conformists, and this is the reason why monocultures are more easily established than a world of many actually diverse ones. It is my relatively inexpert understanding that many of the agricultural monocultures we have established throughout the arable lands of the planet today are disasters waiting to happen on a massive scale whenever some new pathogen finds a weakness in the handful of principal strains of crops we have bet our future as a species on. Monocultures of the civilizational sort, ones whose lack of any sense of balance or restraint is as thoroughgoing as their uniformity, are perhaps equally unsustainable on account of their extreme exceptionalism and the insane scale on which they occur, which exponentially expands the potential array of their consequences.

Maybe I am being hyperbolic when I compare culture to cancer but it seems they are both monomaniacally obsessed with *building*. For example, I have always been intrigued at how rarely the core capitalist notion that "growth" *must always* occur is challenged. There can be no times of rest, or even simply the adoption of an economy that exactly matches the material, actual needs of the human species (neither growth nor contraction), which would only grow as a material necessity in proportion to the population.

Even this wouldn't address the unfortunately essential consideration that we humans have already, by any realistic measure, far exceeded our physically, ecologically sustainable, limits (nearly 7 *billion* of us (!), and not shrinking), so even if we suddenly became "responsible" and instituted draconian population controls and enforced an economy that did nothing more than maintain us materially, (calorically), we still would probably not last. Unfortunately, as far as I can tell (based on strictly *a posteriori* considerations), there are simply way too many of us, and barring a similar scenario to the one depicted in P.D. James' *The Children of Men*, whereby we simply stop proliferating, a lasting vision of a human future seems unrealistic. And that's just addressing the material side of things.

Lately (historically), pan-capitalism, the turbo-charging retrofit capping off the West's historical tumescence, can be pointed to as a significant part of the problem. We could speak of the intrinsic and historical failings of other systems, but capitalism is all that we now have. It is another of our creations that we have disowned as an excuse to avoid facing the tasks involved in reckoning with our existence as a society, and now as a species. God forbid we simply use the *science* and *technology* that we so brilliantly came up with and *ardently love* to figure out how to manage needs and risks without resort to the magical thinking that is the dogmatic capitalist ideology (duh!, again).

We created this system, but we assume that we are powerless to change or replace it because it is conceptually underwritten by our metaphysics. That metaphysical anchoring has always served to displace our responsibility for having brought it, like every other system we have devised, into existence. We misrecognize it as the product not of our own doing, but of some extra-human process, power, or principle. It is but another example of us playing God and

Welcome to the Fragmentorium! **151**

then disavowing responsibility for what we have wrought. You say capitalists are rational? Well, a few of them have a lot of material wealth anyway, but does this wealth translate proportionally into an improved mental life? Not as far as I've seen. Idiot billionaires compete with each other based on the size of their yachts, just as today's Republican presidential hopefuls compete on the basis of the size of their "hands." Give an ape a bunch of money and he will remain that same ape, only with more means to demonstrate it.

Building, which is what (empirically) civilization does, looks to escape time and materiality through the erection of monuments and the cultivation of legacies, which take what appears as enduring form in the serialized iterations of the collective consciousnesses of human beings. In *practice*, the final result of post-modern, technologically mediated civilization (and its aftermath) has been globalization and the promotion of a monocultural "multiculturalism" that stands for everything and nothing all at once.

Ironically, the anti-Kantian approach taken by the pre-golden age Greeks and others, like the Mongols, may have been the technique with the greatest likelihood of actually saving the species from extinction. Kantianism, which won the battle for "perpetual peace" between civilization and savagery (although not at all in the way it envisioned that victory), will surely kill us all, eventually, one way or another. It is ironic that the human practice of making themselves ends-in-themselves appears to be the best way they have found to simply end themselves.

We brilliantly idiotic bonobo-chimpanzees have availed ourselves of the capacity to re-write the material rules of nature at every step of the game, which has enabled our exponential expansion as a species. Civilization does not merely create the *material* problem of the destruction of life on the planet in a multitude of ways with its incessant interventionism, i.e., it is not all about quantity. It is also about *quality*. Our culture has raced toward the erasure of everything real about human life by creating an arena in which people have been able to substitute increasingly imaginary forms of living for the actual ones we used to have no choice but to accept.

Civilization (at least in the modern West), as Irving Babbitt says, lacks a robust self-restraining mechanism, and he wrote that thought in 1932. Unchecked appetitivism has now become a characteristic not just of the culture at large, but of the individual people who make up our civilization. This is evidenced, among other ways, in the fact that the growing epidemic of obesity has now been exported even to relatively extremely poor countries. I have read that overweight people in some of these countries are at once overweight and malnourished, likely because all they can get their hands on is things like Coca-Cola and other such nutritionally empty "food" products. Babbitt's concerns had not to do principally with material, physical limits as a preventive against ecological destruction, but rather with the diminution in the quality of life that occurs proportionally with the voracity of the entity under consideration. Empirically, the *frein vital* is an idea(l) only, at least for civilization writ large. Individuals can practice it, living inside the madhouse, but not "drinking the kool-ade," with the benefit of a little perspective and a sense of humor of cosmic proportions. We will likely never see a civilization that takes to heart Babbitt's recommendations. This is the un-Kantian view of the end of history.

Our shared system of consciousness is designed to minimize, even do away with, the kind of higher consciousness involved in philosophical reflection that would be required to properly understand the situation into which we have gotten ourselves, much less extricate ourselves from. This is to say nothing about the vital capacity and psychological wherewithal that turning around the aircraft carrier that is civilization would entail. Such a project would involve far more dedication and sacrifice than was required to build the thing in the first place. When we are not consuming some actual object, we have our faces down, looking at our phones. When we are doing neither, we are thinking about doing both. I know that's hyperbole, but barely. On a daily basis, I almost run over people on the streets who no longer bother looking for traffic because they are absorbed in their phones. The medical branch of orthopedics is going to have a gold mine on its hands in twenty years or so when all the millennials go in to have their cervical vertebrae repaired for all the downward craning they will have been doing over those years.

The durability of the Donald Trump candidacy signifies the true end of the concern for reality in America. Finally, we have achieved the *total* disengagement from both reality and the quaint old practice of adherence to a semblance of rationality and decency in the election season. Perhaps, in this light, it is in fact *no longer cynical*: we have returned to a state of pre-sagacity to which the capacity for cynicism does not apply, like Nietzsche's image of the child, but not at all in the way he envisaged it. With the legitimation of all culture in the globalized world of today, there is *no outside* of culture (the text) (except in outlying minds). *Everyone* is infected with the madness—it can only work if that is the case; it ensures that there will be no uninfected jury to whom to appeal for a "reasonable" evaluation and diagnosis.

It is the cultivation of technology in the West and the rise of the culture of interventionism that has made possible this broadly shared delusionality and the concomitant near universal misunderstanding that we are all acting relatively practically and rationally and that nothing is amiss. If a problem results from one of our interventions, rather than re-think our myopic, audacious, and Franken-steinian mania for interventionism *itself* (not the purported *raison d'être* for any individual intervention), our first thought is: "There's got to be some other intervention we can make to 'correct' the unforeseen consequences of the preceding one." Never do we step back for a moment to gain perspective on the situation because we know that doing so would reveal that interventionism is the madness that must be done away with itself if we are to return to reality at all *and we don't want to give it up.* Freud was right, reality bites! We remain in the thinking that sees interventions as the only path forward, the only path *anywhere* from here,

Welcome to the Fragmentorium! 153

which is exactly where we want to go. This is what Baudrillard means when he claims that virtuality is our only horizon. We are living in our own psycho-drama and reference to reality is not only out of place, but has become a joke.

In the mediated world of contemporary Western consciousness, we find ourselves in a fragmentorium made up of an infinite number of possible interests, identities, and ideologies,[1] an imaginarium peopled with quasi-monadic vehicles of cultural signification in which individual minds reside and fight for their legitimacy with little regard for anything else. The only point of rhetorical convergence between this infinity of identities promoting themselves in the culture wars of today is a shared sense of outrage born of the paranoid, narcissistic "experience" of persecution and victimization. It is a perpetual culture war carried out under the Bush doctrine of (actually) universally offensive pre-emption-as-(imaginative) defense.

It is unfortunate for those nostalgic for the idea of actuality, who wish to really do something about things like poverty, racism, violence against women, the loss of American "greatness," or any such actual issue, that we have replaced the critical practice of de-legitimizing the oppressive practices and master-narratives of the Euro-legacy with the easier goal of simply legitimizing *all* narratives. This solves the problem of hegemony, but at the cost of trivializing *everything*.

We have attempted in this work to provide another lens through which to consider the human being and its mind both in empirical, material terms and in ideational, cultural terms, as the kind of being whose current and past behaviors can at least in part be explained by thinking of them as apes who crave significance in any form they can find it. The anthropological upshot is not so much that every person, every group, every identity, has as much claim to legitimacy as any other in a world bereft of ultimaticity. It is rather that they all *pine so* for it. This pining for significance is the engine of narrativism. Couple together that engine with *any kind of machine*, and it will do something for sure. We humans are a wily lot and we will take any action that serves our immediate purpose, usually with an enthusiasm that matches proportionally our lack of foresight into, or care for, its likely consequences.

Serio-Comic Relief? *(TY)*

Everywhere in virtual society identities, the units of imaginative significance that make up the material of the fragmentorium onto which human minds glom, are more important themselves than the practical benefits one would assume they are (or were once) valued for. Asserting their "rights" to share the road with cars, cyclists are willing to risk their lives by defensively riding abreast on the streets in protest of (potential or actual) unaccommodating motorists. Many in the deaf community have faced their own struggle with deciding whether or not to be fitted with cochlear implants that would restore or establish the capacity to hear. In the cases where they are refusing such treatments, it is because of the fact that they *value their deafness as part of their identity*, and that perhaps that identity matters more than physical function. There is no need to make individual value judgments as to the wisdom or folly of these and other examples of identity-mania, just to note that they form the topography of our virtual social world.

The quest for legitimacy and normative recognition is a function of the fact that the will to power, as Nietzsche understood it, no longer holds sway (if it ever did), except in as much as perceived power, for the average meaningless person like you or me, is now figurative and cultural rather than principally material. Power, or, more accurately, "feeling empowered," comes now from rhetorical status in a given social situation with little connection to materiality. The Nietzschean idea of the will to power is much more simplistic and far too literal to be applicable in today's social world, as it anachronistically assumes an autochthonous ego at the center of its idea of the human subject. The victim culture is the reverse—an *a posteriori* refutation of Nietzsche's idea. We appear to have lost the "instinct" for *actual* self-promotion and we can only do it with the (at least imaginative) help of others. Today, no one simply seeks to take anything for themselves on their own terms. Instead, to have one's rights to something enshrined formally in public discourse and practice is infinitely more important than the actual enjoyment of the original, ostensible object of that right itself. Everyone wants his or her sacred identity respected. The will to power is perhaps something still in effect, but it is not practiced by individual humans. It is practiced, rather *on* humans, by *human creations*—world-views and cultures. Absurdly, *these* are asserting their will to power over us meaningless blobs of minded flesh who provide occupation-settings for their proliferation and durability.

The serio-comic attitude is put forth here as an antidote to the lust for meaning and the wars, actual and virtual, that it spawns, which make up the fragmentorium. The serio-comic attitude is *practical* because it arises from the overcoming or refusal of the quest for transcendent meaning of any kind. It is a fundamental alternative to the regnant attitude of today because it is erosive of the seductive power of fascistic demagoguery, ideological intolerance, and dogmatism of *every* kind. It is part of an idiosyncratic culture whose purpose is the cultivation of practical rational hedonism ("impure" practical reason), and the acceptance of reality rather than ignoring or fighting against it. It is the approach to life that succeeds what is now an anachronistic ego-philosophy, the last legacy of modernism as embodied in existentialism, which, one notes, conspicuously lacked an ascendant sense of humor. The serio-comic successor to ego philosophy that is being adopted here is based on something much more akin to the Buddhist quest for self-overcoming and the sense of not taking oneself so seriously that that effort can foment, as an alternative to the high-stakes, mindless dramatism of Euro-romantic anthropo-narcissism.

The serio-comic attitude says that one of the worst mistakes one can make is to take *anything* too seriously, but *especially* to take *at all* seriously others who themselves take things too seriously. It is not your fault, but by apparent virtue of your

Welcome to the Fragmentorium! **155**

bonobo-chimpanzee nature, you are much more than likely, at least on occasion, somewhat *ridiculous*. So am I. One is incapable of truly not taking others too seriously until one understands that we are *ourselves* all at least a little ridiculous.

We have on the whole lost what trace of a sense of humor we may have had, and it is not the *actual things* that people take seriously that are of significance, but instead the fact that generally speaking we seem to need *something, anything* to take seriously as a condition for living. It is hard to understand how anyone who turns on a television or logs on to the internet does not see this.

The serio-comic attitude is the best possible defense against the risk of self- or other-induced suffering that one may experience at the hands of mere ideas. In the words of exemplary radical phenomenologist of mind George Clinton, "Free your mind [from the spirit of seriousness] and your ass will follow!" Buddhism had this figured out a long time ago: forget yourself and there is nothing to defend or hold up in any way. I know that's infinitely more easily said than done, but it is what it is ... If you are not satisfied with the anthropological approach to the scourge of excessive seriousness, consider it from the practical angle, and ask yourself, in the words of my now late co-author from the opening of this chapter: "What can I do? (nothing) This is the way it is. *What the hell can I do about it? (nothing): Who cares?* (not me)."

Note

1 I owe the formulation of these concepts in this triadic form to my student, Lauren Heintz.

BIBLIOGRAPHY

Adorno, Theodor and Max Horkheimer. *Dialectic of Enlightenment*. Translated by John Cumming. New York: Continuum, 1995.

Alexander, Samuel. *Space, Time and Deity*, 2 vols. New York: Humanities Press, 1950.

Al-Ghazālī. *The Incoherence of the Philosophers*. Translated by Michael E. Marmura. Provo: Brigham Young University Press, 1997.

Al-Ghazālī. *Deliverance from Error*. Translated by R.J. McCarthy. Louisville: Fons Vitae, 1999.

Althusser, Louis. *For Marx*. Translated by Ben Brewster. London: Verso, 1965.

Althusser, Louis. *Lenin and Philosophy and Other Essays*. Translated by Ben Brewster. New York: Monthly Review, 1971.

Althusser, Louis and Etienne Balibar. *Reading Capital*. Translated by Ben Brewster. London: Verso, 1997.

Babbitt, Irving. "What I Believe." *Forum* 83(1930): 80–87.

Battaille, Georges. *The Accursed Share*, 2 vols. Translated by Robert Hurley. New York: Zone Books, 1991.

Baudelaire, Charles. *The Flowers of Evil*. Edited by Marthiel Matthews and Jackson Matthews. New York: New Directions, 1989.

Baudrillard, Jean. *Symbolic Exchange and Death*. Translated by Iain Hamilton Grant. London: Sage, 1976.

Baudrillard, Jean. *Fatal Strategies*. Translated by Phillipe Beitchman and W.G.J. Nieslu- chowski. Los Angeles: Semiotext(e), 1990.

Baudrillard, Jean. *The Transparency of Evil*. Translated by James Benedict. London: Verso, 1993.

Baudrillard, Jean. *Simulacra and Simulations*. Translated by Sheila Faria Glaser. Ann Arbor: The University of Michigan Press, 1994.

Baudrillard, Jean. *The Perfect Crime*. Translated by Chris Turner. London: Verso, 1996.

Benjamin, Walter. *Illuminations*. Translated by Harry Zohn. New York: Schocken Books, 1969.

Bergson, Henri. *Time and Free Will: An Essay on the Immediate Data of Consciousness*. Translated by F.L. Pogson. Mineola: Dover, 2001.

Bibliography **157**

The Bhagavad-Gita. Translated by Eknath Easwaran. Tomales: Niligri Press, 2007.

Blanchot, Michel. *Writing the Disaster.* Translated by Ann Smock. Lincoln: University of Nebraska Press, 1995.

Buchler, Justus. *Toward a General Theory of Human Judgment.* New York: Columbia University Press, 1951.

Camus, Albert. *The Stranger.* Translated by Matthew Ward. New York: Kopf Doubleday, 1993.

Camus, Albert. *The Myth of Sisyphus.* Translated by Justin O'Brien. London: Penguin, 2000.

Cawley, A.C., ed., *Everyman.* In *Everyman and Medieval Miracle Plays,* 195–225. London: J. M. Dent, 1993.

Cioran, E.M. *The Fall into Time.* Chicago: Quadrangle Books, 1970.

Cioran, E.M. *The Temptation to Exist.* Translated by Richard Howard. London: Quartet Books, 1987.

Darwin, Charles. *On the Origin of the Species by Means of Natural Selection.* New York: Dover, 2006.

DeBord, Guy. "Theory of the Dérive." First published 1956. Translated by Ken Knabb. *Situationist International Online.* Accessed July 25, 2016. www.cddc.vt.edu/sionline/si/theory.html.

DeBord, Guy. *The Society of the Spectacle.* Translated by Donald Nicholson-Smith. New York: Zone Books, 1994.

Derrida, Jacques. *Speech and Phenomena and Other Essays.* Translated by David B. Allison. Evanston: Northwestern University Press, 1973.

Derrida, Jacques. *Of Grammatology.* Translated by Gayatri Chakravorty Spivak. Baltimore: The Johns Hopkins University Press, 1976.

Derrida, Jacques. *Writing and Difference.* Translated by Alan Bass. Chicago: University of Chicago Press, 1978.

Derrida, Jacques. "Force of Law: The 'Mystical Foundation of Authority.'" In *Deconstruction and the Possibility of Justice.* Edited by Drucilla Cornell, Michael Rosenfeld, and David Gray Carlson, 3–67. New York: Routledge, 1992.

Descartes, Rene. *Meditations on First Philosophy.* Translated by Laurence J. Lafleur. New York: Macmillan, 1960.

deWaal, Frans. *Our Inner Ape.* New York: Riverhead Books, 2005.

deWaal, Frans and Robert Wright, Christine M. Korsgaard, Phillip Kitcher, and Peter Singer. *Primates and Philosophers: How Morality Evolved.* Princeton: Princeton University Press, 2006.

deWaal, Frans. *The Bonobo and the Atheist: In Search of Humanism Among the Primates.* New York: W.W. Norton, 2013.

Dewey, John. *Experience and Nature.* New York: Dover, 1958.

Dewey, John. *The Quest for Certainty.* Vol. 4 of *John Dewey: The Later Works, 1925–1953.* Carbondale: Southern Illinois University Press, 1988.

Donne, John. "Now, This Bell Tolling Softly for Another, Tells Me: Thou Must Die." In *Devotions Upon Emergent Occasions and Death's Duel, 102–107.* New York: Vintage, 1999.

Dostoevsky, Feodor. *The Brothers Karamazov.* Translated by Andrew H. MacAndrew. Toronto: Bantam, 1981.

Dostoevsky, Feodor. *Notes from Underground.* Translated by Richard Pevear and Larissa Volokhonsky. New York: Vintage, 1994.

Eco, Umberto. "Postmodernism, Irony, the Enjoyable." In *Reflections on The Name of the Rose.* Translated by William Weaver, 65–72. London: Secker and Warburg, 1985.

158 Bibliography

Foucault, Michel. *The Order of Things: An Archaeology of the Human Sciences.* New York: Vintage, 1970.

Foucault, Michel. *The Archaeology of Knowledge.* Translated by A.M. Sheridan Smith. New York: Pantheon, 1972.

Foucault, Michel. *Discipline and Punish.* Translated by Alan Sheridan. New York: Vintage, 1977.

Foucault, Michel. *The Essential Works of Foucault*, 3 vols. Edited by Paul Rabinow. New York: The New Press, 2000.

Freud, Sigmund. *Totem and Taboo.* Translated by James Strachey. New York: W.W. Norton, 1950.

Freud, Sigmund. *Beyond the Pleasure Principle.* Translated by James Strachey. New York: Bantam Books, 1959.

Freud, Sigmund. *Sigmund Freud: Collected Papers*, 5 vols. Edited by Ernest Jones. New York: Basic Books, 1959.

Freud, Sigmund. *The Ego and the Id.* Translated by Joan Riviere. New York: W.W. Norton, 1960.

Freud, Sigmund. *The Future of an Illusion.* Translated by James Strachey. New York: W. W. Norton, 1961.

Freud, Sigmund. "Transference." In *Introductory Lectures on Psychoanalysis.* Translated by James Strachey, 431–447. New York: W.W. Norton, 1966.

Grant, George. *Time as History.* Toronto: CBC Learning Systems, 1969.

Groddeck, Georg. *The Book of the It.* Translated by V.M.E. Collins. New York: Vintage, 1961.

Habermas, Jurgen. *Legitimation Crisis.* Translated by Thomas A. McCarthy. Boston: Beacon Press, 1975.

Habermas, Jurgen. *The Theory of Communicative Action*, 2 vols. Translated by Thomas A. McCarthy. Boston: Beacon Press, 1984.

Hegel, G.W.F. *Phenomenology of Spirit.* Translated by A.V. Miller. Oxford: Oxford University Press, 1977.

Heidegger, Martin. *Being and Time.* Translated by John Macquarrie and Edward Robinson. San Francisco: Harper, 1962.

Heidegger, Martin. "Only a God Can Save Us: Der Spiegel's Interview with Martin Heidegger." *Philosophy Today* 20(1976): 267–283.

Heidegger, Martin. *The Question Concerning Technology and Other Essays.* Translated by William Lovitt. San Francisco: Harper, 1977.

Heidegger, Martin. *Nietzsche Volume 4: Nihilism.* Translated by Frank A. Capuzzi. San Francisco: Harper Collins, 1982.

Heraclitus. "Fragments." In *The Presocratics.* Edited by Phillip Wheelwright, 64–89. New York: Macmillan, 1966.

Hobbes, Thomas. *Man and Citizen (De Homine and De Cive).* Edited by Bernard Gert. Indianapolis: Hackett, 1991.

Hobbes, Thomas. *Leviathan.* Edited by Richard Flathman. New York: Norton, 1997.

Holmes, Oliver Wendell, Sr. *The Professor at the Breakfast Table.* Boston: Houghton Mifflin, 1891.

Hume, David. *An Enquiry Concerning Human Understanding.* Indianapolis: Hackett, 1977.

Huntington, Samuel. *The Clash of Civilizations.* New York: Simon and Schuster, 1996.

Huppke, Rex W. 2015. "'The Comedians' – a Fine Show About Work." *Chicago Tribune* (July 10, 2015). www.chicagotribune.com/business/careers/ct-huppke-work-advi ce-0713-biz-20150710-column.html.

Husserl, Edmund. *Ideas: General Introduction to Pure Phenomenology*. Translated by W.R. Boyce Gibson. New York: Collier, 1962.

Husserl, Edmund. "Philosophy as a Rigorous Science." In *Phenomenology and the Crisis of Philosophy*. Translated by Quentin Lauer, 71–147. New York: Harper, 1965.

Husserl, Edmund. *Logical Investigations*, 2 vols. Translated by J. N. Findlay. New York: Routledge, 1982.

James, P.D. *The Children of Men*. New York: Alfred A. Knopf, 1992.

James, William. *The Principles of Psychology*, 2 vols. New York: Dover, 1950.

James, William. *Essays in Radical Empiricism*. New York: Dutton, 1971.

James, William. *The Meaning of Truth*. Amherst: Prometheus, 1997.

Kant, Immanuel. *Critique of Pure Reason*. Translated by Norman Kemp Smith. Boston: Bedford/St. Martin's, 1929.

Kant, Immanuel. *Critique of Practical Reason*. Translated by Lewis White Beck. Indianapolis: Bobbs-Merrill, 1956.

Kant, Immanuel. *Religion within the Limits of Reason Alone*. Translated by Theodore M. Greene and Hoyt Hudson. New York: Harper Torchbooks, 1960.

Kant, Immanuel. *Kant: Political Writings*. Edited by Hans Reiss. Cambridge: Cambridge University Press, 1991.

Kazantzakis, Nikos. *Zorba the Greek*. New York: Simon and Schuster, 1959.

Kierkegaard, Søren. *The Concept of Dread*. Translated by Walter Lowrie. Princeton: Princeton University Press, 1957.

Kierkegaard, Søren. *Philosophical Fragments*. Translated by Howard V. Wong. Princeton: Princeton University Press, 1962.

Kierkegaard, Søren. *Concluding Unscientific Postscript*. Translated by David F. Swenson. Princeton: Princeton University Press, 1974.

Kierkegaard, Søren. *Fear and Trembling*. Translated by Sylvia Walsh. Cambridge: Cambridge University Press, 2006.

Kristeva, Julia. *Strangers to Ourselves*. Translated by Leon S. Roudiez. New York: Columbia University Press, 1991.

Kuhn, Thomas. *The Structure of Scientific Revolutions*. Chicago: University of Chicago Press, 1962.

Leibniz, Gottfried W. "The Principles of Philosophy, or the Monadology." In *Leibniz: Philosophical Essays*, translated by Roger Ariew, 213–224. Indianpolis: Hackett, 1989.

Levinas, Emmanuel. *Otherwise Than Being, or Beyond Essence*. Translated by Alphonso Lingis. Dordrecht: Kluwer, 1974.

Locke, John. *An Essay Concerning Human Understanding*. New York: J.M. Dent, 1961.

Lyotard, Jean-Francois. *The Postmodern Condition: A Report on Knowledge*. Translated by Geoff Bennington and Brian Massumi. Minneapolis: University of Minnesota Press, 1984.

Machiavelli, Niccolo. *The Prince*. Translated by Luigi Ricci. Revised by E.R.P. Vincent. New York: Penguin, 1952.

Marcuse, Herbert. *Eros and Civilization*. New York: Vintage, 1962.

Marcuse, Herbert. *One Dimensional Man*. Boston: Beacon Press, 1964.

Martin, George R.R. *A Game of Thrones*. New York: Bantam, 1996.

Marx, Karl. "The Eighteenth Brumaire of Louis Bonaparte." In *Marx: Later Political Writings*. Edited by Terrell Carver, 31–127. Cambridge: Cambridge University Press, 1996.

160 Bibliography

Marx, Karl and Friedrich Engels. *The German Ideology*. Amherst, New York: Prometheus Books, 1998.

Meillassoux, Quentin. *After Finitude*. Translated by Ray Brassier. London: Bloomsbury, 2006.

Newman, John Henry. *An Essay in Aid of a Grammar of Assent*. New York: Doubleday, 1958.

Nietzsche, Friedrich. *Twilight of the Idols*. In *The Portable Nietzsche*. Edited by Walter Kaufmann, 463–563. New York: Viking Press, 1954.

Nietzsche, Friedrich. *Beyond Good and Evil*. Translated by Walter Kaufmann. New York: Vintage, 1966.

Nietzsche, Friedrich. *The Will to Power*. Translated by Walter Kaufmann and R.J. Hollingdale. New York: Vintage, 1968.

Nietzsche, Friedrich. *On the Genealogy of Morals*. Translated by Walter Kaufmann. New York: Vintage, 1969.

Nietzsche, Friedrich. *The Gay Science*. Translated by Walter Kaufmann. New York: Penguin, 1974.

Nietzsche, Friedrich. *Human, All Too Human*. Translated by Marion Faber. Lincoln: University of Nebraska Press, 1984.

Nietzsche, Friedrich. *Daybreak*. Translated by R.J. Hollingdale. Cambridge: Cambridge University Press, 1997.

Ortega y Gasset, José. "The Self and the Other." In *The Dehumanization of Art and Other Essays on Art, Culture, and Literature*. Translated by Willard R. Trask, 175–204. Princeton: Princeton University Press, 1968.

Perry, Ralph Baron. *The Moral Economy*. New York: Charles Scribner's and Sons, 1909.

Pierce, C.S. *Philosophical Writings of Pierce*. Edited by Justus Buchler. New York: Dover, 1955.

Plato. *The Republic*. Translated by B. Jowett. Garden City: Anchor Press, 1973.

Poniewozik, James. "Caitlyn Jenner and Jazz Jennings Reveal Remarkable Women Living Amid the Mundane." *Time* vol. 186, 8(2015).

Rorty, Richard. *Philosophy and the Mirror of Nature*. Princeton: Princeton University Press, 1979.

Santayana, George. *Dominations and Powers: Reflections on Liberty, Society, and Government*. New York: Scribner's, 1951.

Santayana, George. *Scepticism and Animal Faith*. New York: Dover, 1955.

Sartre, Jean-Paul. *Nausea*. Translated by Lloyd Alexander. New York: New Directions, 1949.

Sartre, Jean-Paul. *Being and Nothingness: A Phenomenological Essay on Ontology*. Translated by Hazel E. Barnes. New York: Washington Square Press, 1956.

Sartre, Jean-Paul. *The Words: The Autobiography of Jean-Paul Sartre*. Translated by Bernard Frechtman. New York: Vintage, 1981.

Scheler, Max. *Man's Place in Nature*. Translated by Hans Meyerhoff. New York: Noonday, 1961.

Scheler, Max. *Problems of a Sociology of Knowledge*. Translated by Manfred S. Frings. London: Routledge and Kegan Paul, 1980.

Schopenhauer, Arthur. *The World as Will and Representation*, 2 vols. Translated by E.F.J. Payne. New York: Dover, 1968.

Shestov, Lev. *Athens and Jerusalem*. Translated by Bernard Martin. New York: Clarion, 1966.

Simmel, Georg. "How is Society Possible?" *American Journal of Sociology* 16 (November, 1910): 372–391.

Solanas, Valerie. *SCUM Manifesto*. London: Verso, 2004.

Spinoza, Benedict de. *Ethics*. Translated by R.H.M. Elwes. Amherst: Prometheus Books, 1989.

Stekel, Wilhelm. *The Autobiography of Wilhelm Stekel*. Edited by Emil A. Gutheil. New York: Liveright, 1950.

Stirner, Max. *The Ego and its Own*. Translated by Steven T. Byington. Mineola: Dover, 2005.

Unamuno, Miguel de. *Tragic Sense of Life*. Translated by J.E. Crawford Fitch. New York: Dover, 1954.

Vasconcelos, José. *Pesimismo Alegre*. Madrid: M. Aguilar, 1931.

Weinstein, Michael A. *Structure of Human Life: A Vitalist Ontology*. New York: New York University Press, 1979.

Weinstein, Michael A. *Unity and Variety in the Philosophy of Samuel Alexander*. West Lafayette, IN: Purdue University Press, 1984.

Weinstein, Michael A. *Culture/Flesh: Explorations of Postcivilized Modernity*. Lanham, Maryland: Rowman and Littlefield, 1995.

Whitehead, Alfred N. *Science and the Modern World*. New York: Macmillan, 1925.

Whitehead, Alfred N. *The Function of Reason*. Beacon Hill: Beacon, 1929.

Whitehead, Alfred N. *Modes of Thought*. New York: The Free Press, 1938.

Whitehead, Alfred N. *Dialogues of Alfred North Whitehead*. Edited by Lucien Price. New York: Mentor, 1954.

Whitehead, Alfred N. *Process and Reality: The Corrected Edition*. Edited by David Ray Griffin and Donald W. Sherburne. New York: The Free Press, 1978.

Other Media

Amenabar, Alejandro. *The Others*. Directed by Alejandro Amenabar. 2001. Cruise/Wagner Productions. Dimension Films 2001. DVD.

Clinton, George, Edward Hazel and Raymond Davis. "Free Your Mind and Your Ass Will Follow." Performed by Funkadelic. 1970. Detroit: Westbound Records.

de Grasse-Tyson, Neil. *Cosmos: A Spacetime Odyssey*. Hosted by Neil de Grasse-Tyson. Cosmos Productions and Fuzzy Door Productions. Washington, D.C.: National Geographic Channel. 2014.

Jones, Terry, and Terry Gilliam. *Monty Python and the Holy Grail*. Directed by Terry Jones and Terry Gilliam. 1975. London: Michael White Productions and National Film Trustee Company. Sony Pictures Home Entertainment. 2005. DVD.

Judge, Mike. *Idiocracy*. Directed by Mike Judge. 2006. Los Angeles: Twentieth Century Fox Home Entertainment. 2007. DVD.

INDEX

Adorno, Theodore 37, 53–4
adversity 16–17, 21–3
Alexander, Samuel 66, 74
Al-Ghazālī 18, 36, 48, 106, 150; and
 deconstruction 63n4; and skepticism
 40–2
alteracion 65–6
Althusser, Louis 36, 43, 107, 110, 116; as
 phenomenologist of mind 37, 61
anthropo-narcissism 8, 10, 13, 115;
 and Euro-romance 14, 29, 34–5, 50;
 and postmodernism 56; and serio-
 comedy 154

Babbitt, Irving 151–2
Battaille, Georges 149, 156
Baudrillard, Jean: as critic of modernity 8,
 27, 39, 43, 54–6; and deterrence
 machine 129; and loss of the real
 8–9, 111, 147, 153; and nostalgia 49,
 52, 56
Bedlam of Ideals 68, 72, 85, 98; *see also*
 phantasmagoria
Benjamin, Walter 53, 156
Bergson, Henri 5, 62, 75
Bin Laden, Osama 136–7, 140
bonobo-chimpanzee (BC): as bipolar ape
 105, 113–16, 118, 137; humans as
 hybrid of 57, 112, 121, 144,150–1; and
 media culture 55, 57; and privileging of
 mental life 56, 115, 148
Buddhism 16, 62, 119, 155; *see also* Zen

Camus, Albert 8, 17, 95, 32; and absurd
 51–3, 72, 78, 97, 100
capitalism 27, 37, 150
Charlie Hebdo 139–40
Cioran, E.M. 13, 74
civilization 13–14, 16–17, 37, 111;
 cancer-like logic of in West 148–53;
 moribund 9–10, 58–9, 143, Western
 25–7, 31, 49, 53
critique of ideology 37, 61, 110, 147, 150

Darwinism 27, 43–4, 46, 115, 119
DeBord, Guy 81–2
deconstruction 8, 37, 63n4, 74; *see also*
 postmodernism
demystification 46, 50
dérive 81–4
Derrida, Jacques 8, 31, 37, 56, 93, 135
Descartes, René 5, 35, 47, 81; and modern
 rationalism 39–42, 86
deWaal, Frans 113–14, 119
Dewey, John 4–5, 16, 74, 104
Dostoevsky, Feodor 8, 17–18, 50–1, 103
drop of experience 69, 77, 80–1, 83, 87

Eco, Umberto 73
ego-centered discourse 72–6, 87, 91,
 95, 102
ego-philosophy 95–9, 154
embeddedness 90–5, 111, 118, 122;
 embedded existence 89–90, 94,
 96–102

ensimismamiento 65
existentialism 12, 21, 61, 71, 119, 131; as part of Euro-romance 92, 154; and ultimate meaning 41, 51–4, 95

fatalism 28–34, 36, 49, 57, 119; *see also* tragedy
fetishization 39, 45, 60–1
finitude 25, 46, 51–2, 62; and consciousness 66–7, 73, 79, 85, 90
Foucault, Michel 8, 36–8, 42–3, 158
fragmentorium 54, 104, 111, 125, 142; and fluidity of meaning 46, 129–32; and identity 136, 153–4; and social disconnection 57, 121–3, 145, 147–8
Freud, Sigmund 8, 18, 61, 111, 152; psychoanalytic concepts 9–10, 12, 23, 98, 105; resistance to differing approaches 45; as student of mind 4, 6, 24, 107, 136

Grand Inquisitor 17, 119, 140
Groddeck, Georg 108–10

happy pessimism (*pesimismo alegre*) 70, 161
Hegel, G.W.F. 6, 124, 130, 135; as Euro-romantic 31, 33, 35
Heidegger, Martin 5, 7, 13, 19, 35–6; and existentialism 8, 17, 62, 74, 79, 92; and meaning 51–3, 108; and nihilism 10, 49, 54, 57; and technology 26, 149
Heraclitus 27–8, 36
Hobbes, Thomas: and civilization 58; and self-preservation 13, 17, 35; and shared meaning 12, 17, 21; and veneer theory 113–14
Holmes, Oliver Wendell, Sr. 67–8, 70, 85, 91
home discourse 66, 71–2, 87, 99
Homer 15, 25, 27
Horkheimer, Max 53–4
human maladaptivity 33, 104, 118–20
Hume, David 44, 47, 50
Husserl, Edmund 6, 19, 42, 74; and phenomenology; 1, 3, 5, 20, 60; and transcendence 8, 61–2

identity: individual 100, 110–11; socio-political 135–6, 143–8, 153–4
immediacy 1, 3, 7, 9, 14, 102
integral consciousness 76–81; compresent 79–80 83–5; and embeddedness 90, 94; and reflective review 87, 89, 99

James, William 5, 62, 64, 66–7, 84; as phenomenologist of mind 6, 10n1
Jenner, Bruce/Caitlyn 134–5, 160

Kant, Immanuel 3, 30, 43, 65, 82, 119; as edifying thinker 31–5; as erosive critical thinker 34, 47–8, 92; on the origins of mind 33, 103–5
Kazantzakis, Nikos 74, 159
Kierkegaard, Søren 17–18, 39, 48, 74; as critic of rationalism 8, 50–2, 57; and faith 40, 119; and freedom; 24, 41–2

Leibniz, Gottfried W. 31, 98
Levinas, Emmanuel 28, 56
lex talionis 28, 31, 119, 147
logos 17, 28, 31, 43–4, 49
love piracy 61
Lyotard, Jean-François 8, 71

Marx, Karl 9, 37, 56
Mohammed 10, 139–40
mythos 30–1, 54

NASCAR 124–7
necessity, concept of 44: ancient 29, 33; modern 31–2, 39, 42–3
Nietzsche, Friedrich 4–5, 18, 74, 103, 124; as critic of modernity 29–30, 38, 46–51, 152; and moral idealism 106; and nihilism 10, 32, 49, 53, 57, 60; and nostalgia 56; and will to power 24, 154; and will to truth 17, 21
nihilism 20, 42, 56, 106–7, 110; as value-neutral datum 58–61, 96, 114; as ground of radical phenomenology 8, 102–3, 110–11, 116; negative (as disaster) 10, 47, 49–52, 54; ontological 1–2, 17, 32, 73–4; and Zen 77–8
nostalgia 20, 26, 49, 101; and modernism 92–3; and postmodernism 54, 56–7, 135

omnipotence of thoughts 9, 107–8, 111; *see also* power of mind
ontology 26, 61–2, 64, 74, 108; fundamental (Heideggerian) 52; in Western thought 28, 37, 51
onto-theology 31, 41, 50, 93
Ortega y Gasset, José 65, 70, 73–4, 92

164 Index

particularity 2, 4, 17, 56, 85; and embeddedness 90–1; and existentialism 51–2; and freedom 19; as immediate fact of experience 11–12, 21, 56; and ontological nihilism 20, 38, 60

phantasmagoria 28, 33, 69, 76–7, 82; and embeddedness 89, 91, 98; as indeterminate contents of experience 68, 78–9, 87; and public discourse 111, 123–4; and leveling of importance 69, 81–2, 84–5, 102; and serio-comedy 71–2, 74

phenomenology 1, 20, 44, 48–9, 90

phenomenology of mind (radical) 2–3, 6–8, 16, 98; and Euro-romantic discourse 18–19, 56–9, 60–2; and contemporary discourse 130, 135; and critique of ideology 37–8; and immediate experience 85, 89–90, 122; and ontological nihilism 42, 49, 51, 108; and philosophical anthropology 102–4, 84, 116–18

philosophy 7, 18, 26–8, 53, 118; modernist 72, 74, 78, 86–7; postmodernist 92; as Socratic vital practice; 75–6, 81–2, 84, 112; as Western institution 4, 9, 13, 40–1, 58, 73

philosophical anthropology *see* phenomenology of mind (radical)

philosophical autobiography 73–4, 79

Pierce, Charles Sanders 1–2, 12

Plato 27–31, 34–6, 40, 43

postmodernism 13, 37, 49, 53–7; critique of modernity 61, 72–3, 134–5, 144

power of mind: as creative 6, 9, 46; as liberating power 16; as oppressive force 23–4, 105, 107–11, 154

primatological view 102, 105, 111–16, 123

progress, modern myth of 32–3, 140

psychoanalysis 23, 45, 109

rationalism, modern 7–8, 36, 40, 47, 52; and anthropo-narcissism 41, 48; and criticism 39, 49–50, 63n4; and necessity; 32–4, 42

relativism 36, 42–4, 57, 61, 107

Rorty, Richard 35, 50

Rousseau, Jean-Jacques 35, 113

Santayana, George 1, 74–5, 85; and phantasmagoria 62–3, 69, 78–9, 86

Sartre, Jean-Paul 18, 71, 74, 95, 98; and the desire to be God 22–3; and existentialism 8, 17, 51–2, 92–3; and freedom 32, 67

Scheler, Max 33, 61, 102, 116, 118

scientism (culture of science) 36–7, 48; ontological assumptions of 7–8; and aesthetics 43–6, 86; sacralization of science in 60

sciousness (James) 66–7

serio-comedy 55, 58 100–2; and contemporary situation 122–4, 132, 135–6; and *dérive* 81–3; and integral consciousness 84–5, 89, 91; and spirit of seriousness 49–50, 61, 154–5; and tragic sense 67–74, 76–7

Shestov, Lev 26, 31, 57

Simmel, Georg 70, 97

Sisyphus 92, 100, 123–4, 126

Socrates 4, 27

Stirner, Max 18, 74, 106; and mind as empowering 96–7; and mind as oppressive 109–12, 117

technology 6, 60; and nihilism 52, 54–6; and Western *ethos*; 26–7; and present-day culture 120–2, 138, 150–2

tragedy 26, 32, 73; ancient 27–31, 57, 109, 119, 147; and modern loss of meaning 84, 91

tragic sense of life 63, 69–72, 76, 78, 136

transcendence 32, 89, 98, 103, 108; and Husserl 60–2; and meaning, 24–5, 49–50, 57, 92; and Western metaphysics 39–40, 46–7, 51–3

Trump, Donald (The Donald) 55, 124, 127, 129, 133–4; and media culture 137, 140–1, 143–5, 152

ultimate meaning (ultimaticity) 20, 24, 54, 80, 110, 153; and modern thought 8, 35, 46, 50, 57–9; and existentialism 51–2; and postmodernism 53–6

Unamuno, Miguel de 74–5, 97; and tragic sense 63, 69–70, 136

undead 27, 55, 58, 128, 137–8

Vasconcelos, José 70, 74

Weinstein, Michael A. 61, 63n1, 63n6

Whitehead, Alfred North 1, 4–7, 36, 62; critique of scientism 69–70, 74, 78, 85, 118

will to truth 17, 21, 38, 50, 104

Zen 57, 62, 77

zombies *see* undead